BILLY *THE* KID'S
OLD TIMEY ODDITIES

writer *artist*
Eric Powell **Kyle Hotz**

colorist
Eric Powell

letterer
Michael Heisler

story and characters created by
Eric Powell and Kyle Hotz

DARK HORSE BOOKS™

publisher
Mike Richardson

editor
Matt Dryer
with Dave Marshall

designer
Lia Ribacchi

featuring
Scott Allie as Pat Garrett

special thanks to
Gina Gagliano

This volume collects issues 1-4 of the Dark Horse Comics miniseries
Billy the Kid's Old Timey Oddities.

Published by
Dark Horse Books
A division of
Dark Horse Comics, Inc.
10956 SE Main Street
Milwaukie, OR 97222

First Edition: January 2006
ISBN: 1-59307-448-4

1 3 5 7 9 10 8 6 4 2
Printed in China

INTRODUCTION

Wild, wicked Western weirdness, starring Western legend Billy the Kid. I got to tell you, trail mates, this is the best weird western I've read in many a blue Western moon. I'm partial to the form, and have taken a crack at it myself, as novelist, short-story writer, screenplay writer, and comic scripter. Making these two genres blend is harder than it looks. And *Billy the Kid's Old Timey Oddities* has got a bit of everything, and then some with mustard. And you know what? It tastes pretty good, though I'm not sure what it's doing to my stomach.

It's got one of the West's premier gunfighters for a start. It's got strange characters. Man, I'll say. You got your alligator man, your wolf boy, your tattooed woman with tattoos that provide messages, reminiscent of Bradbury's "Illustrated Man", and all of this is just in the first issue!

What are these guys drinking? This is the coolest, weirdest Western character since Jonah Hex. And, frankly, I think *Billy the Kid's Old Timey Oddities* may have more range and possibilities.

So what do these comics have that makes them so special?

Damn good scripts, for one. This, of course, includes a wild and interesting plot, written by Eric Powell. Way he writes, it's as if Billy the Kid was born under the pen of Edgar Allen Poe, then farted on by H. P. Lovecraft. Yeah, Eric writes that creepy.

Instead of just a series of events, the story draws out Billy's character, and touches on what strikes me as something closer to the real Billy the Kid, though the real Billy the Kid had a much more mundane life. I hope.

Really, I'm not kidding. There have been numerous depictions of Billy, from misunderstood, to psychopath, to just plain old downtrodden. This one has hints of them all rolled into one seriously messed-up, and as far as weirdness goes, unlucky cowpoke. This version makes him what he may have been. A very confused, abused child done grown up into a luckless man trying to deal with life.

Eric, you da man.

And the art. Kyle Hotz is drinking from the same contaminated well as Eric. This stuff seems to have been painted by Lovecraft's Pickman. Pickman, a character in Lovecraft's great story "Pickman's Models," was an artist who painted very strange and horrible characters. They were so unsettling, that people questioned his sanity. It turns out, gulp, that his models were real.

So, uh, Kyle, I won't be visiting you anytime soon.

Let's go cowboy and simplify this here message.

Please read this dadburn book. It's a jalopena-laced kick in the pants.

— Joe R. Lansdale

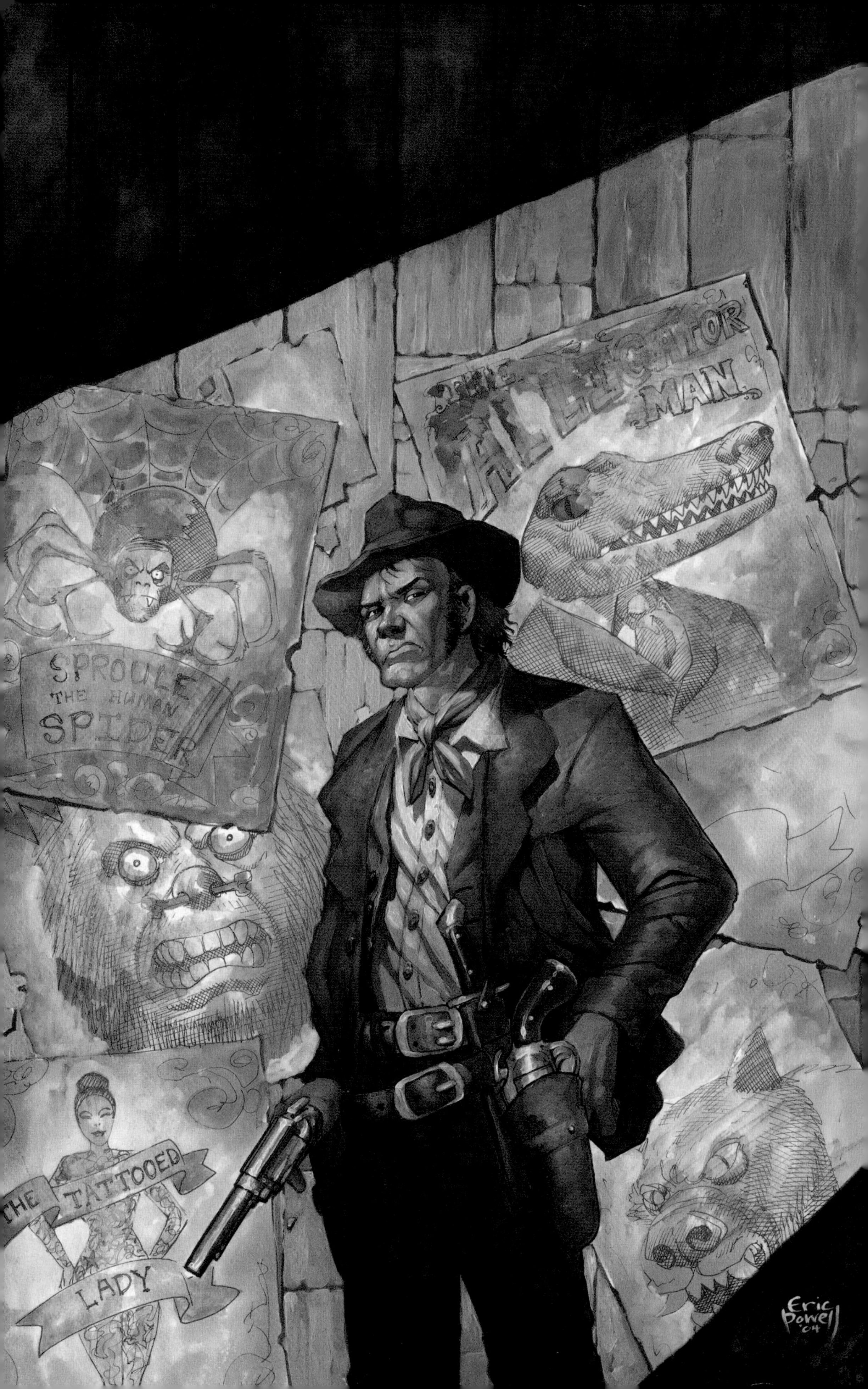

SPROULE
THE HUMAN
SPIDER
MAN
THE TATTOOED
LADY
Eric Powell '04

FUGITIVE KILLER SLAIN IN DESPERATE GUN BATTLE

WILLIAM HENRY McCARTY (AKA William H. Bonney), known to the world as Billy the Kid, has finally been brought to justice by lawman Pat Garrett.

Wanted for murder, theft, and rustling, McCarty had evaded many traps and ambushes, and was often rumored to have an animal-like instinct warning him of danger. Yet, rumor had not kept him from eventual capture and jailing in Mesilla.

After only a single day of deliberation at court, McCarty was convicted of murdering Sheriff William Brady. On April 13, 1881, the honorable Judge Warren Bristol sentenced him to hang in one month's time.

Transported to Lincoln for his execution, McCarty was kept under guard by James Bell and Robert Ollinger in the building known as "the House" before the Lincoln County War. Yet, on April 28, he somehow managed to escape, killing both of his guards.

It is widely believed that a friend or Regulator sympathizer had hidden a pistol in the privy that McCarty was escorted to daily. McCarty shot Bell with the pistol from the top of a flight of stairs in "the House." After that, he stole Ollinger's 10-gauge double-barrel shotgun and waited for his other captor to return. McCarty then shot Ollinger as he paused from running across the street upon hearing McCarty call, "Hello, Bob" from his window.

"The Kid" was back on the run and Garrett took his escape as a personal shot to his pride. On July 14, Garret's search brought him to the home of McCarty's friend, Pete Maxwell in Old Fort Sumner. While Garret questioned Maxwell in his darkened bedroom, McCarty unexpectedly entered the room. Not recognizing his pursuer in the poor lighting conditions, McCarty asked, "Quien es? Quien es?" (Spanish for "Who is it? Who is it?"), to which Garrett responded with two shots from his revolver. The first shot hit McCarty in the heart. The second went astray.

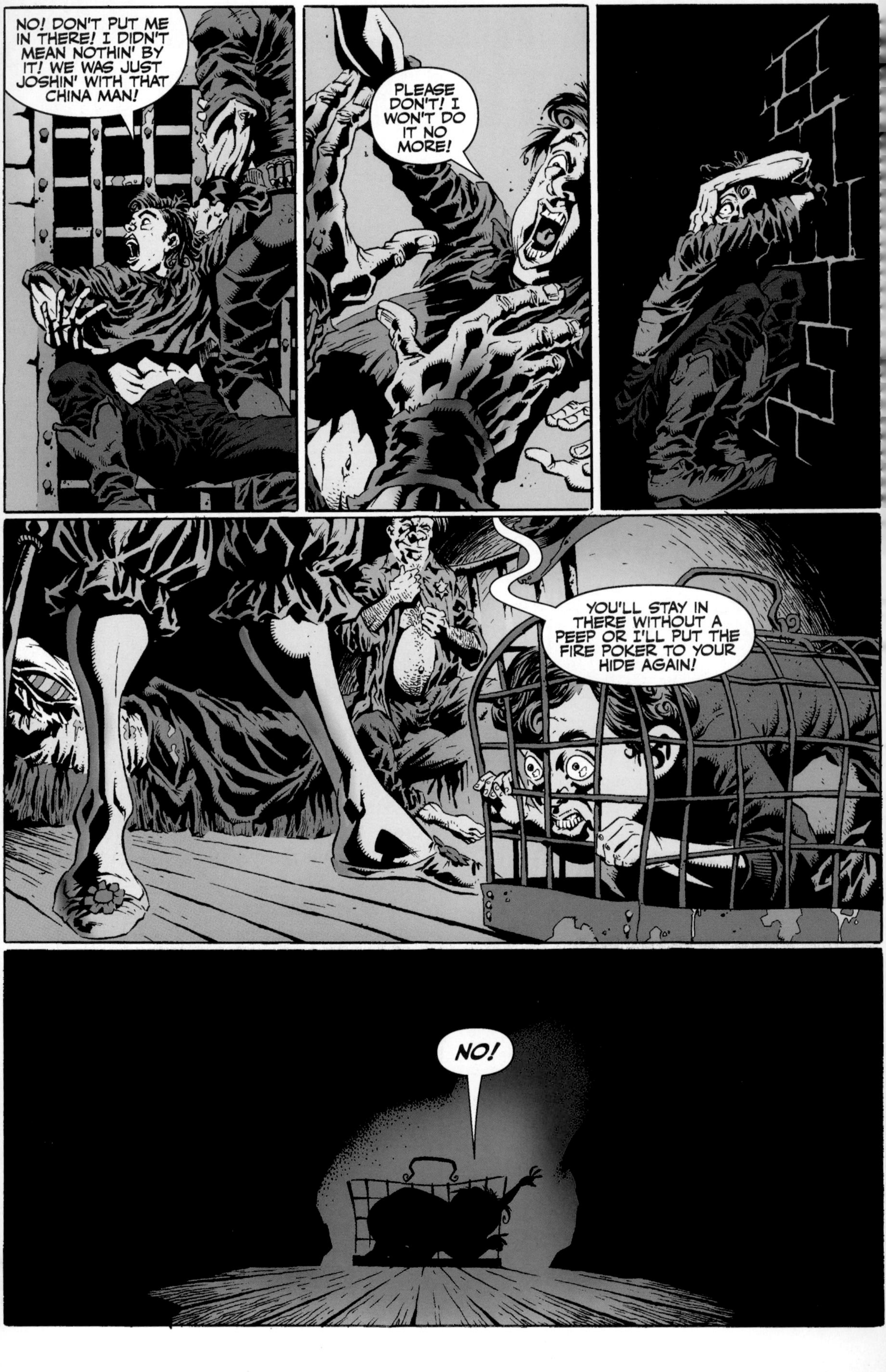
NO! DON'T PUT ME IN THERE! I DIDN'T MEAN NOTHIN' BY IT! WE WAS JUST JOSHIN' WITH THAT CHINA MAN!
PLEASE DON'T! I WON'T DO IT NO MORE!
YOU'LL STAY IN THERE WITHOUT A PEEP OR I'LL PUT THE FIRE POKER TO YOUR HIDE AGAIN!
NO!

WHOOOOO!

NO!

BAD DREAM?

HUH?

HAVING A NIGHTMARE?

MIND YOUR OWN BUSINESS, SPIFFY!

SOUNDED LIKE A NIGHTMARE. YOU WERE MUMBLING SOMETHING ABOUT BEING LOCKED UP.

YOU GOT A PROBLEM, BOY? WHEN DID YOU GET ON HERE, ANYHOW?

WHILE YOU WERE SLEEPING.

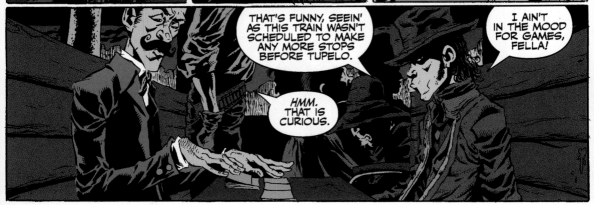

THAT'S FUNNY, SEEIN' AS THIS TRAIN WASN'T SCHEDULED TO MAKE ANY MORE STOPS BEFORE TUPELO.

HMM. THAT IS CURIOUS.

I AIN'T IN THE MOOD FOR GAMES, FELLA!

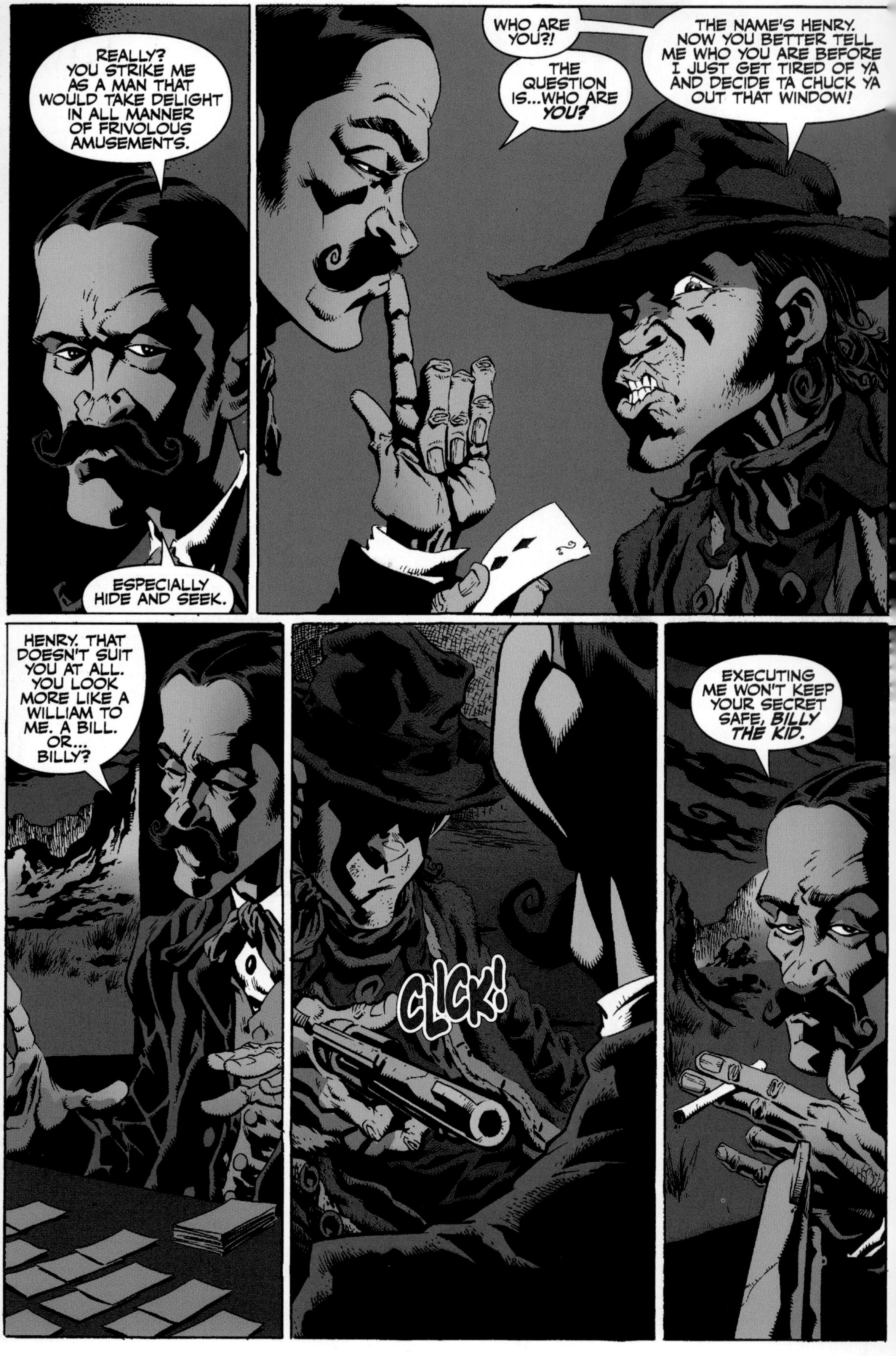
REALLY? YOU STRIKE ME AS A MAN THAT WOULD TAKE DELIGHT IN ALL MANNER OF FRIVOLOUS AMUSEMENTS.
ESPECIALLY HIDE AND SEEK.
WHO ARE YOU?!
THE QUESTION IS...WHO ARE *YOU?*
THE NAME'S HENRY. NOW YOU BETTER TELL ME WHO YOU ARE BEFORE I JUST GET TIRED OF YA AND DECIDE TA CHUCK YA OUT THAT WINDOW!
HENRY. THAT DOESN'T SUIT YOU AT ALL. YOU LOOK MORE LIKE A WILLIAM TO ME. A BILL. OR... BILLY?
CLICK!
EXECUTING ME WON'T KEEP YOUR SECRET SAFE, *BILLY THE KID.*

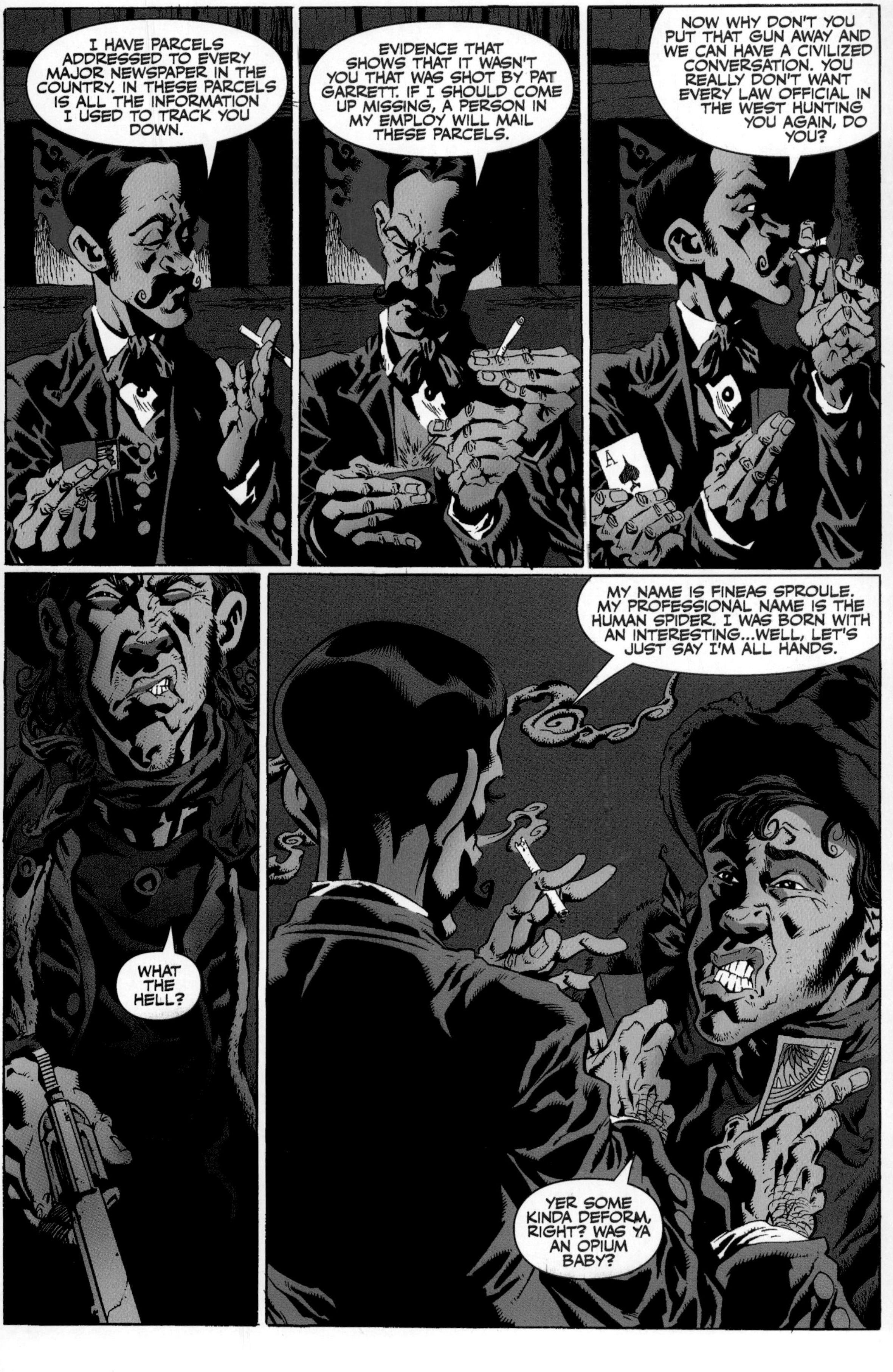
I HAVE PARCELS ADDRESSED TO EVERY MAJOR NEWSPAPER IN THE COUNTRY. IN THESE PARCELS IS ALL THE INFORMATION I USED TO TRACK YOU DOWN.
EVIDENCE THAT SHOWS THAT IT WASN'T YOU THAT WAS SHOT BY PAT GARRETT. IF I SHOULD COME UP MISSING, A PERSON IN MY EMPLOY WILL MAIL THESE PARCELS.
NOW WHY DON'T YOU PUT THAT GUN AWAY AND WE CAN HAVE A CIVILIZED CONVERSATION. YOU REALLY DON'T WANT EVERY LAW OFFICIAL IN THE WEST HUNTING YOU AGAIN, DO YOU?
WHAT THE HELL?
MY NAME IS FINEAS SPROULE. MY PROFESSIONAL NAME IS THE HUMAN SPIDER. I WAS BORN WITH AN INTERESTING...WELL, LET'S JUST SAY I'M ALL HANDS.
YER SOME KINDA DEFORM, RIGHT? WAS YA AN OPIUM BABY?

AS I WAS SAYING, I RUN A TRAVELING SPECTACLE CALLED SPROULE'S BIOLOGICAL CURIOSITIES.

YA MEAN A FREAK SHOW?

NO. A TRAVELING SPECTACLE OF BIOLOGICAL CURIOSITIES.

STYLE IT UP ALL YA WANT, FELLA. SOUNDS LIKE A FREAK SHOW TA ME.

≋SIGH≋ I'M HERE TO MAKE YOU A VERY GENEROUS OFFER, MR. KID. MY COLLEAGUES AND I ARE IN NEED OF A MAN OF YOUR ABILITIES FOR A RATHER UNSCRUPULOUS ENDEAVOR. I SUPPOSE YOU COULD CALL IT A TREASURE HUNT.

WE WILL OFFER YOU ASYLUM IN OUR BAND OF TRAVELERS, YOUR TRUE IDENTITY WILL BE CLOSELY GUARDED, AND AN EQUAL PERCENTAGE OF ANY ACQUISITION THAT MAY FALL INTO OUR HANDS. NO OFFENSE, BUT YOU LOOK AS IF YOU COULD USE THE EMPLOYMENT.

THAT SOUNDS ALL WELL AND GOOD, MISTER, BUT WHY DO I DESERVE SUCH GENEROSITY? WHAT YOU WANT FROM ME?

THIS IS NO SUNDAY AFTERNOON STROLL I'M ASKING YOU TO TAKE PART IN, MR. KID. IN ALL LIKELIHOOD THE WHOLE EXPEDITION WILL MEET A MOST DISAGREEABLE END.

AND WHAT IF I SAY NO?

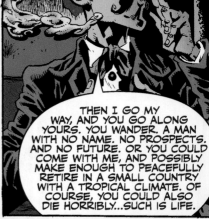

THEN I GO MY WAY, AND YOU GO ALONG YOURS. YOU WANDER. A MAN WITH NO NAME. NO PROSPECTS. AND NO FUTURE. OR YOU COULD COME WITH ME, AND POSSIBLY MAKE ENOUGH TO PEACEFULLY RETIRE IN A SMALL COUNTRY WITH A TROPICAL CLIMATE. OF COURSE, YOU COULD ALSO DIE HORRIBLY...SUCH IS LIFE.

I RECKON I COULD TRAVEL WITH YOU A WAYS. LEAST HEAR MORE ABOUT THIS JOB.

SO WHO ARE WE RIPPIN' OFF? I LIKE TO KNOW WHO I'M STEALIN' FROM.

THE GENTLEMAN'S NAME...

...IS FRANKENSTEIN.

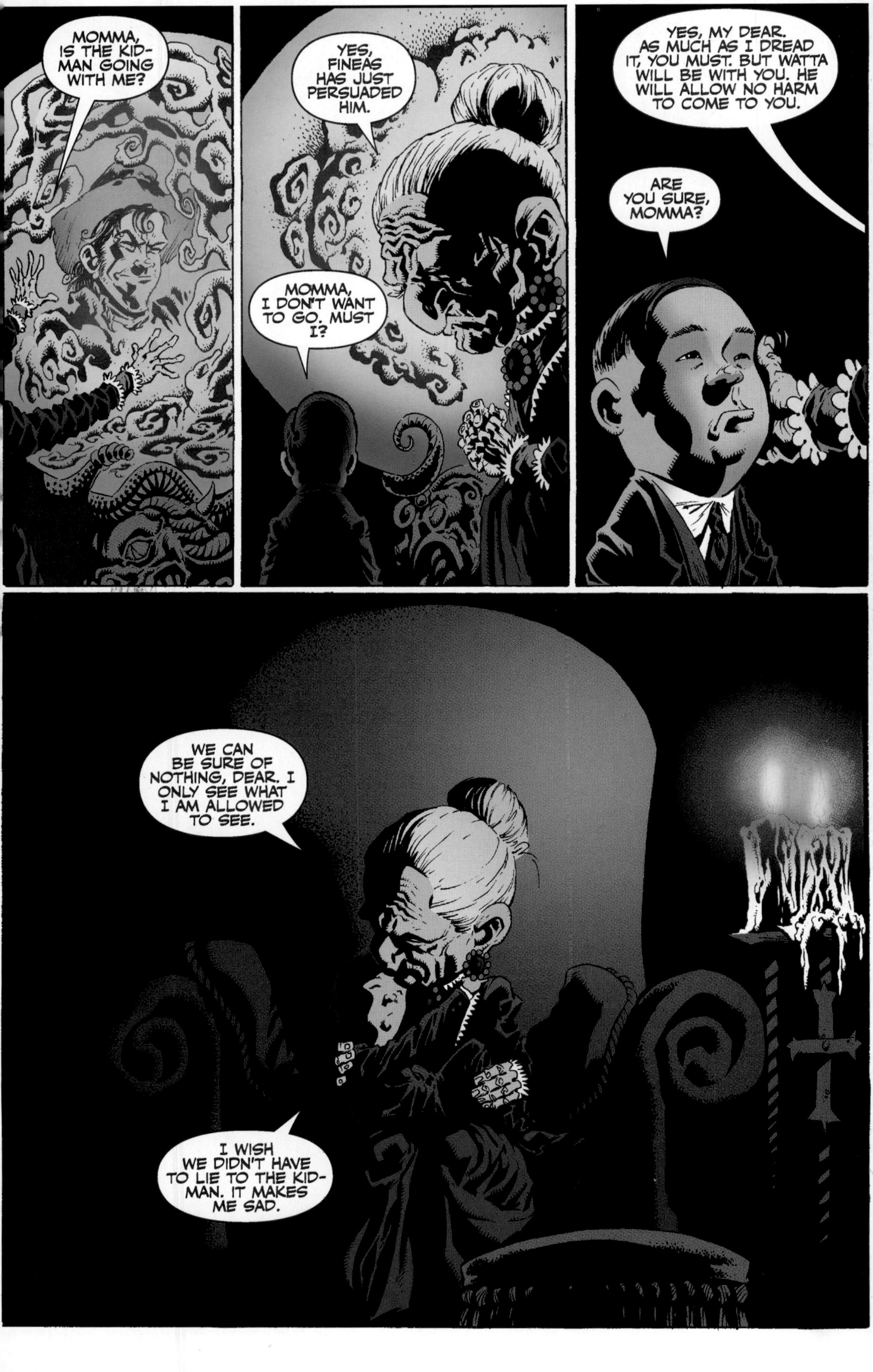

MOMMA, IS THE KID-MAN GOING WITH ME?
YES, FINEAS HAS JUST PERSUADED HIM.
MOMMA, I DON'T WANT TO GO. MUST I?
YES, MY DEAR. AS MUCH AS I DREAD IT, YOU MUST. BUT WATTA WILL BE WITH YOU. HE WILL ALLOW NO HARM TO COME TO YOU.
ARE YOU SURE, MOMMA?
WE CAN BE SURE OF NOTHING, DEAR. I ONLY SEE WHAT I AM ALLOWED TO SEE.
I WISH WE DIDN'T HAVE TO LIE TO THE KID-MAN. IT MAKES ME SAD.

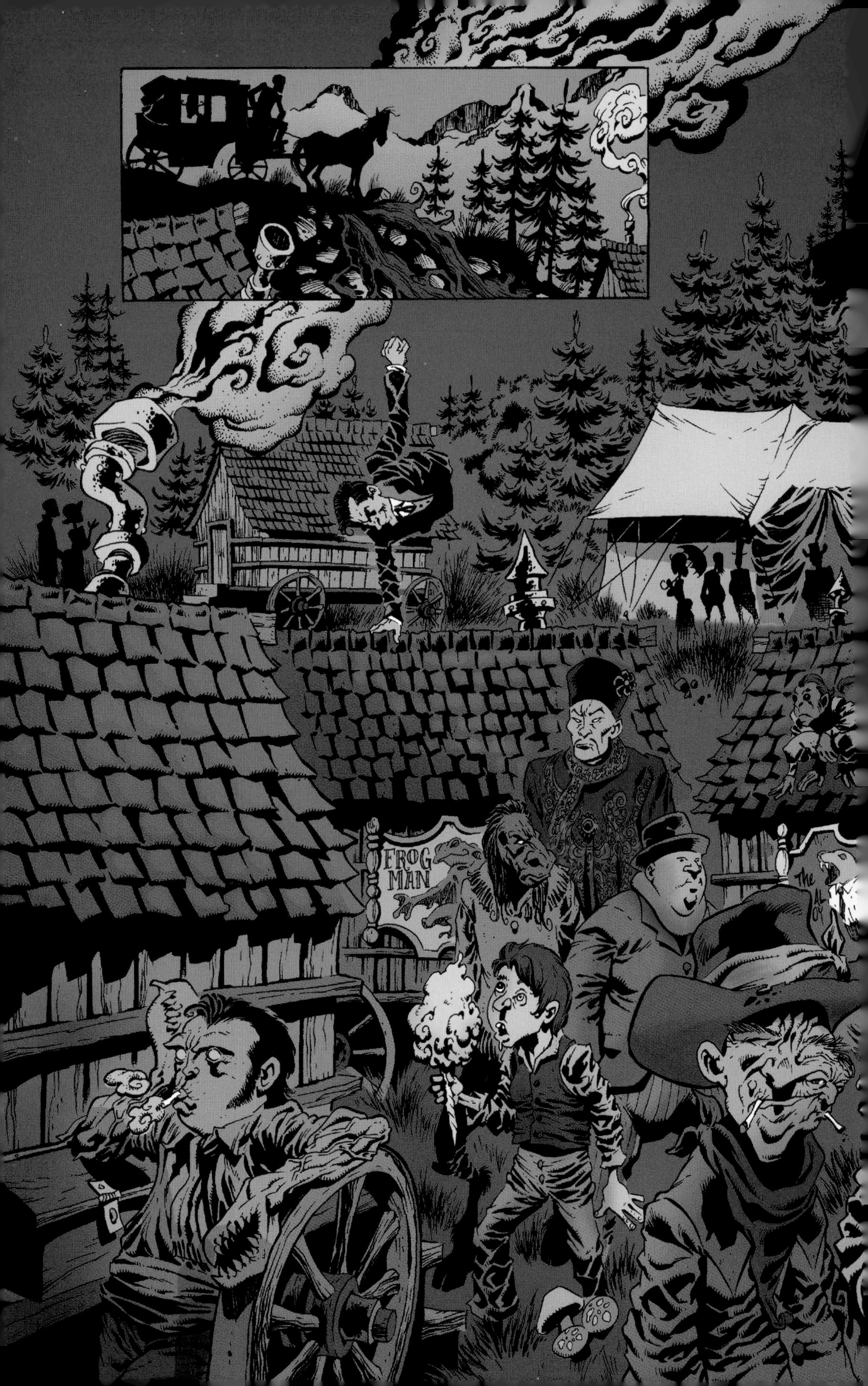
FROG MAN

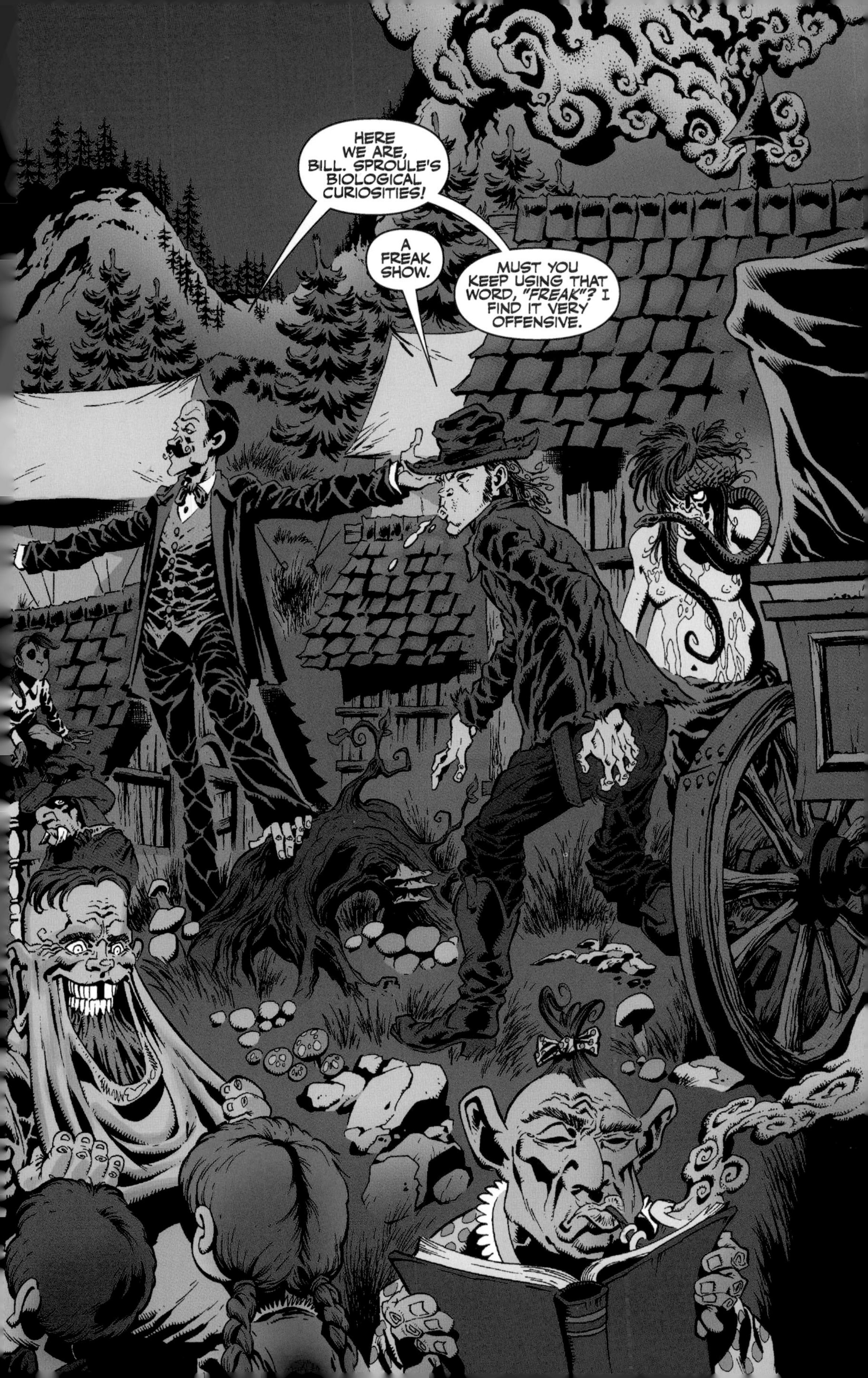
HERE WE ARE, BILL. SPROULE'S BIOLOGICAL CURIOSITIES!
A FREAK SHOW.
MUST YOU KEEP USING THAT WORD, "FREAK"? I FIND IT VERY OFFENSIVE.

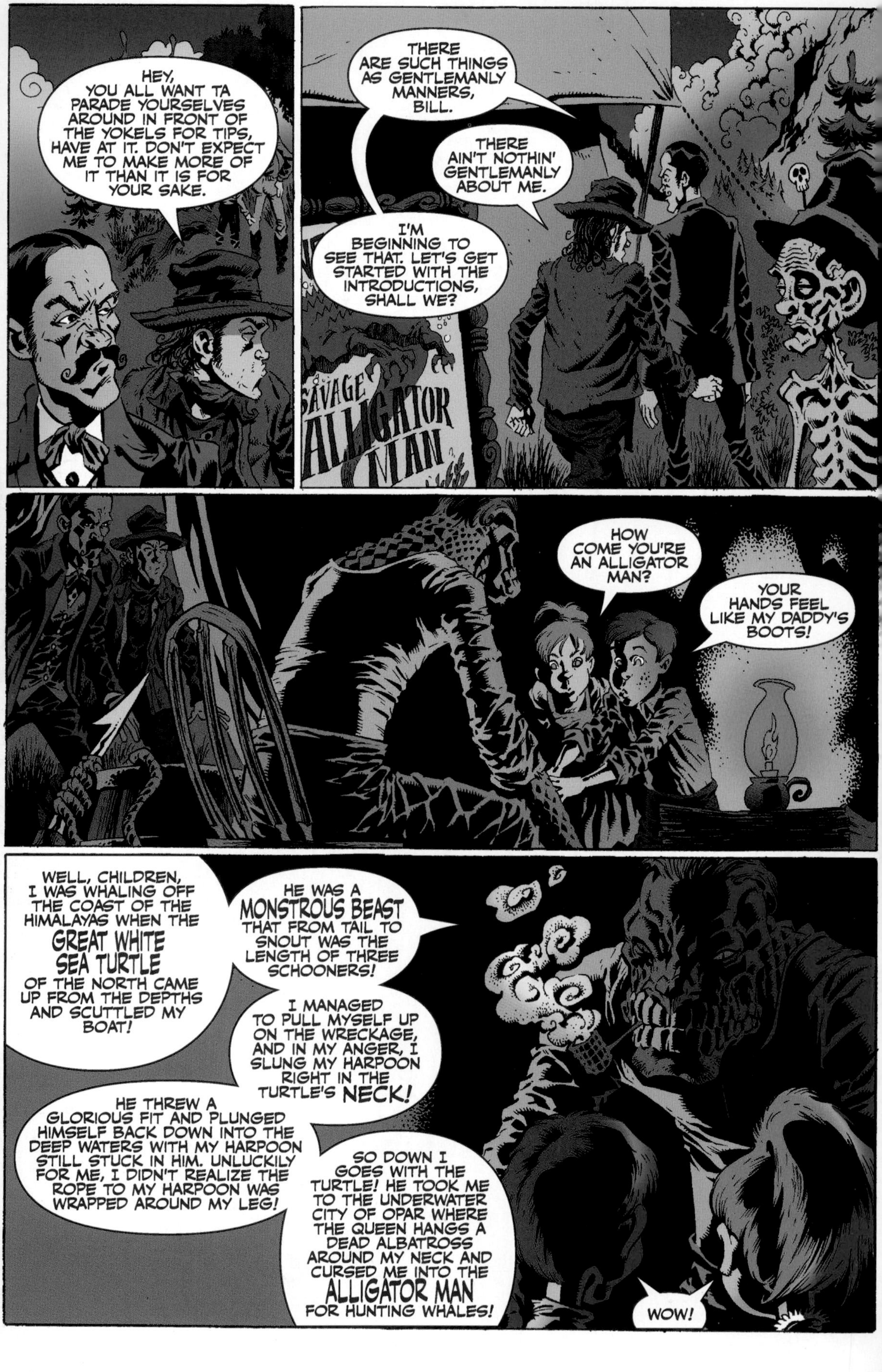
HEY, YOU ALL WANT TA PARADE YOURSELVES AROUND IN FRONT OF THE YOKELS FOR TIPS, HAVE AT IT. DON'T EXPECT ME TO MAKE MORE OF IT THAN IT IS FOR YOUR SAKE.
THERE ARE SUCH THINGS AS GENTLEMANLY MANNERS, BILL.
THERE AIN'T NOTHIN' GENTLEMANLY ABOUT ME.
I'M BEGINNING TO SEE THAT. LET'S GET STARTED WITH THE INTRODUCTIONS, SHALL WE?
SAVAGE ALLIGATOR MAN
HOW COME YOU'RE AN ALLIGATOR MAN?
YOUR HANDS FEEL LIKE MY DADDY'S BOOTS!
WELL, CHILDREN, I WAS WHALING OFF THE COAST OF THE HIMALAYAS WHEN THE GREAT WHITE SEA TURTLE OF THE NORTH CAME UP FROM THE DEPTHS AND SCUTTLED MY BOAT!
HE WAS A MONSTROUS BEAST THAT FROM TAIL TO SNOUT WAS THE LENGTH OF THREE SCHOONERS!
I MANAGED TO PULL MYSELF UP ON THE WRECKAGE, AND IN MY ANGER, I SLUNG MY HARPOON RIGHT IN THE TURTLE'S NECK!
HE THREW A GLORIOUS FIT AND PLUNGED HIMSELF BACK DOWN INTO THE DEEP WATERS WITH MY HARPOON STILL STUCK IN HIM. UNLUCKILY FOR ME, I DIDN'T REALIZE THE ROPE TO MY HARPOON WAS WRAPPED AROUND MY LEG!
SO DOWN I GOES WITH THE TURTLE! HE TOOK ME TO THE UNDERWATER CITY OF OPAR WHERE THE QUEEN HANGS A DEAD ALBATROSS AROUND MY NECK AND CURSED ME INTO THE ALLIGATOR MAN FOR HUNTING WHALES!
WOW!

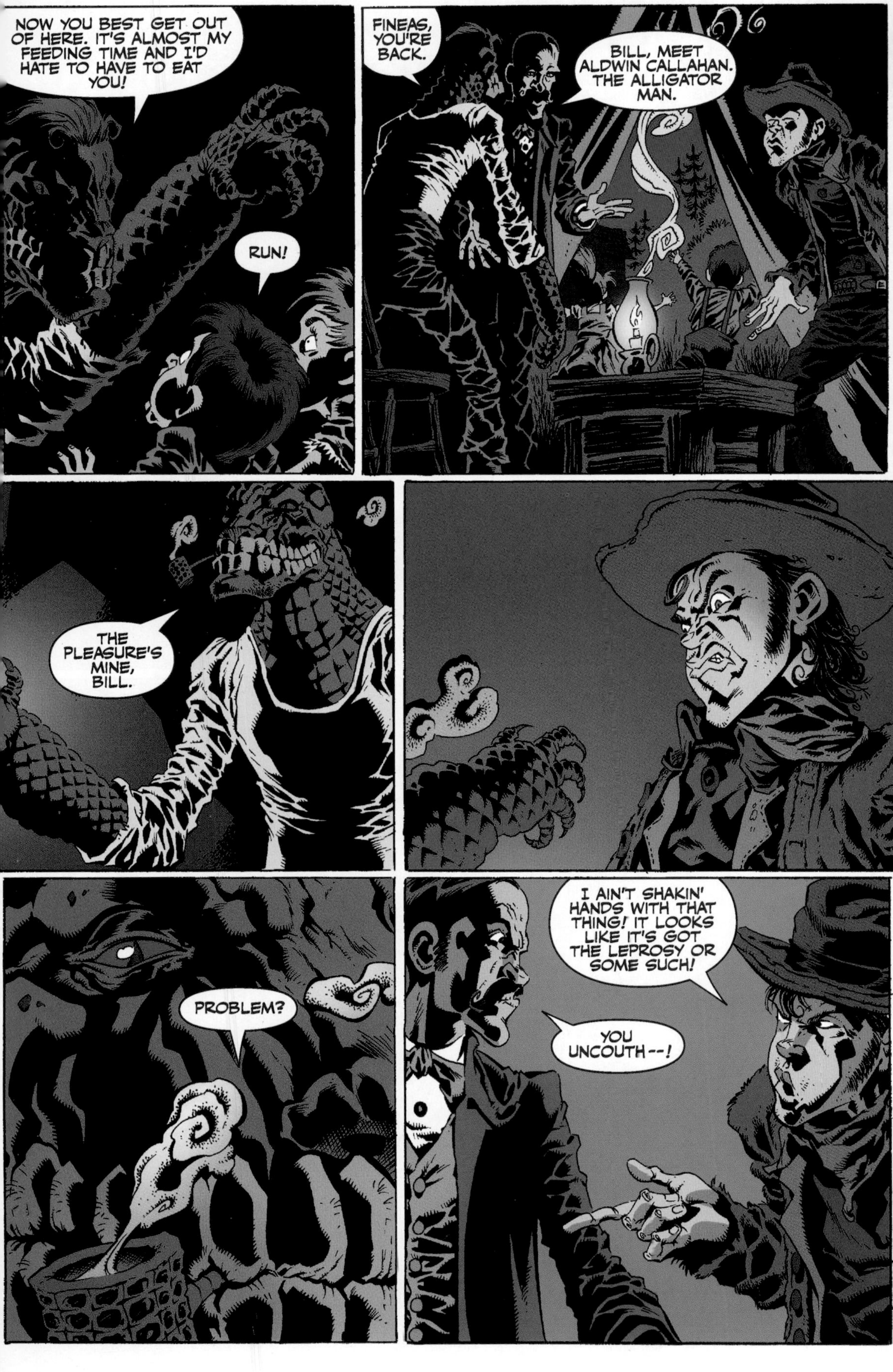
NOW YOU BEST GET OUT OF HERE. IT'S ALMOST MY FEEDING TIME AND I'D HATE TO HAVE TO EAT YOU!
RUN!
FINEAS, YOU'RE BACK.
BILL, MEET ALDWIN CALLAHAN. THE ALLIGATOR MAN.
THE PLEASURE'S MINE, BILL.
PROBLEM?
I AIN'T SHAKIN' HANDS WITH THAT THING! IT LOOKS LIKE IT'S GOT THE LEPROSY OR SOME SUCH!
YOU UNCOUTH--!

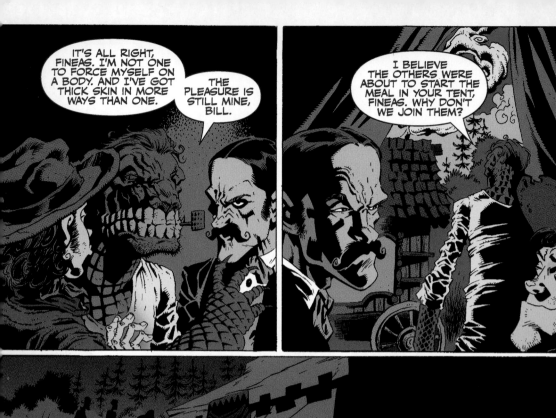

IT'S ALL RIGHT, FINEAS. I'M NOT ONE TO FORCE MYSELF ON A BODY. AND I'VE GOT THICK SKIN IN MORE WAYS THAN ONE.

THE PLEASURE IS STILL MINE, BILL.

I BELIEVE THE OTHERS WERE ABOUT TO START THE MEAL IN YOUR TENT, FINEAS. WHY DON'T WE JOIN THEM?

EVERYONE, I'D LIKE TO INTRODUCE YOU TO OUR MISSING PIECE. MEET WILLIAM H. BONNEY, OTHERWISE KNOWN AS BILLY THE KID.

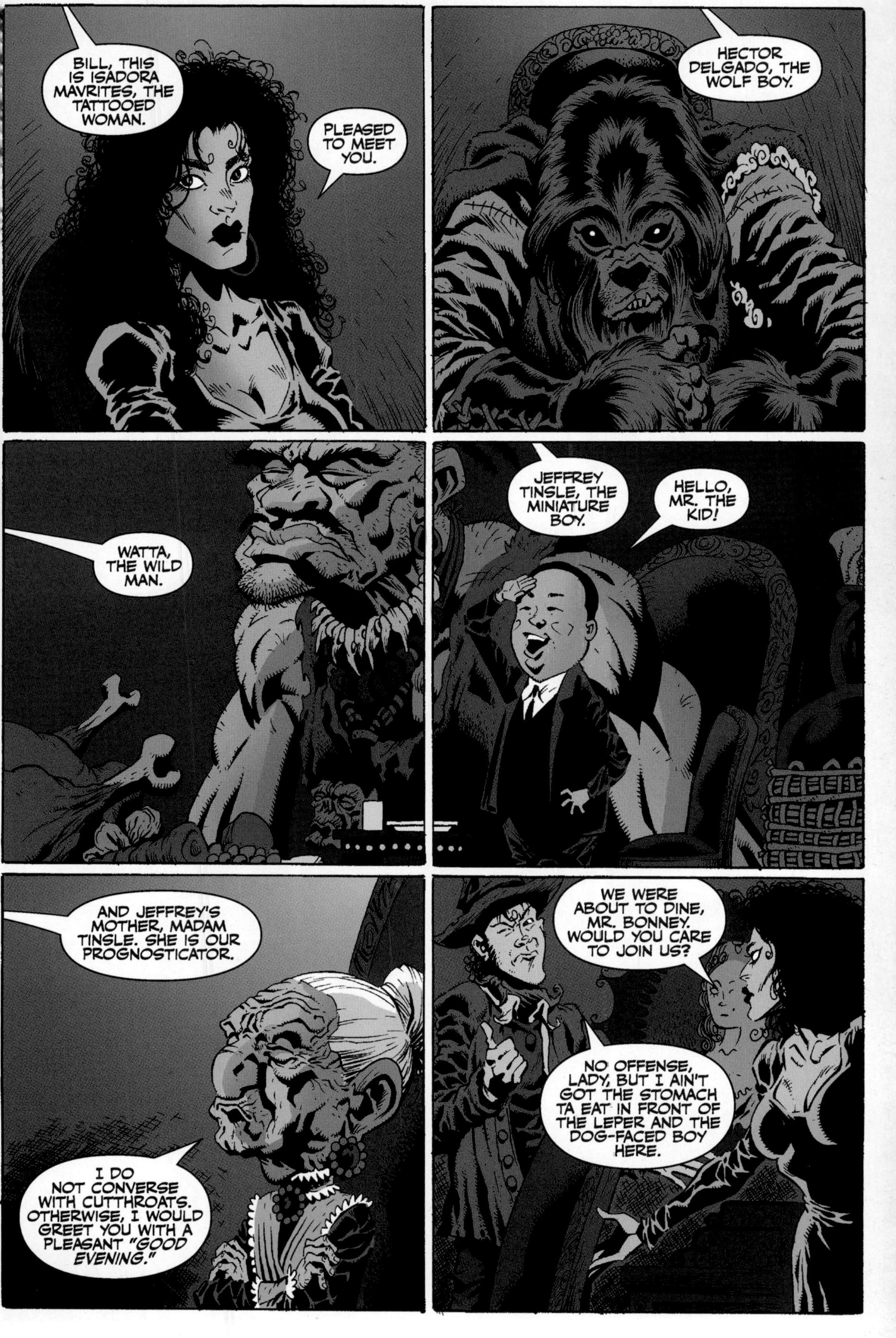

BILL, THIS IS ISADORA MAVRITES, THE TATTOOED WOMAN.
PLEASED TO MEET YOU.
HECTOR DELGADO, THE WOLF BOY.
WATTA, THE WILD MAN.
JEFFREY TINSLE, THE MINIATURE BOY.
HELLO, MR. THE KID!
AND JEFFREY'S MOTHER, MADAM TINSLE. SHE IS OUR PROGNOSTICATOR.
I DO NOT CONVERSE WITH CUTTHROATS. OTHERWISE, I WOULD GREET YOU WITH A PLEASANT *"GOOD EVENING."*
WE WERE ABOUT TO DINE, MR. BONNEY. WOULD YOU CARE TO JOIN US?
NO OFFENSE, LADY, BUT I AIN'T GOT THE STOMACH TA EAT IN FRONT OF THE LEPER AND THE DOG-FACED BOY HERE.

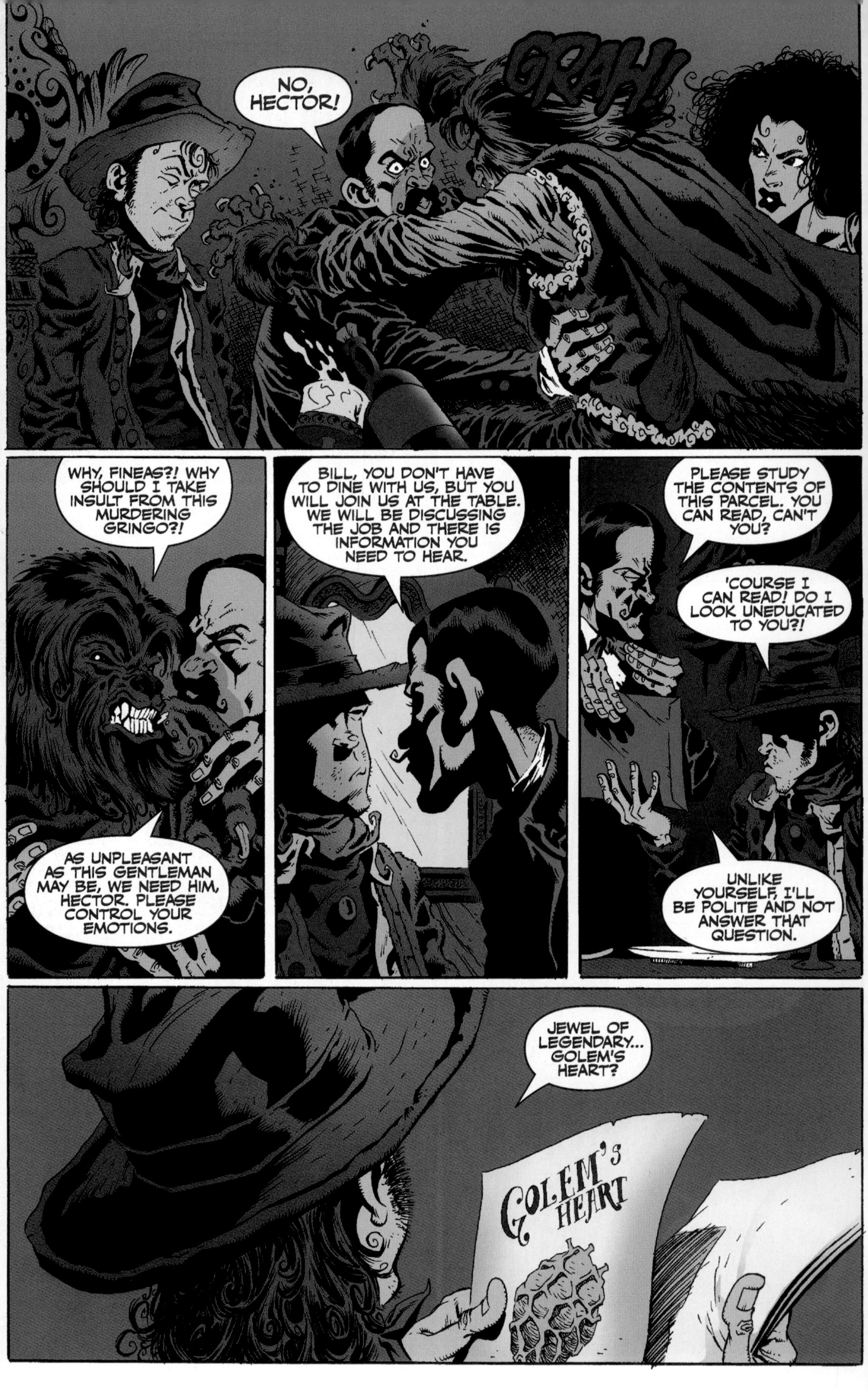
NO, HECTOR!
GRAH!
WHY, FINEAS?! WHY SHOULD I TAKE INSULT FROM THIS MURDERING GRINGO?!
AS UNPLEASANT AS THIS GENTLEMAN MAY BE, WE NEED HIM, HECTOR. PLEASE CONTROL YOUR EMOTIONS.
BILL, YOU DON'T HAVE TO DINE WITH US, BUT YOU WILL JOIN US AT THE TABLE. WE WILL BE DISCUSSING THE JOB AND THERE IS INFORMATION YOU NEED TO HEAR.
PLEASE STUDY THE CONTENTS OF THIS PARCEL. YOU CAN READ, CAN'T YOU?
'COURSE I CAN READ! DO I LOOK UNEDUCATED TO YOU?!
UNLIKE YOURSELF, I'LL BE POLITE AND NOT ANSWER THAT QUESTION.
JEWEL OF LEGENDARY... GOLEM'S HEART?
GOLEM'S HEART

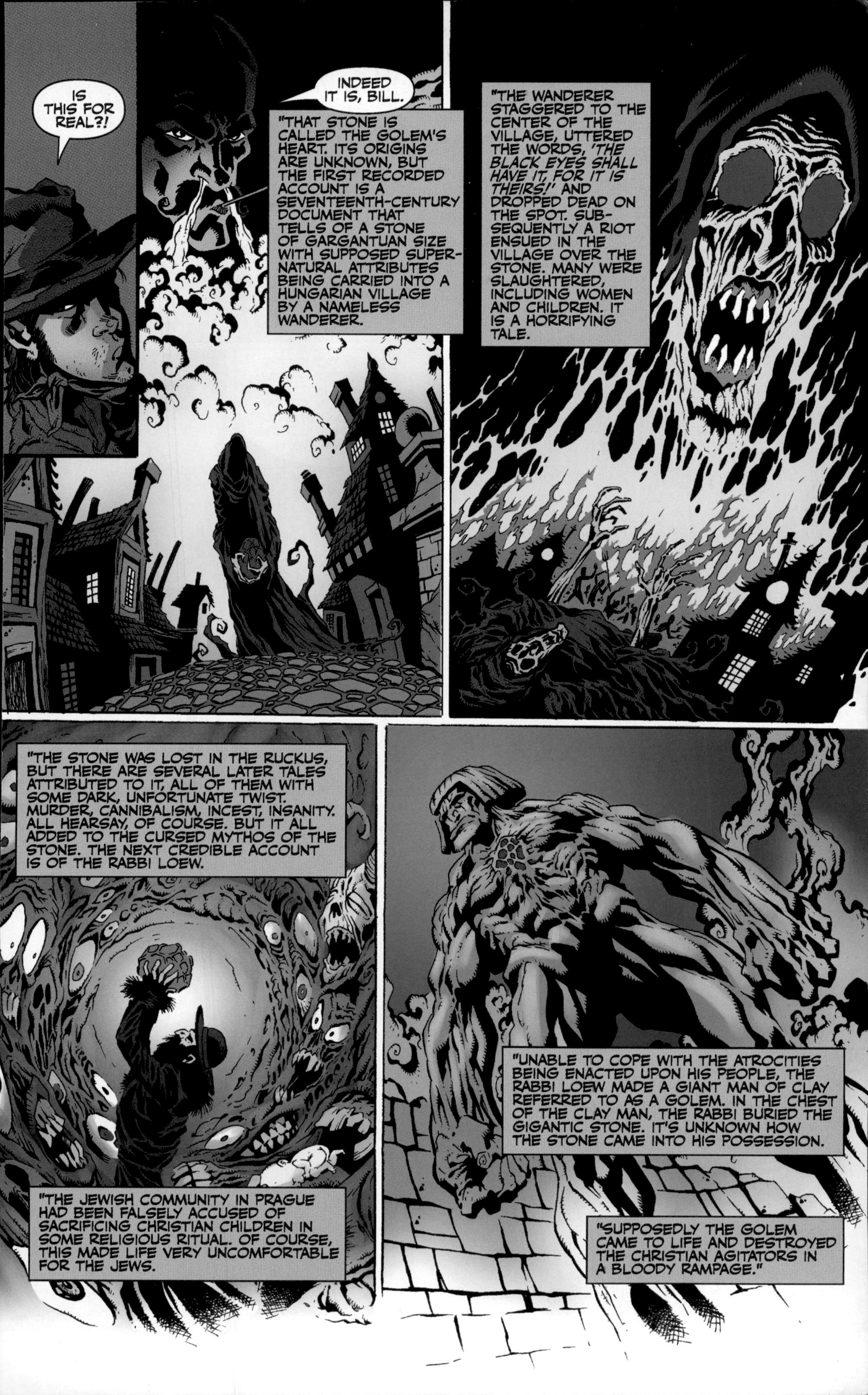
IS THIS FOR REAL?!
INDEED IT IS, BILL.
"THAT STONE IS CALLED THE GOLEM'S HEART. IT'S ORIGINS ARE UNKNOWN, BUT THE FIRST RECORDED ACCOUNT IS A SEVENTEENTH-CENTURY DOCUMENT THAT TELLS OF A STONE OF GARGANTUAN SIZE WITH SUPPOSED SUPER-NATURAL ATTRIBUTES BEING CARRIED INTO A HUNGARIAN VILLAGE BY A NAMELESS WANDERER.
"THE WANDERER STAGGERED TO THE CENTER OF THE VILLAGE, UTTERED THE WORDS, *'THE BLACK EYES SHALL HAVE IT, FOR IT IS THEIRS!'* AND DROPPED DEAD ON THE SPOT. SUB-SEQUENTLY A RIOT ENSUED IN THE VILLAGE OVER THE STONE. MANY WERE SLAUGHTERED, INCLUDING WOMEN AND CHILDREN. IT IS A HORRIFYING TALE.
"THE STONE WAS LOST IN THE RUCKUS, BUT THERE ARE SEVERAL LATER TALES ATTRIBUTED TO IT, ALL OF THEM WITH SOME DARK, UNFORTUNATE TWIST. MURDER, CANNIBALISM, INCEST, INSANITY. ALL HEARSAY, OF COURSE. BUT IT ALL ADDED TO THE CURSED MYTHOS OF THE STONE. THE NEXT CREDIBLE ACCOUNT IS OF THE RABBI LOEW.
"THE JEWISH COMMUNITY IN PRAGUE HAD BEEN FALSELY ACCUSED OF SACRIFICING CHRISTIAN CHILDREN IN SOME RELIGIOUS RITUAL. OF COURSE, THIS MADE LIFE VERY UNCOMFORTABLE FOR THE JEWS.
"UNABLE TO COPE WITH THE ATROCITIES BEING ENACTED UPON HIS PEOPLE, THE RABBI LOEW MADE A GIANT MAN OF CLAY REFERRED TO AS A GOLEM. IN THE CHEST OF THE CLAY MAN, THE RABBI BURIED THE GIGANTIC STONE. IT'S UNKNOWN HOW THE STONE CAME INTO HIS POSSESSION.
"SUPPOSEDLY THE GOLEM CAME TO LIFE AND DESTROYED THE CHRISTIAN AGITATORS IN A BLOODY RAMPAGE."

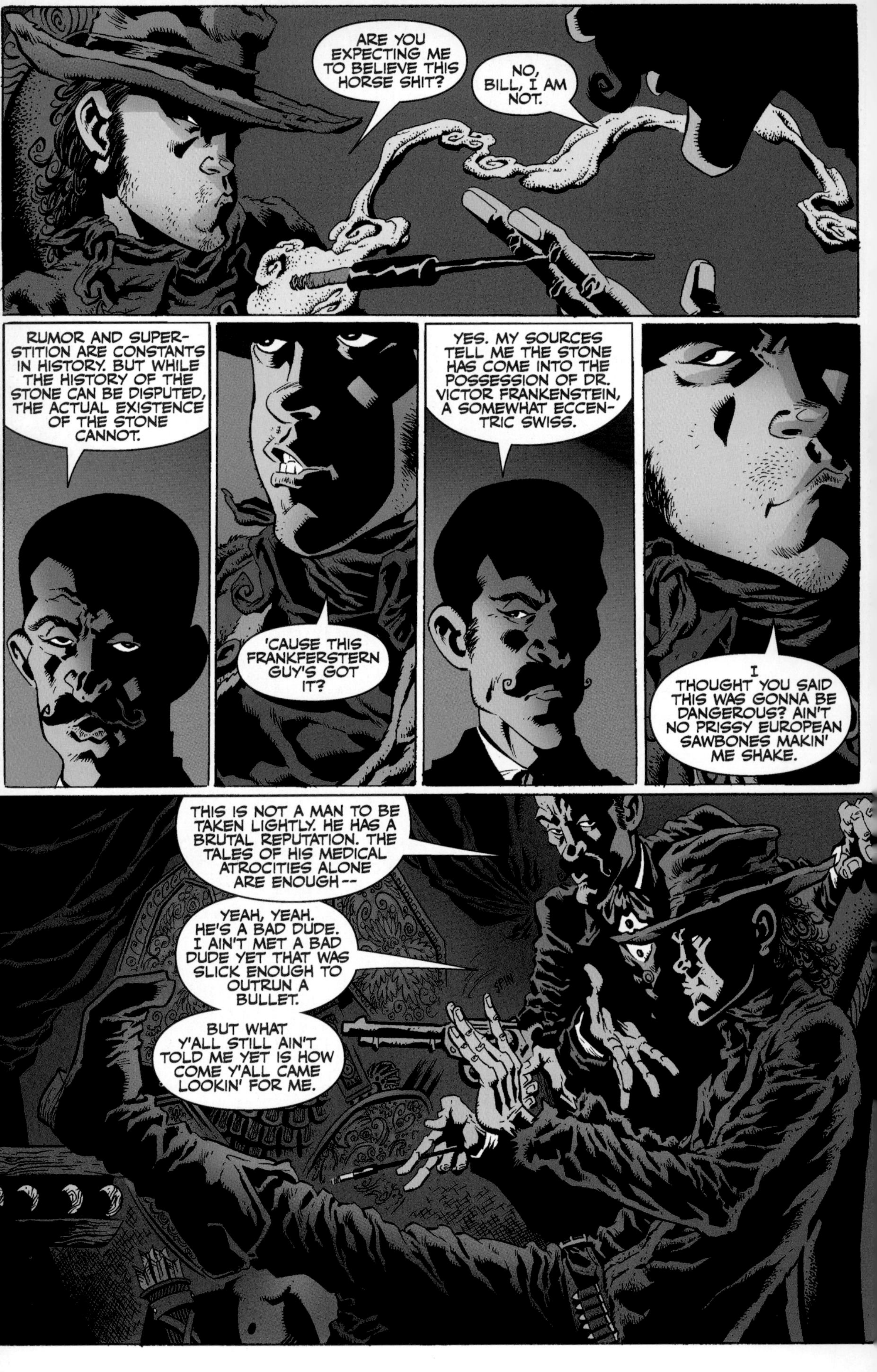
ARE YOU EXPECTING ME TO BELIEVE THIS HORSE SHIT?
NO, BILL, I AM NOT.
RUMOR AND SUPERSTITION ARE CONSTANTS IN HISTORY. BUT WHILE THE HISTORY OF THE STONE CAN BE DISPUTED, THE ACTUAL EXISTENCE OF THE STONE CANNOT.
'CAUSE THIS FRANKFERSTERN GUY'S GOT IT?
YES. MY SOURCES TELL ME THE STONE HAS COME INTO THE POSSESSION OF DR. VICTOR FRANKENSTEIN, A SOMEWHAT ECCENTRIC SWISS.
I THOUGHT YOU SAID THIS WAS GONNA BE DANGEROUS? AIN'T NO PRISSY EUROPEAN SAWBONES MAKIN' ME SHAKE.
THIS IS NOT A MAN TO BE TAKEN LIGHTLY. HE HAS A BRUTAL REPUTATION. THE TALES OF HIS MEDICAL ATROCITIES ALONE ARE ENOUGH--
YEAH, YEAH. HE'S A BAD DUDE. I AIN'T MET A BAD DUDE YET THAT WAS SLICK ENOUGH TO OUTRUN A BULLET.
BUT WHAT Y'ALL STILL AIN'T TOLD ME YET IS HOW COME Y'ALL CAME LOOKIN' FOR ME.

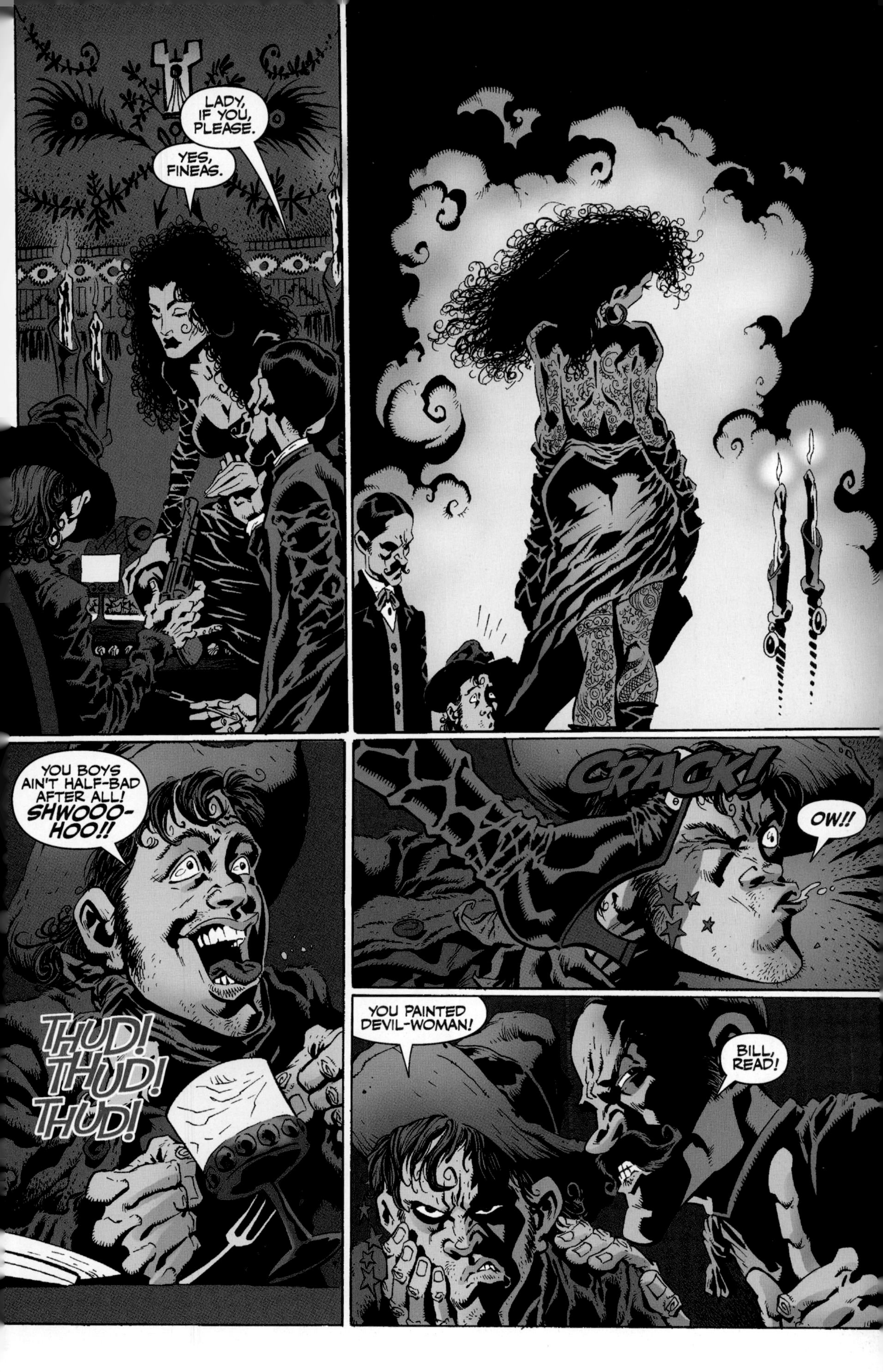
LADY, IF YOU, PLEASE.
YES, FINEAS.
YOU BOYS AIN'T HALF-BAD AFTER ALL! SHWOOO-HOO!!
THUD! THUD! THUD!
CRACK!
OW!!
YOU PAINTED DEVIL-WOMAN!
BILL, READ!

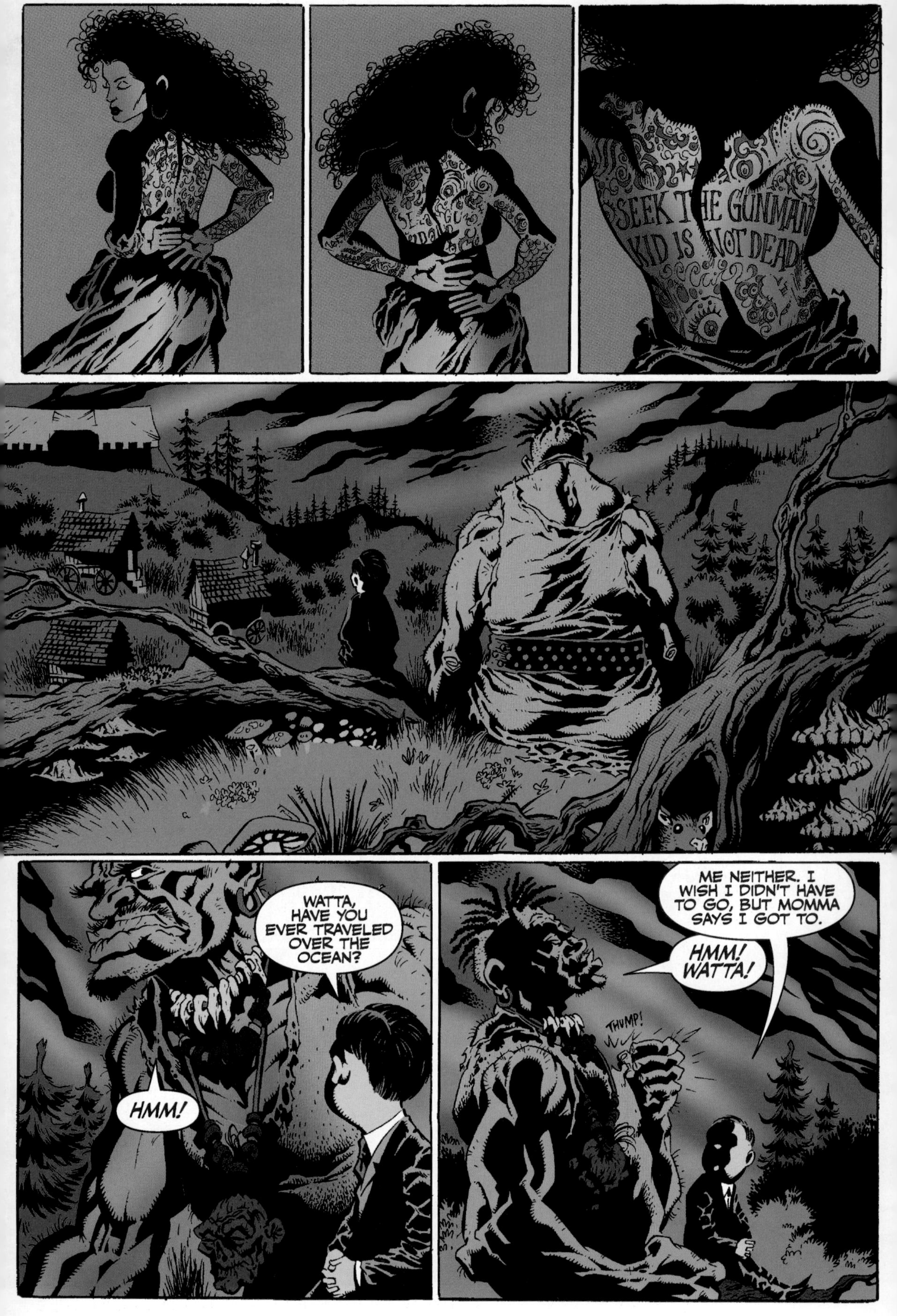
SEEK THE GUNMAN
KID IS NOT DEAD
WATTA, HAVE YOU EVER TRAVELED OVER THE OCEAN?
HMM!
ME NEITHER. I WISH I DIDN'T HAVE TO GO, BUT MOMMA SAYS I GOT TO.
HMM! WATTA!
THUMP!

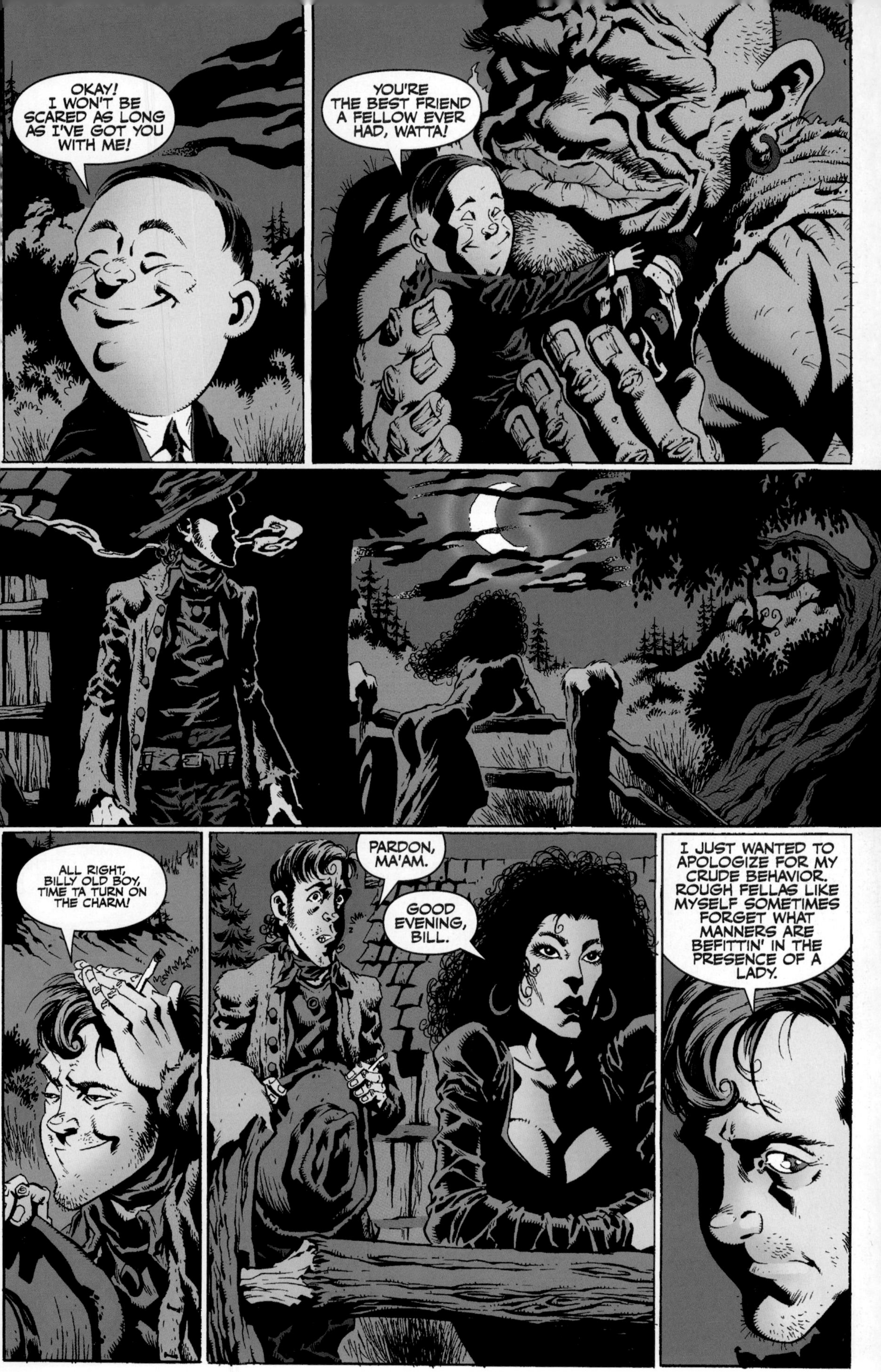
OKAY! I WON'T BE SCARED AS LONG AS I'VE GOT YOU WITH ME!
YOU'RE THE BEST FRIEND A FELLOW EVER HAD, WATTA!
ALL RIGHT, BILLY OLD BOY, TIME TA TURN ON THE CHARM!
PARDON, MA'AM.
GOOD EVENING, BILL.
I JUST WANTED TO APOLOGIZE FOR MY CRUDE BEHAVIOR. ROUGH FELLAS LIKE MYSELF SOMETIMES FORGET WHAT MANNERS ARE BEFITTIN' IN THE PRESENCE OF A LADY.

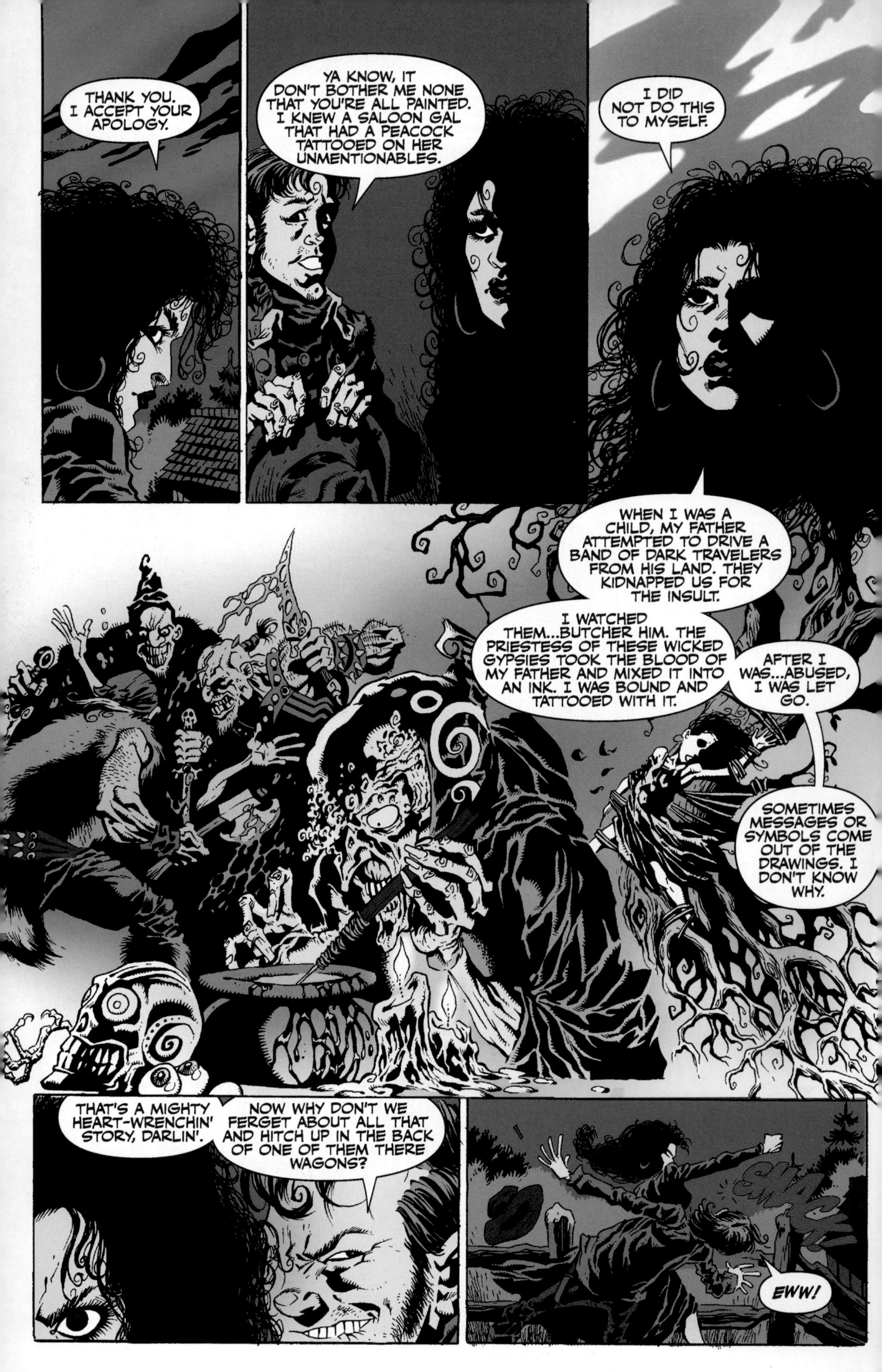
THANK YOU. I ACCEPT YOUR APOLOGY.
YA KNOW, IT DON'T BOTHER ME NONE THAT YOU'RE ALL PAINTED. I KNEW A SALOON GAL THAT HAD A PEACOCK TATTOOED ON HER UNMENTIONABLES.
I DID NOT DO THIS TO MYSELF.
WHEN I WAS A CHILD, MY FATHER ATTEMPTED TO DRIVE A BAND OF DARK TRAVELERS FROM HIS LAND. THEY KIDNAPPED US FOR THE INSULT.
I WATCHED THEM...BUTCHER HIM. THE PRIESTESS OF THESE WICKED GYPSIES TOOK THE BLOOD OF MY FATHER AND MIXED IT INTO AN INK. I WAS BOUND AND TATTOOED WITH IT.
AFTER I WAS...ABUSED, I WAS LET GO.
SOMETIMES MESSAGES OR SYMBOLS COME OUT OF THE DRAWINGS. I DON'T KNOW WHY.
THAT'S A MIGHTY HEART-WRENCHIN' STORY, DARLIN'.
NOW WHY DON'T WE FERGET ABOUT ALL THAT AND HITCH UP IN THE BACK OF ONE OF THEM THERE WAGONS?
SMACK!
EWW!

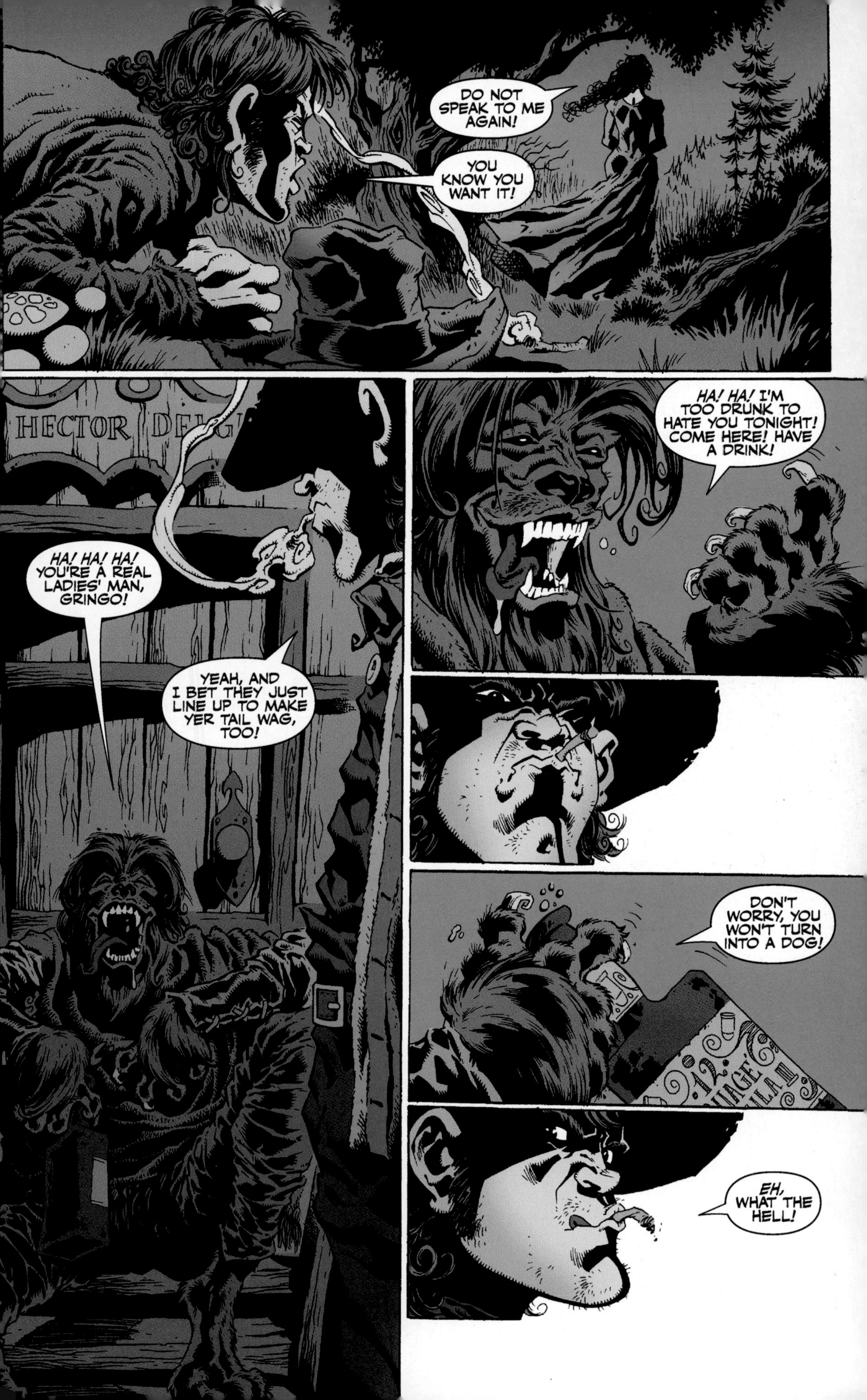
DO NOT SPEAK TO ME AGAIN!
YOU KNOW YOU WANT IT!
HECTOR DELG
HA! HA! HA! YOU'RE A REAL LADIES' MAN, GRINGO!
YEAH, AND I BET THEY JUST LINE UP TO MAKE YER TAIL WAG, TOO!
HA! HA! I'M TOO DRUNK TO HATE YOU TONIGHT! COME HERE! HAVE A DRINK!
DON'T WORRY, YOU WON'T TURN INTO A DOG!
EH, WHAT THE HELL!

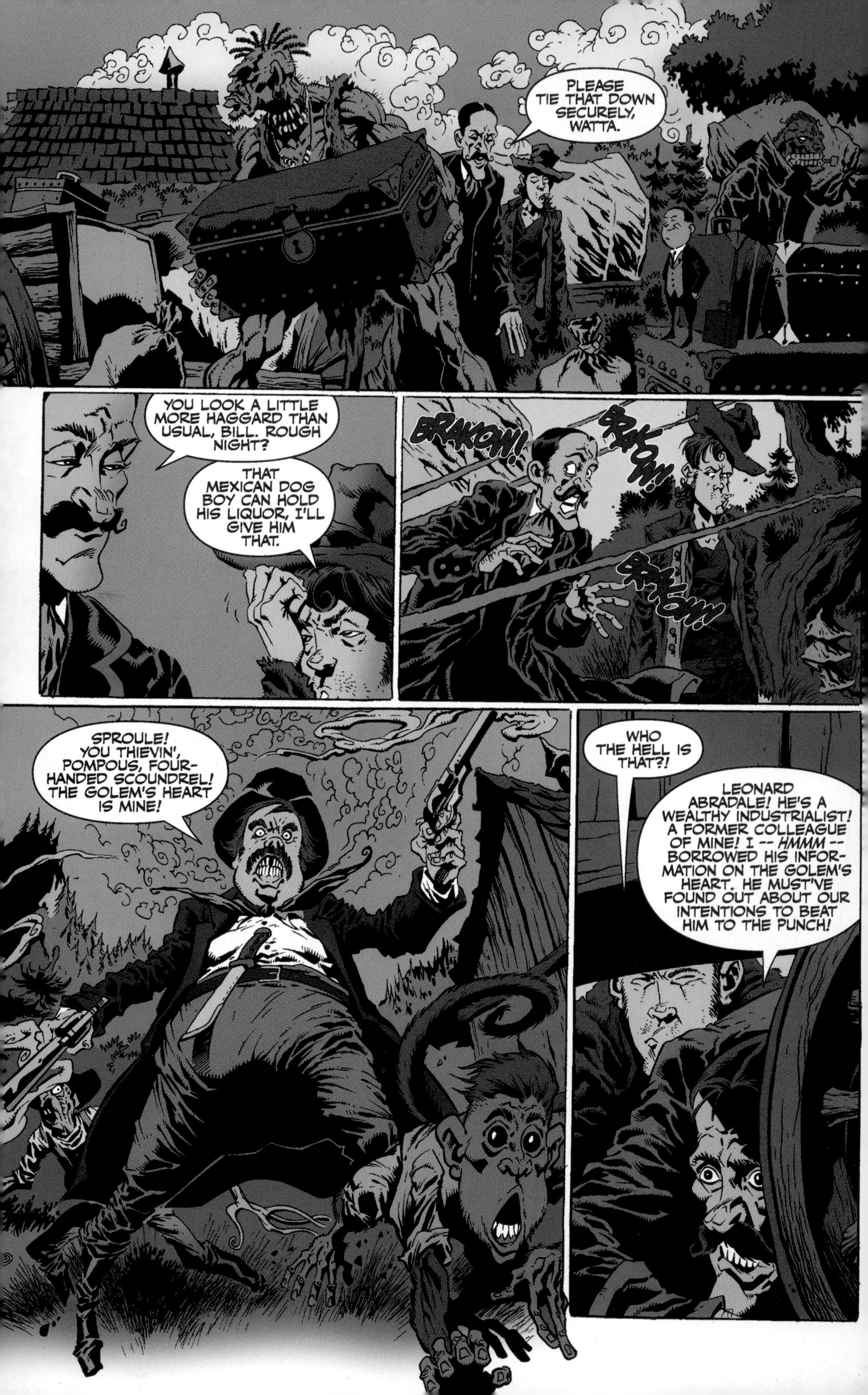
PLEASE TIE THAT DOWN SECURELY, WATTA.
YOU LOOK A LITTLE MORE HAGGARD THAN USUAL, BILL. ROUGH NIGHT?
THAT MEXICAN DOG BOY CAN HOLD HIS LIQUOR, I'LL GIVE HIM THAT.
BRAKOW!
BRAKOW!
BRAKOW!
SPROULE! YOU THIEVIN', POMPOUS, FOUR-HANDED SCOUNDREL! THE GOLEM'S HEART IS MINE!
WHO THE HELL IS THAT?!
LEONARD ABRADALE! HE'S A WEALTHY INDUSTRIALIST! A FORMER COLLEAGUE OF MINE! I -- *HMMM* -- BORROWED HIS INFORMATION ON THE GOLEM'S HEART. HE MUST'VE FOUND OUT ABOUT OUR INTENTIONS TO BEAT HIM TO THE PUNCH!

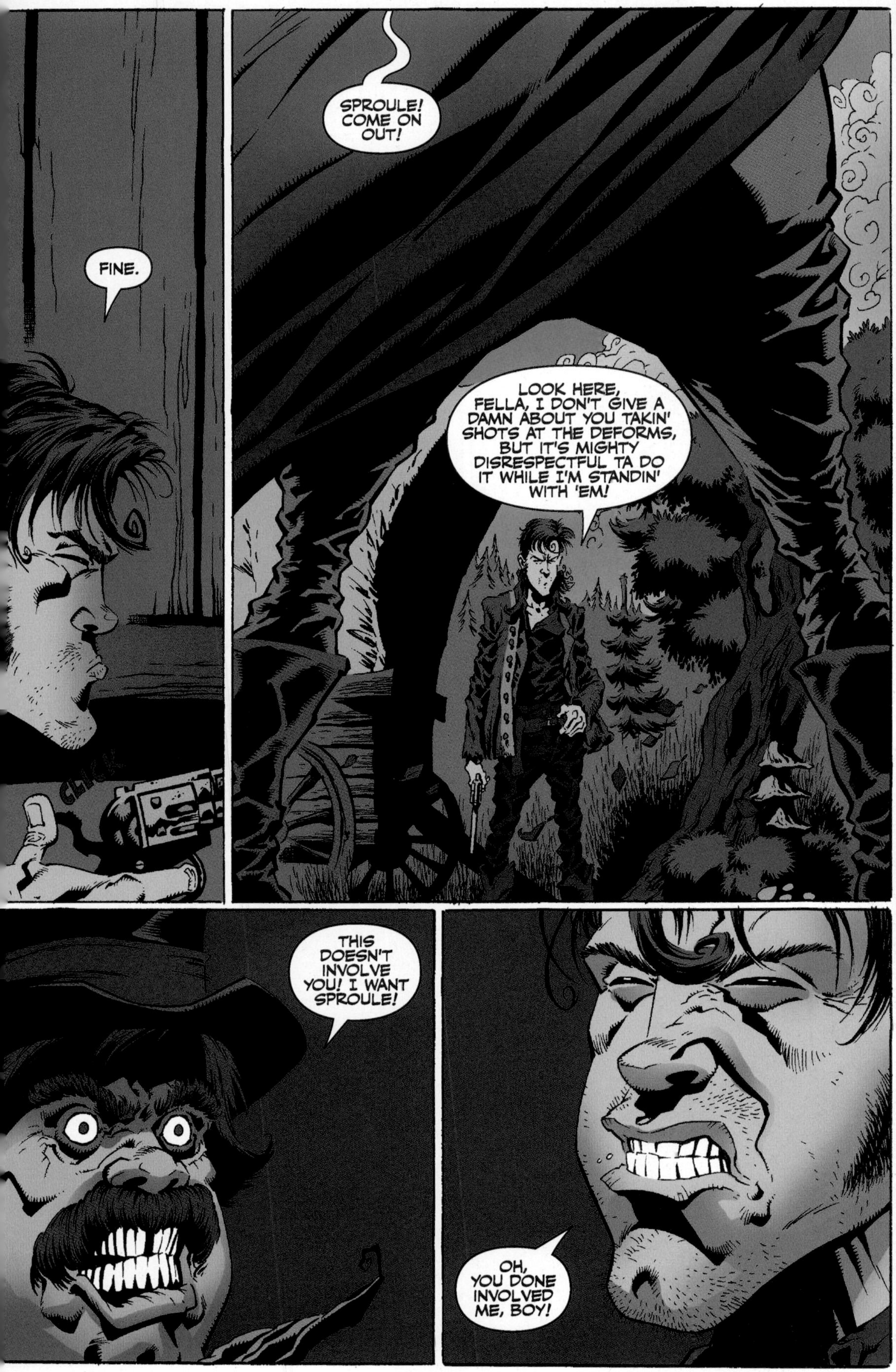
SPROULE! COME ON OUT!
FINE.
CLICK
LOOK HERE, FELLA, I DON'T GIVE A DAMN ABOUT YOU TAKIN' SHOTS AT THE DEFORMS, BUT IT'S MIGHTY DISRESPECTFUL TA DO IT WHILE I'M STANDIN' WITH 'EM!
THIS DOESN'T INVOLVE YOU! I WANT SPROULE!
OH, YOU DONE INVOLVED ME, BOY!

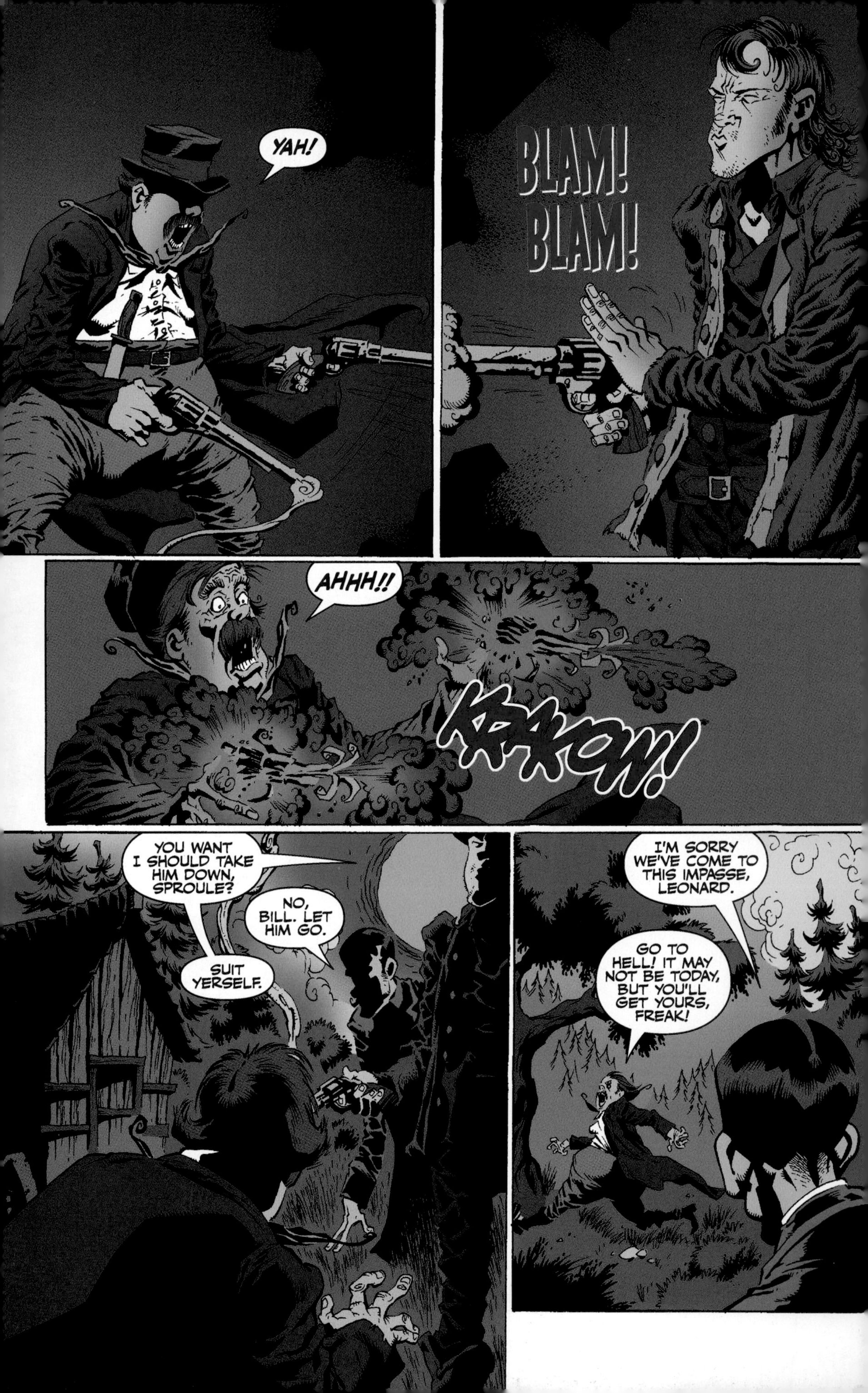
YAH!
BLAM! BLAM!
AHHH!!
KRAKOW!!
YOU WANT I SHOULD TAKE HIM DOWN, SPROULE?
NO, BILL. LET HIM GO.
SUIT YERSELF.
I'M SORRY WE'VE COME TO THIS IMPASSE, LEONARD.
GO TO HELL! IT MAY NOT BE TODAY, BUT YOU'LL GET YOURS, FREAK!

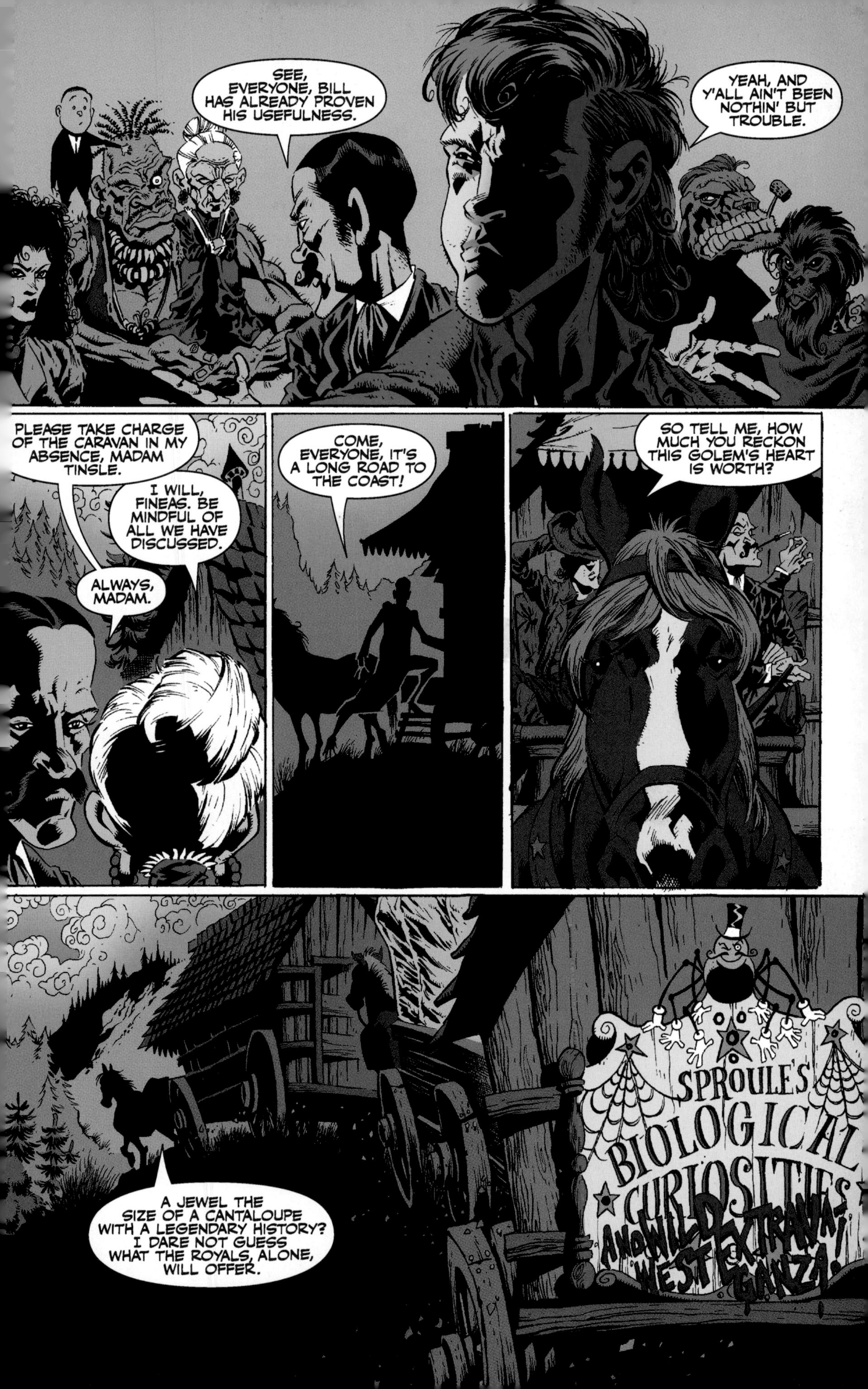
SEE, EVERYONE, BILL HAS ALREADY PROVEN HIS USEFULNESS.
YEAH, AND Y'ALL AIN'T BEEN NOTHIN' BUT TROUBLE.
PLEASE TAKE CHARGE OF THE CARAVAN IN MY ABSENCE, MADAM TINSLE.
I WILL, FINEAS. BE MINDFUL OF ALL WE HAVE DISCUSSED.
ALWAYS, MADAM.
COME, EVERYONE, IT'S A LONG ROAD TO THE COAST!
SO TELL ME, HOW MUCH YOU RECKON THIS GOLEM'S HEART IS WORTH?
SPROULE'S BIOLOGICAL CURIOSITIES AND WILD WEST EXTRAVA-GANZA!
A JEWEL THE SIZE OF A CANTALOUPE WITH A LEGENDARY HISTORY? I DARE NOT GUESS WHAT THE ROYALS, ALONE, WILL OFFER.

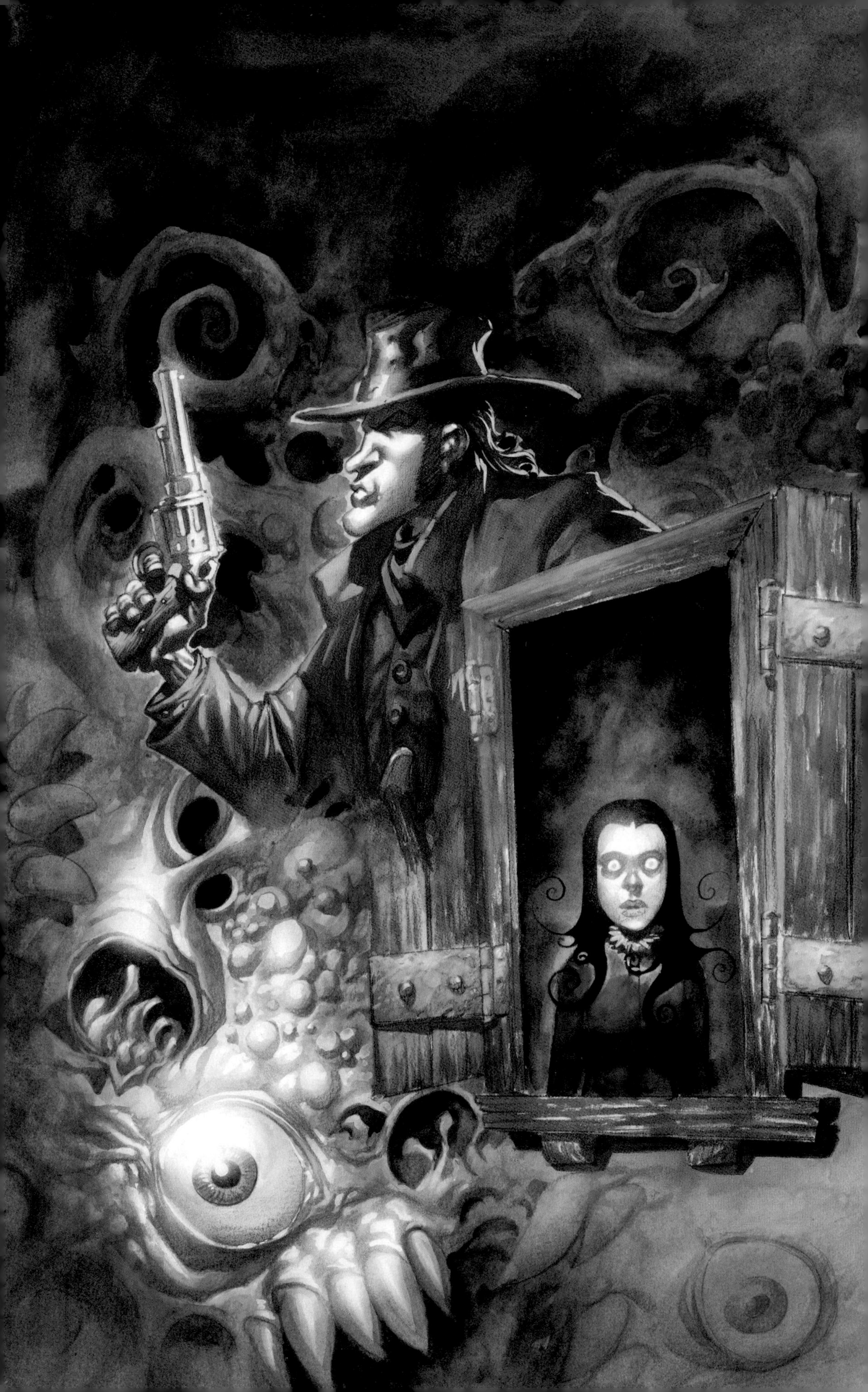

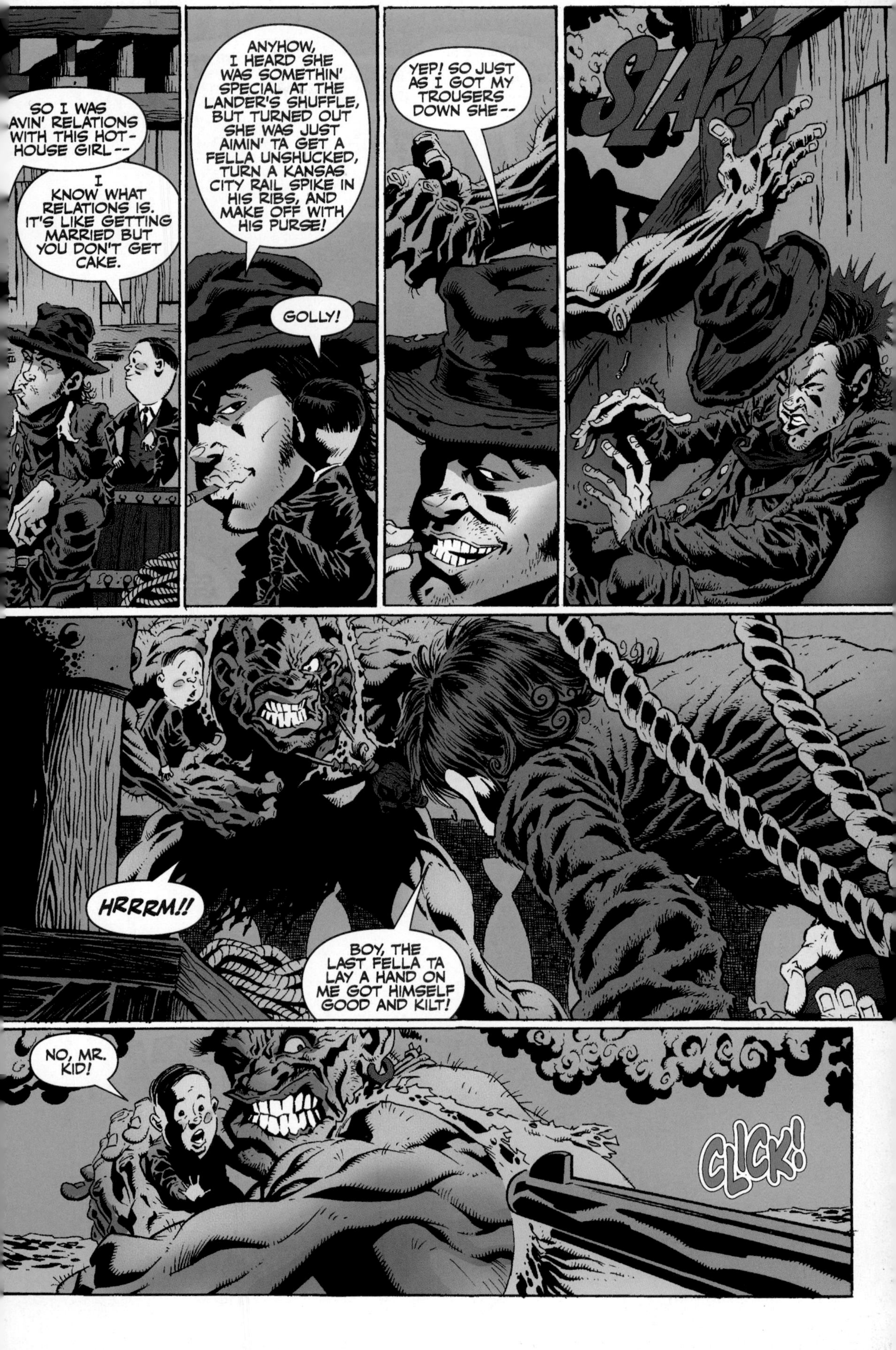
SO I WAS AVIN' RELATIONS WITH THIS HOT-HOUSE GIRL--
I KNOW WHAT RELATIONS IS. IT'S LIKE GETTING MARRIED BUT YOU DON'T GET CAKE.
ANYHOW, I HEARD SHE WAS SOMETHIN' SPECIAL AT THE LANDER'S SHUFFLE, BUT TURNED OUT SHE WAS JUST AIMIN' TA GET A FELLA UNSHUCKED, TURN A KANSAS CITY RAIL SPIKE IN HIS RIBS, AND MAKE OFF WITH HIS PURSE!
GOLLY!
YEP! SO JUST AS I GOT MY TROUSERS DOWN SHE--
SLAP!
HRRRM!!
BOY, THE LAST FELLA TA LAY A HAND ON ME GOT HIMSELF GOOD AND KILT!
NO, MR. KID!
CLICK!

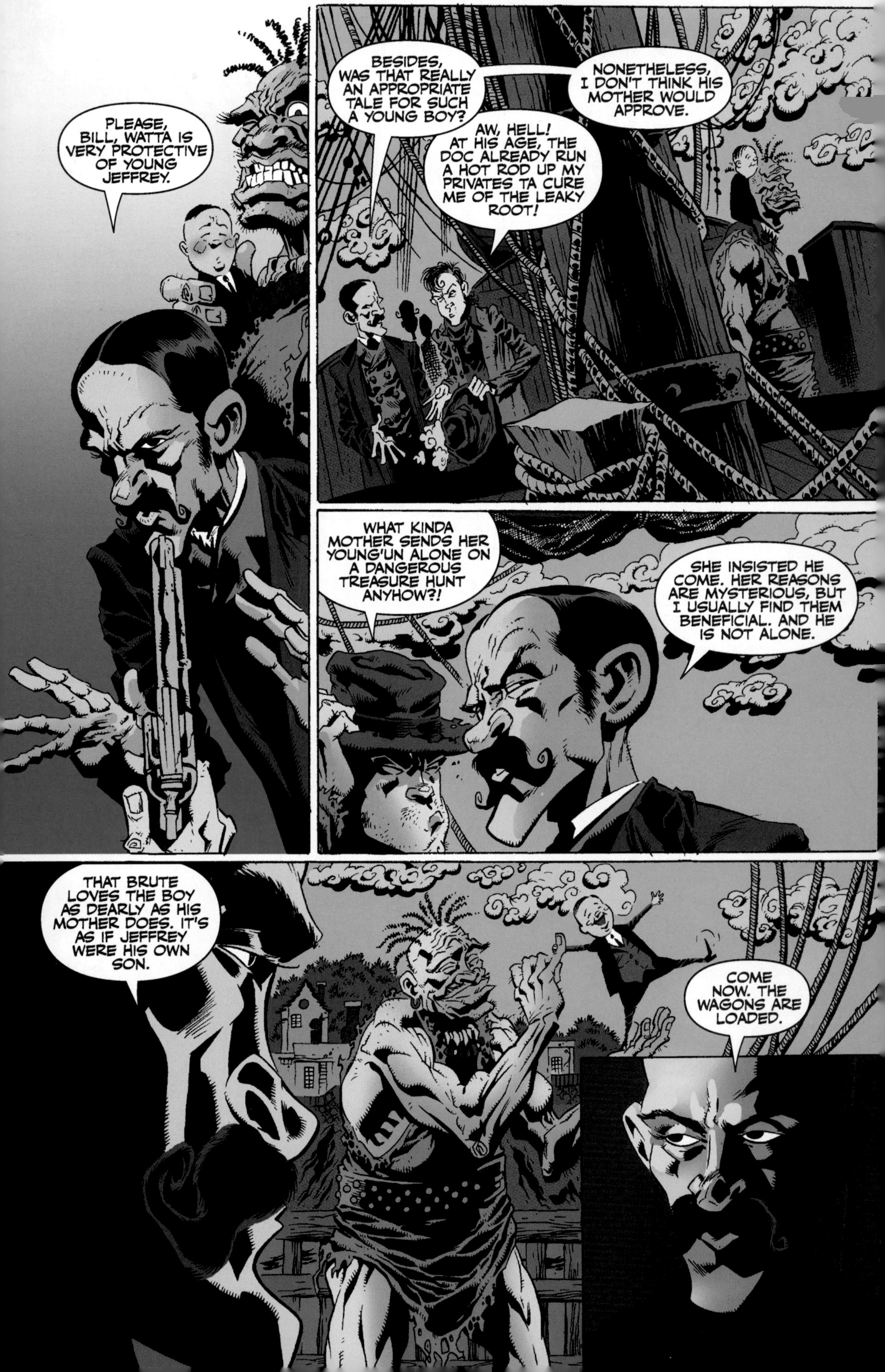
PLEASE, BILL, WATTA IS VERY PROTECTIVE OF YOUNG JEFFREY.
BESIDES, WAS THAT REALLY AN APPROPRIATE TALE FOR SUCH A YOUNG BOY?
NONETHELESS, I DON'T THINK HIS MOTHER WOULD APPROVE.
AW, HELL! AT HIS AGE, THE DOC ALREADY RUN A HOT ROD UP MY PRIVATES TA CURE ME OF THE LEAKY ROOT!
WHAT KINDA MOTHER SENDS HER YOUNG'UN ALONE ON A DANGEROUS TREASURE HUNT ANYHOW?!
SHE INSISTED HE COME. HER REASONS ARE MYSTERIOUS, BUT I USUALLY FIND THEM BENEFICIAL. AND HE IS NOT ALONE.
THAT BRUTE LOVES THE BOY AS DEARLY AS HIS MOTHER DOES. IT'S AS IF JEFFREY WERE HIS OWN SON.
COME NOW. THE WAGONS ARE LOADED.

"TIME FOR OUR LITTLE ADVENTURE TO BEGIN."

WHERE IN THE HELL ARE WE GOIN'?

THERE AIN'T NO VILLAGE ON THIS MAP!

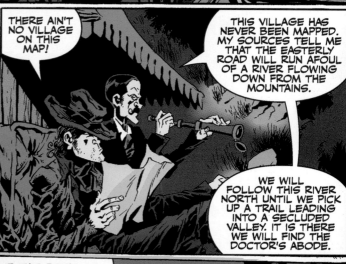

THIS VILLAGE HAS NEVER BEEN MAPPED. MY SOURCES TELL ME THAT THE EASTERLY ROAD WILL RUN AFOUL OF A RIVER FLOWING DOWN FROM THE MOUNTAINS.

WE WILL FOLLOW THIS RIVER NORTH UNTIL WE PICK UP A TRAIL LEADING INTO A SECLUDED VALLEY. IT IS THERE WE WILL FIND THE DOCTOR'S ABODE.

IF THIS DOC'S SO HIGH AND MIGHTY, RICH AND ALL, WHY IS HE LIVIN' IN THE MIDDLE OF NOWHERE?

HIS "INTERESTS" ARE BETTER EXPLORED IN SECLUSION.

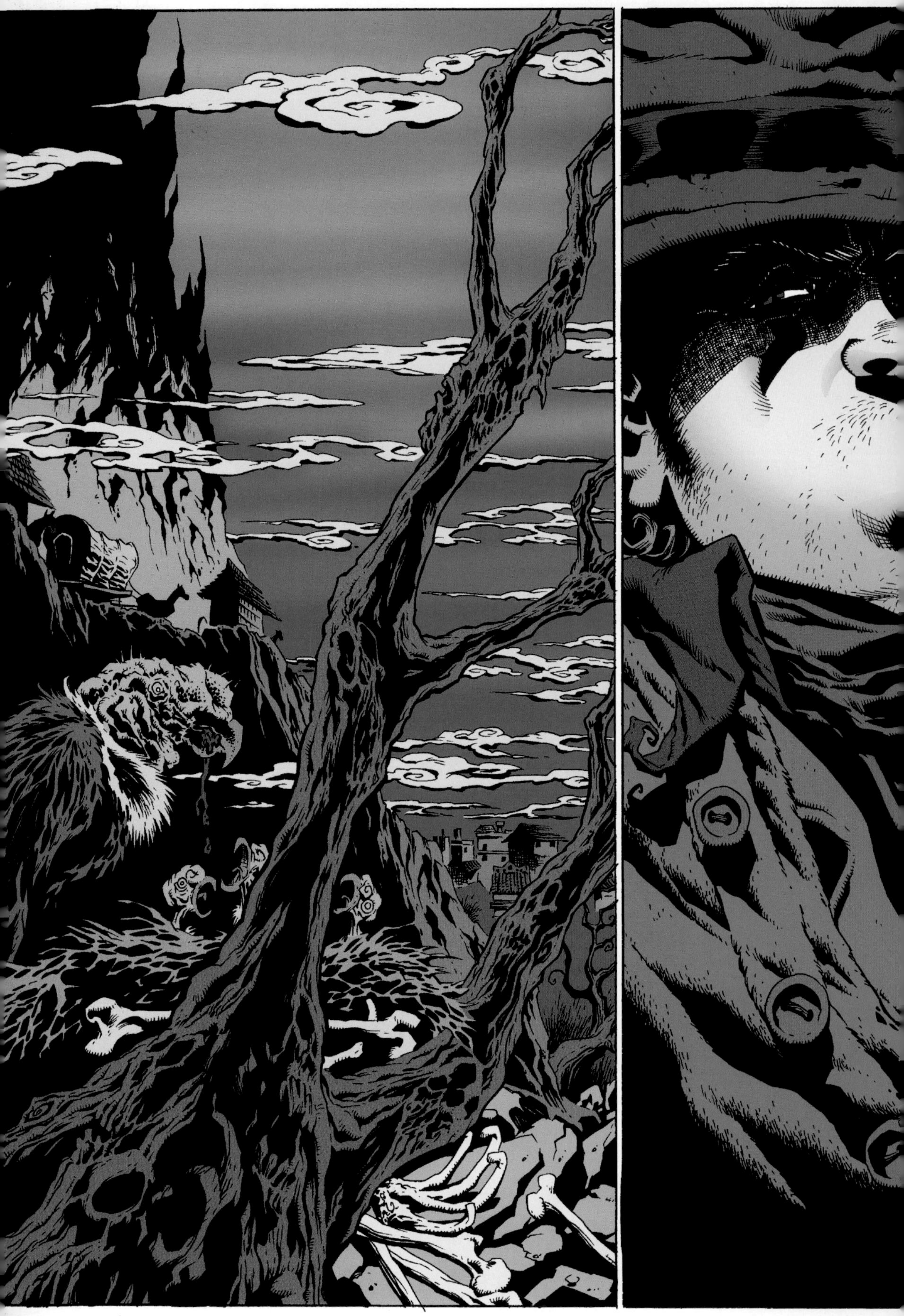

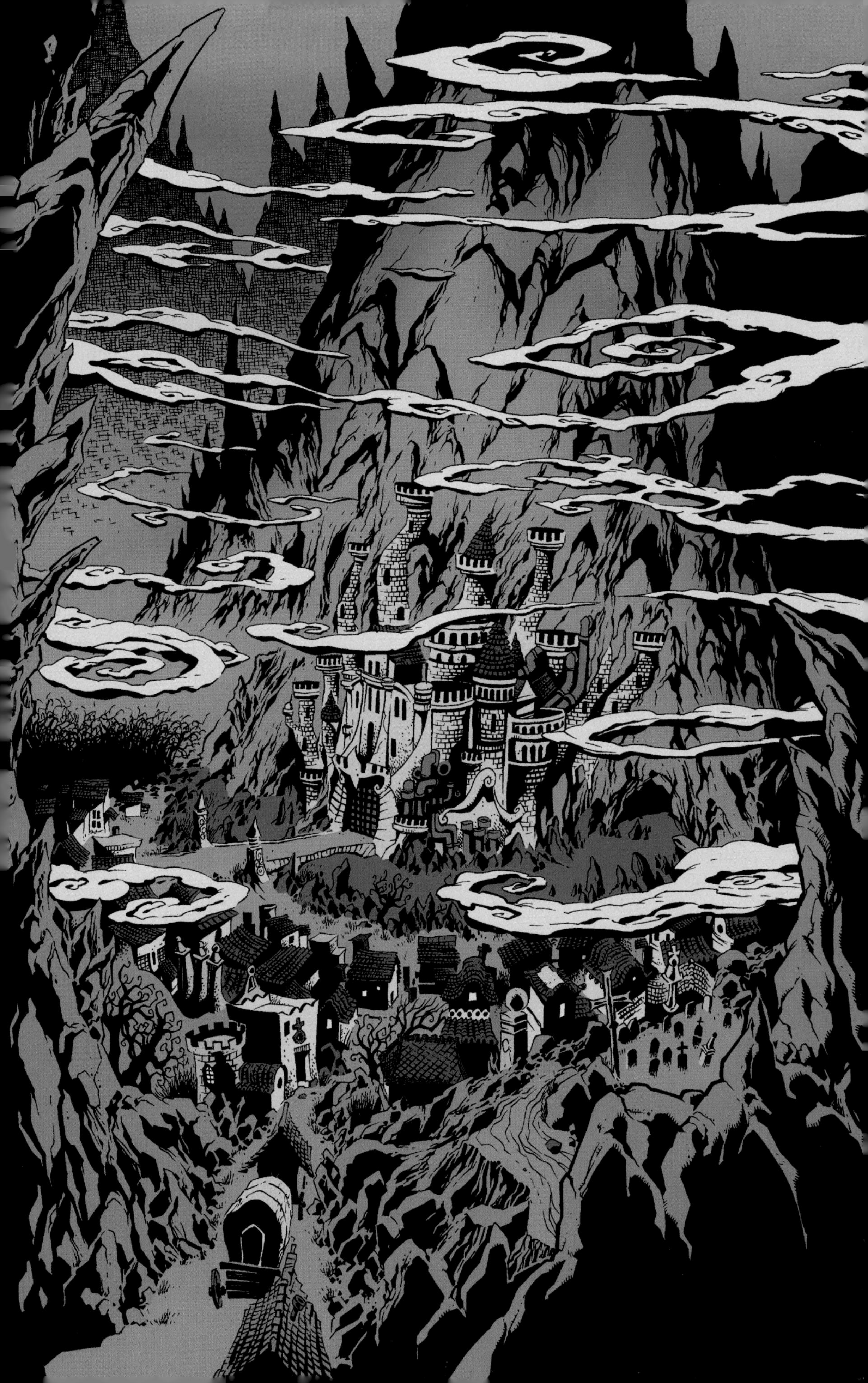

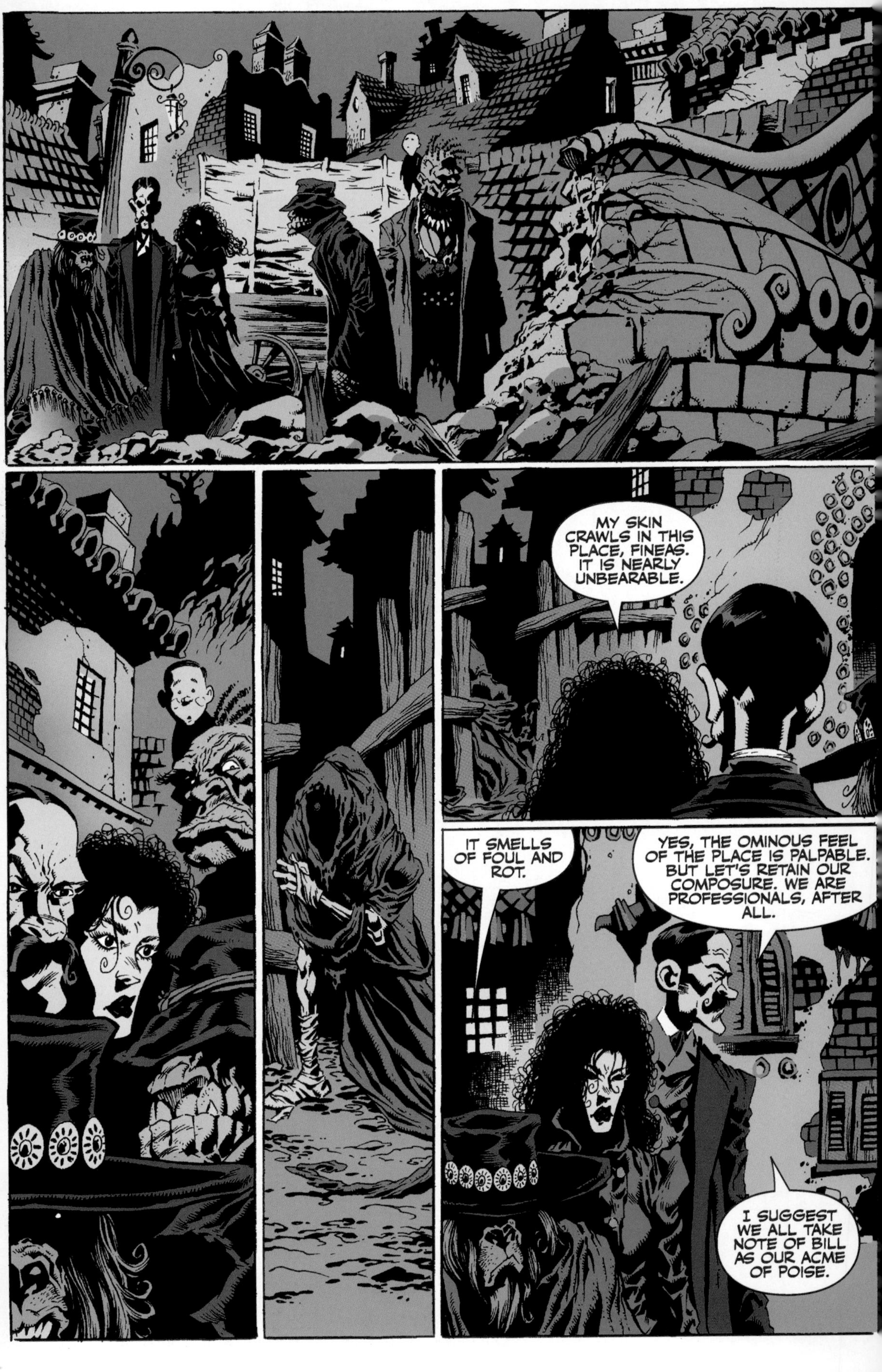
MY SKIN CRAWLS IN THIS PLACE, FINEAS. IT IS NEARLY UNBEARABLE.
IT SMELLS OF FOUL AND ROT.
YES, THE OMINOUS FEEL OF THE PLACE IS PALPABLE. BUT LET'S RETAIN OUR COMPOSURE. WE ARE PROFESSIONALS, AFTER ALL.
I SUGGEST WE ALL TAKE NOTE OF BILL AS OUR ACME OF POISE.

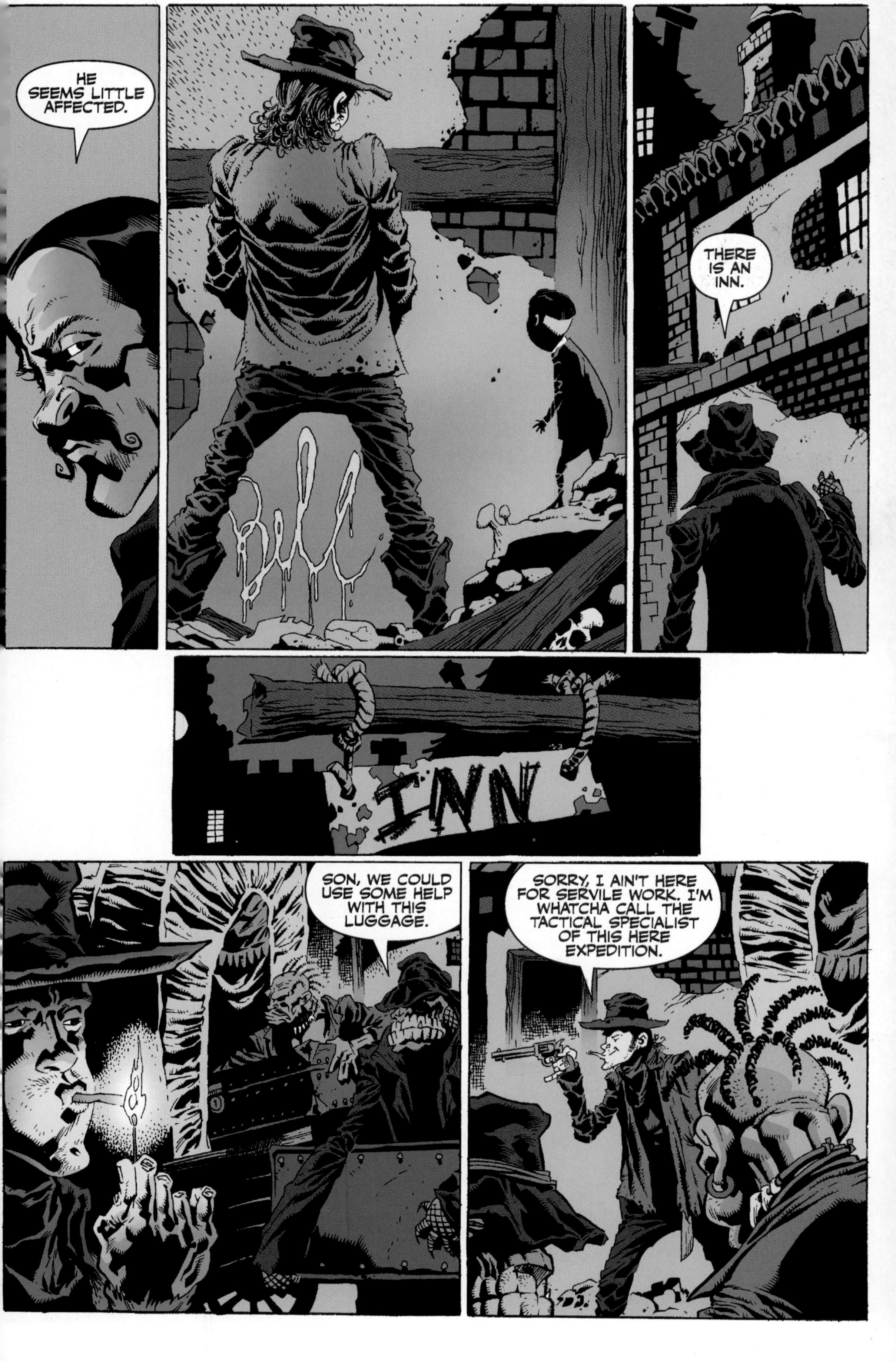
HE SEEMS LITTLE AFFECTED.
THERE IS AN INN.
INN
SON, WE COULD USE SOME HELP WITH THIS LUGGAGE.
SORRY, I AIN'T HERE FOR SERVILE WORK. I'M WHATCHA CALL THE TACTICAL SPECIALIST OF THIS HERE EXPEDITION.

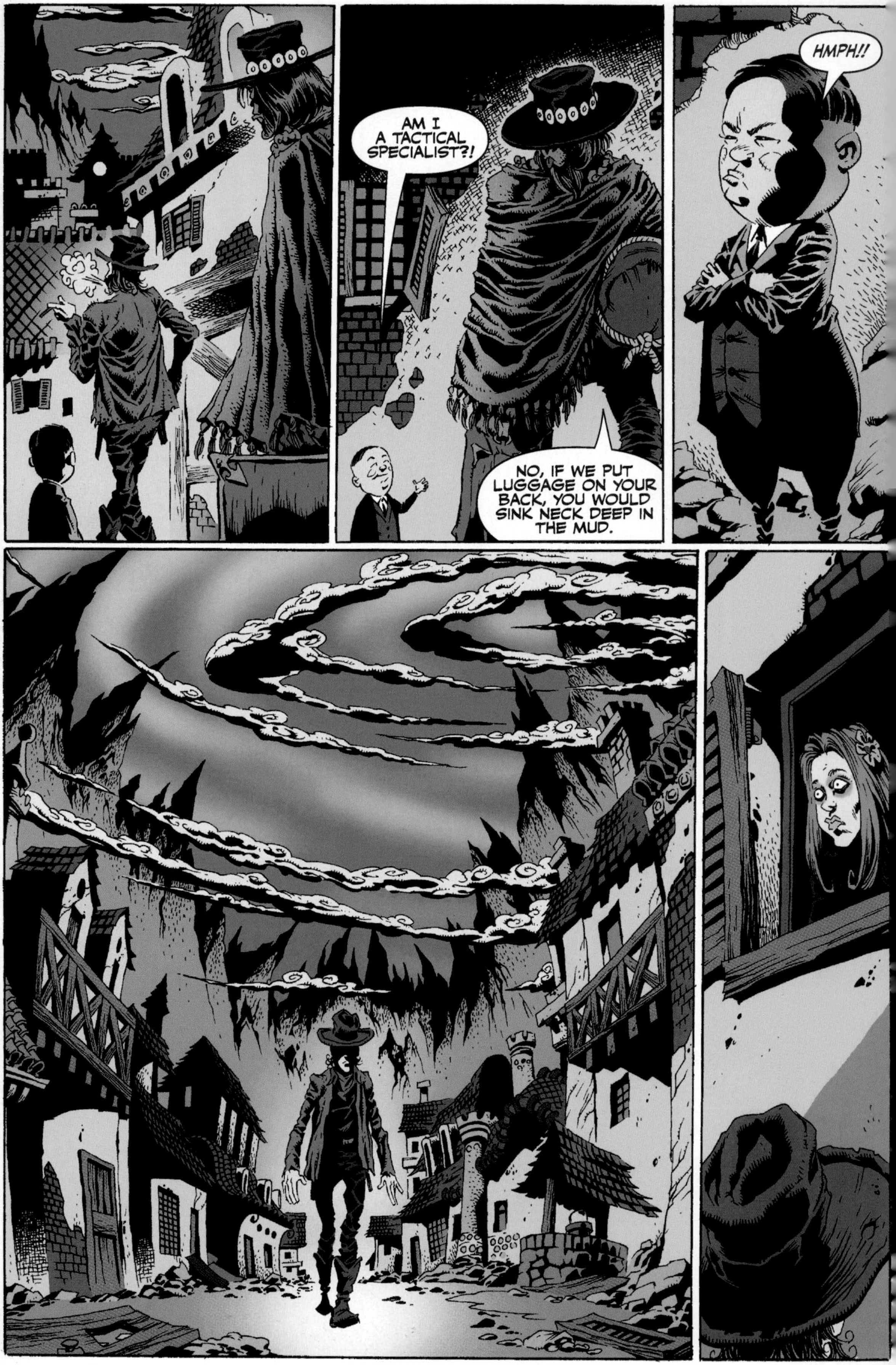
AM I A TACTICAL SPECIALIST?!
NO, IF WE PUT LUGGAGE ON YOUR BACK, YOU WOULD SINK NECK DEEP IN THE MUD.
HMPH!!

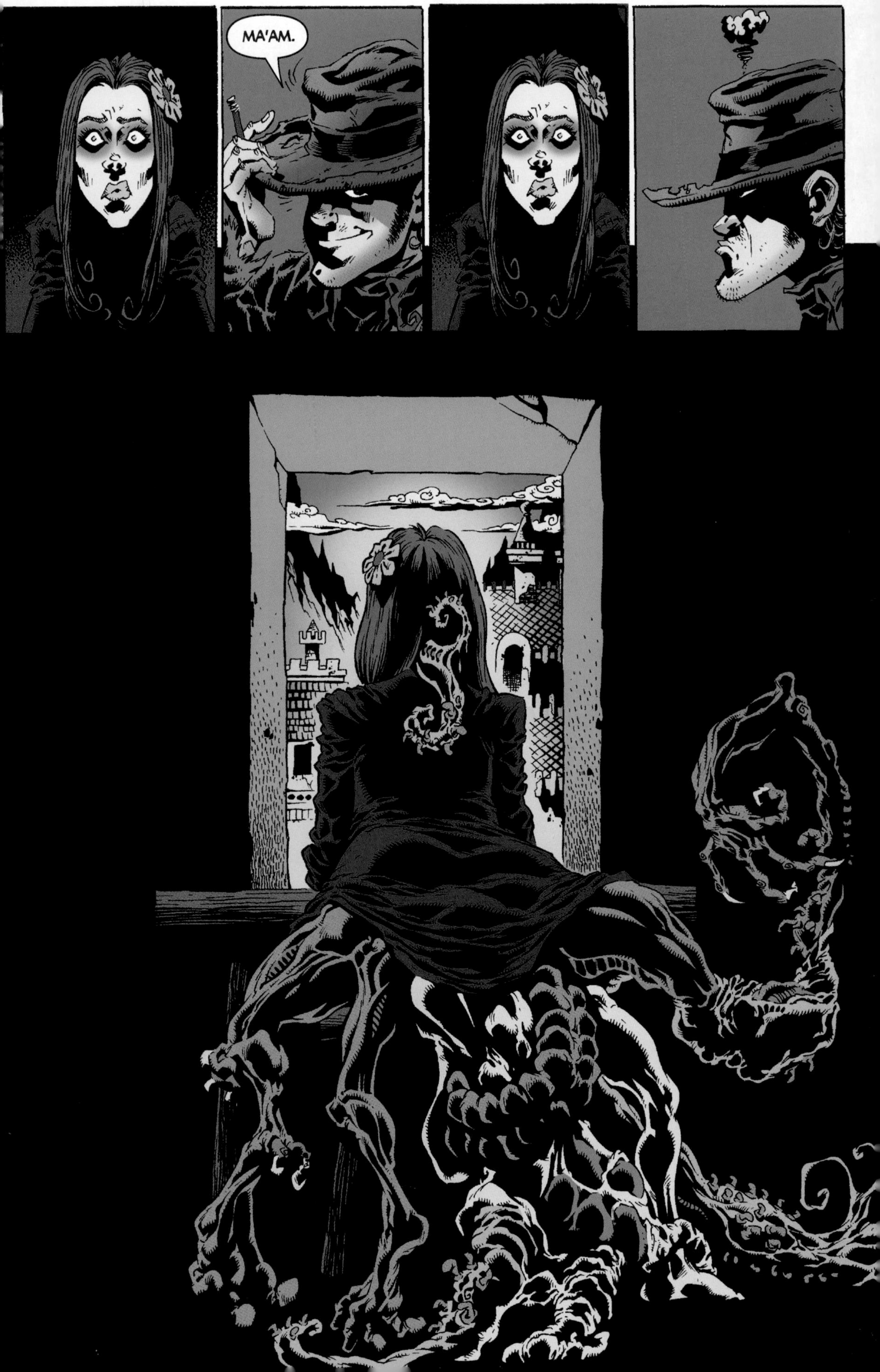
MA'AM.

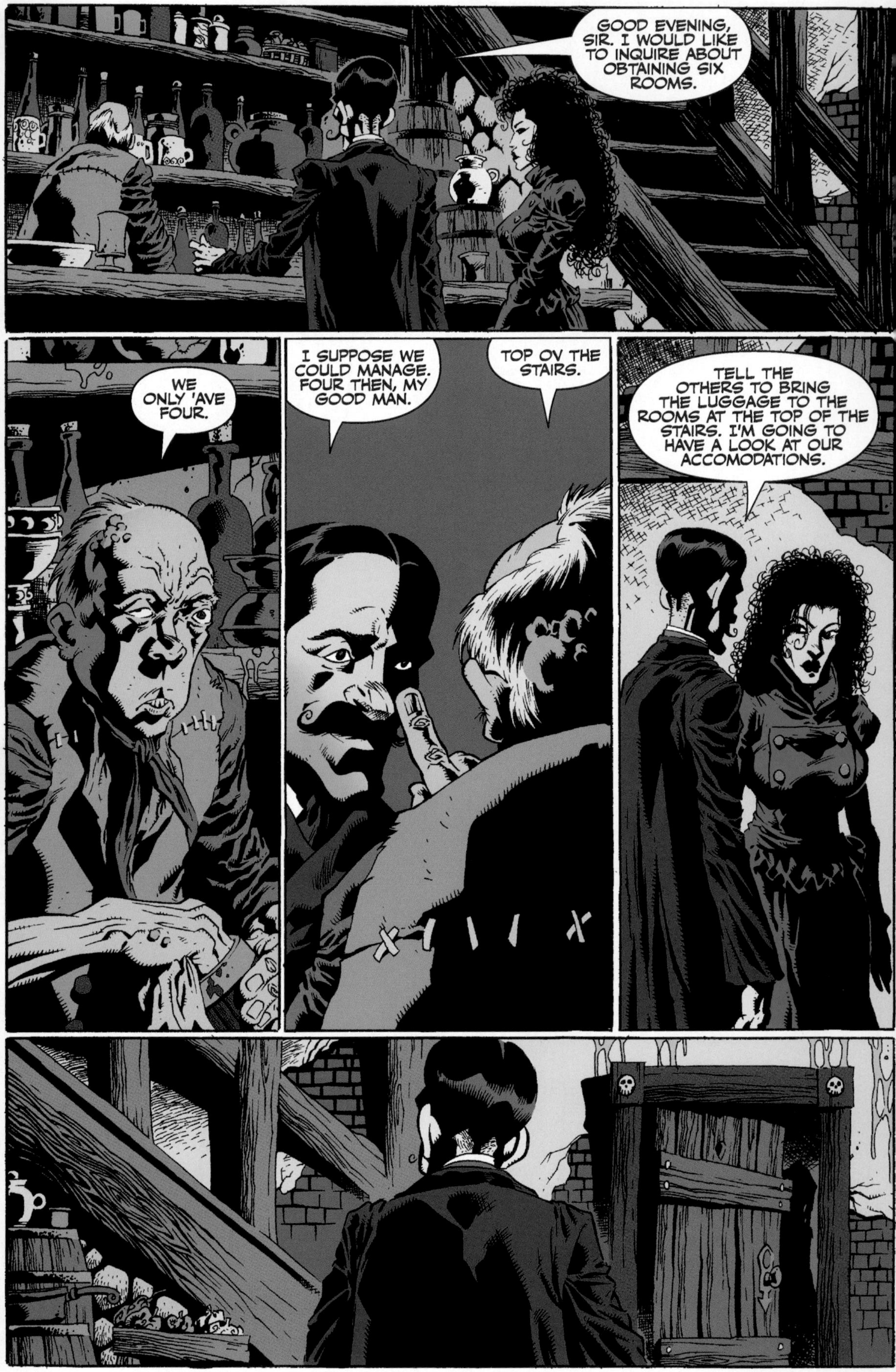
GOOD EVENING, SIR. I WOULD LIKE TO INQUIRE ABOUT OBTAINING SIX ROOMS.
WE ONLY 'AVE FOUR.
I SUPPOSE WE COULD MANAGE. FOUR THEN, MY GOOD MAN.
TOP OV THE STAIRS.
TELL THE OTHERS TO BRING THE LUGGAGE TO THE ROOMS AT THE TOP OF THE STAIRS. I'M GOING TO HAVE A LOOK AT OUR ACCOMODATIONS.

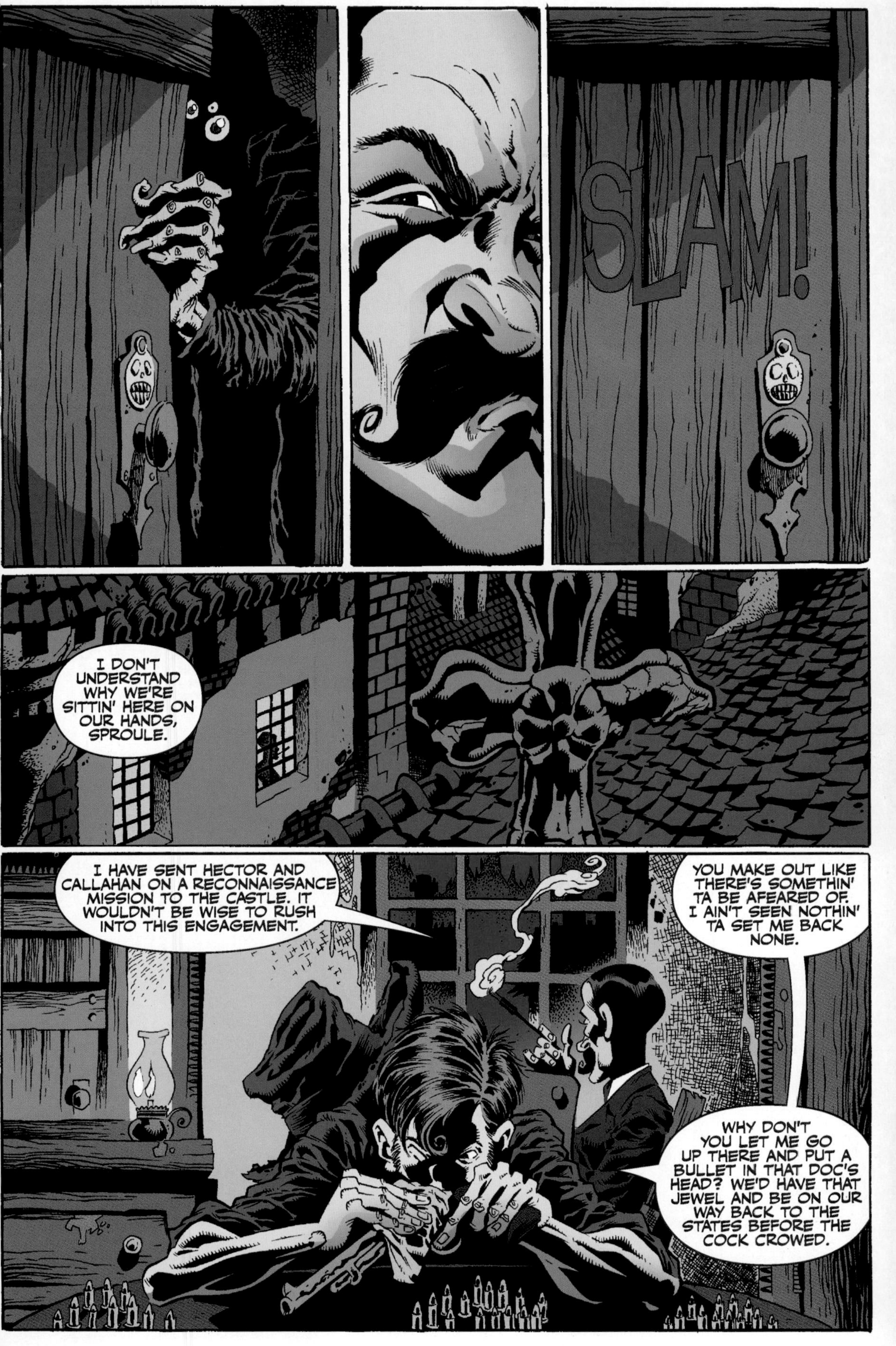
SLAM!
I DON'T UNDERSTAND WHY WE'RE SITTIN' HERE ON OUR HANDS, SPROULE.
I HAVE SENT HECTOR AND CALLAHAN ON A RECONNAISSANCE MISSION TO THE CASTLE. IT WOULDN'T BE WISE TO RUSH INTO THIS ENGAGEMENT.
YOU MAKE OUT LIKE THERE'S SOMETHIN' TA BE AFEARED OF. I AIN'T SEEN NOTHIN' TA SET ME BACK NONE.
WHY DON'T YOU LET ME GO UP THERE AND PUT A BULLET IN THAT DOC'S HEAD? WE'D HAVE THAT JEWEL AND BE ON OUR WAY BACK TO THE STATES BEFORE THE COCK CROWED.

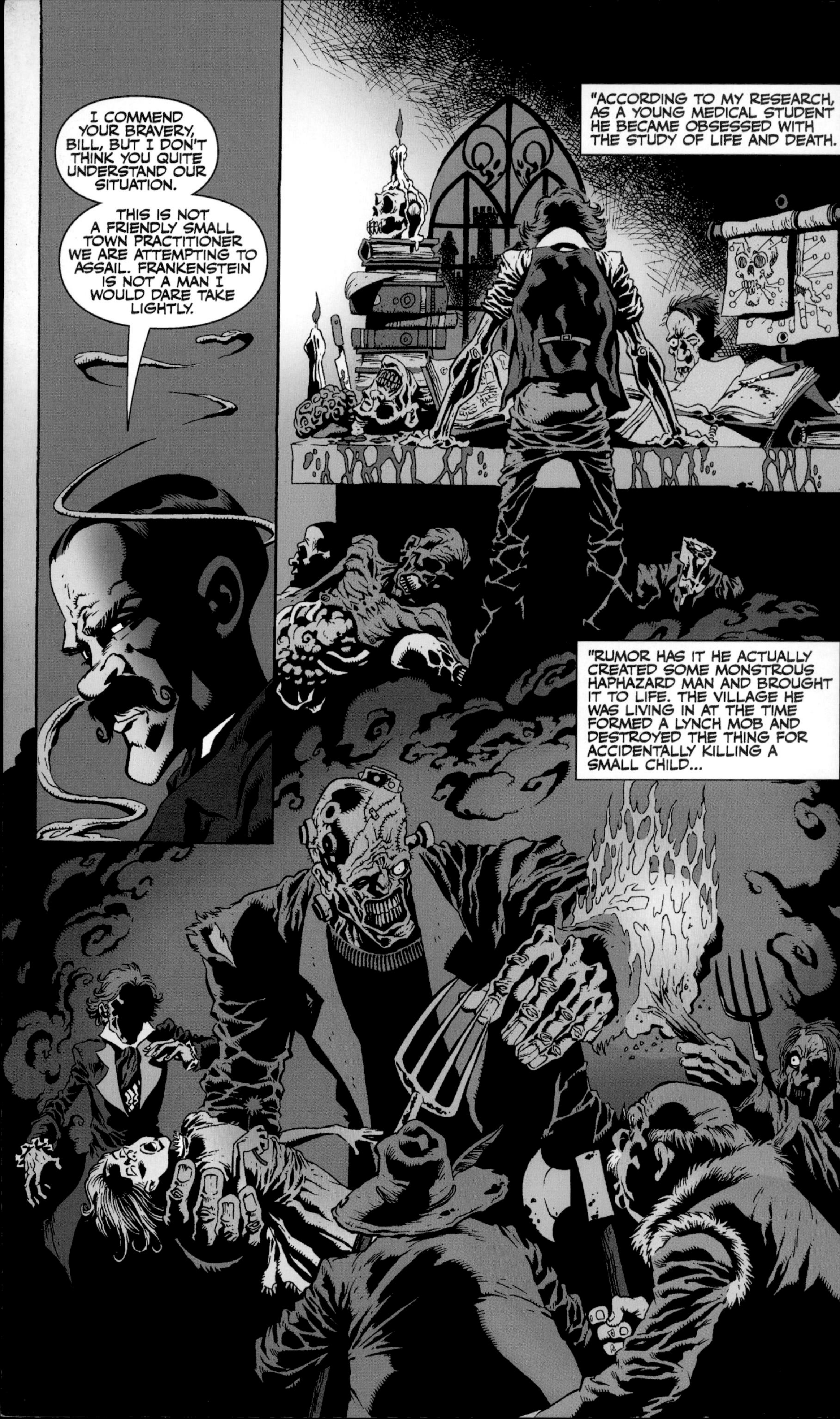
I COMMEND YOUR BRAVERY, BILL, BUT I DON'T THINK YOU QUITE UNDERSTAND OUR SITUATION.
THIS IS NOT A FRIENDLY SMALL TOWN PRACTITIONER WE ARE ATTEMPTING TO ASSAIL. FRANKENSTEIN IS NOT A MAN I WOULD DARE TAKE LIGHTLY.
"ACCORDING TO MY RESEARCH, AS A YOUNG MEDICAL STUDENT HE BECAME OBSESSED WITH THE STUDY OF LIFE AND DEATH.
"RUMOR HAS IT HE ACTUALLY CREATED SOME MONSTROUS HAPHAZARD MAN AND BROUGHT IT TO LIFE. THE VILLAGE HE WAS LIVING IN AT THE TIME FORMED A LYNCH MOB AND DESTROYED THE THING FOR ACCIDENTALLY KILLING A SMALL CHILD...

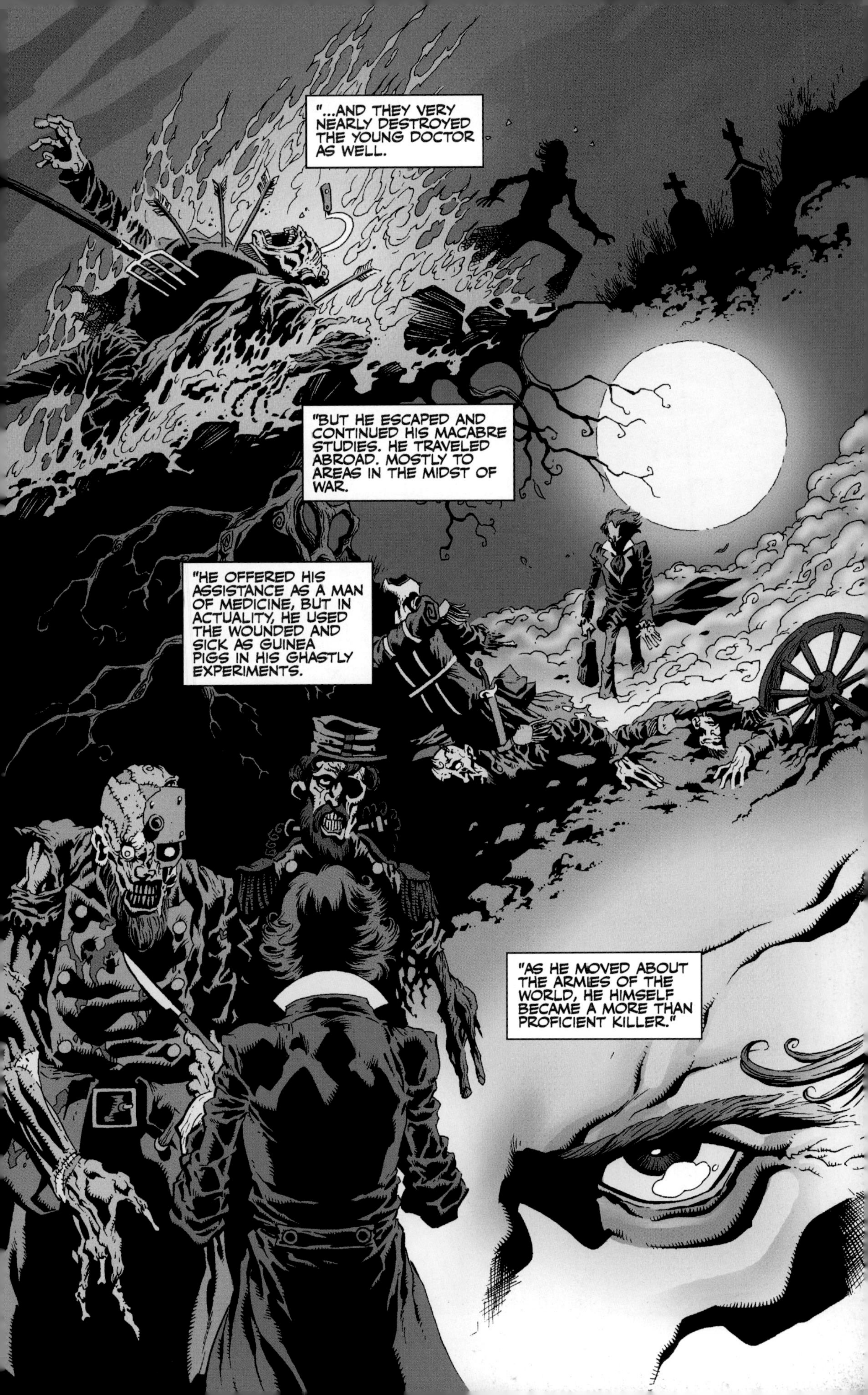
"...AND THEY VERY NEARLY DESTROYED THE YOUNG DOCTOR AS WELL.
"BUT HE ESCAPED AND CONTINUED HIS MACABRE STUDIES. HE TRAVELED ABROAD. MOSTLY TO AREAS IN THE MIDST OF WAR.
"HE OFFERED HIS ASSISTANCE AS A MAN OF MEDICINE, BUT IN ACTUALITY, HE USED THE WOUNDED AND SICK AS GUINEA PIGS IN HIS GHASTLY EXPERIMENTS.
"AS HE MOVED ABOUT THE ARMIES OF THE WORLD, HE HIMSELF BECAME A MORE THAN PROFICIENT KILLER."

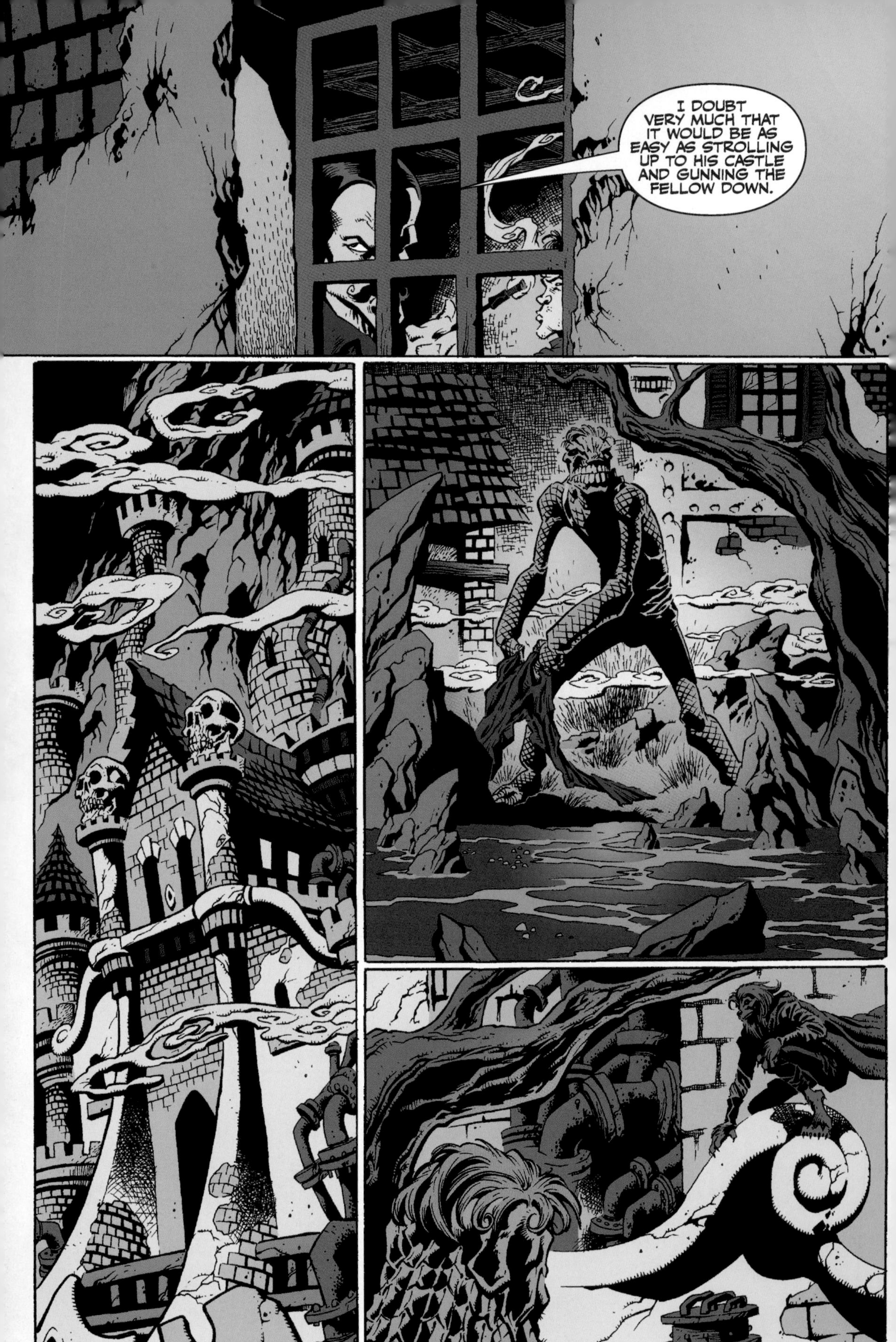
I DOUBT VERY MUCH THAT IT WOULD BE AS EASY AS STROLLING UP TO HIS CASTLE AND GUNNING THE FELLOW DOWN.

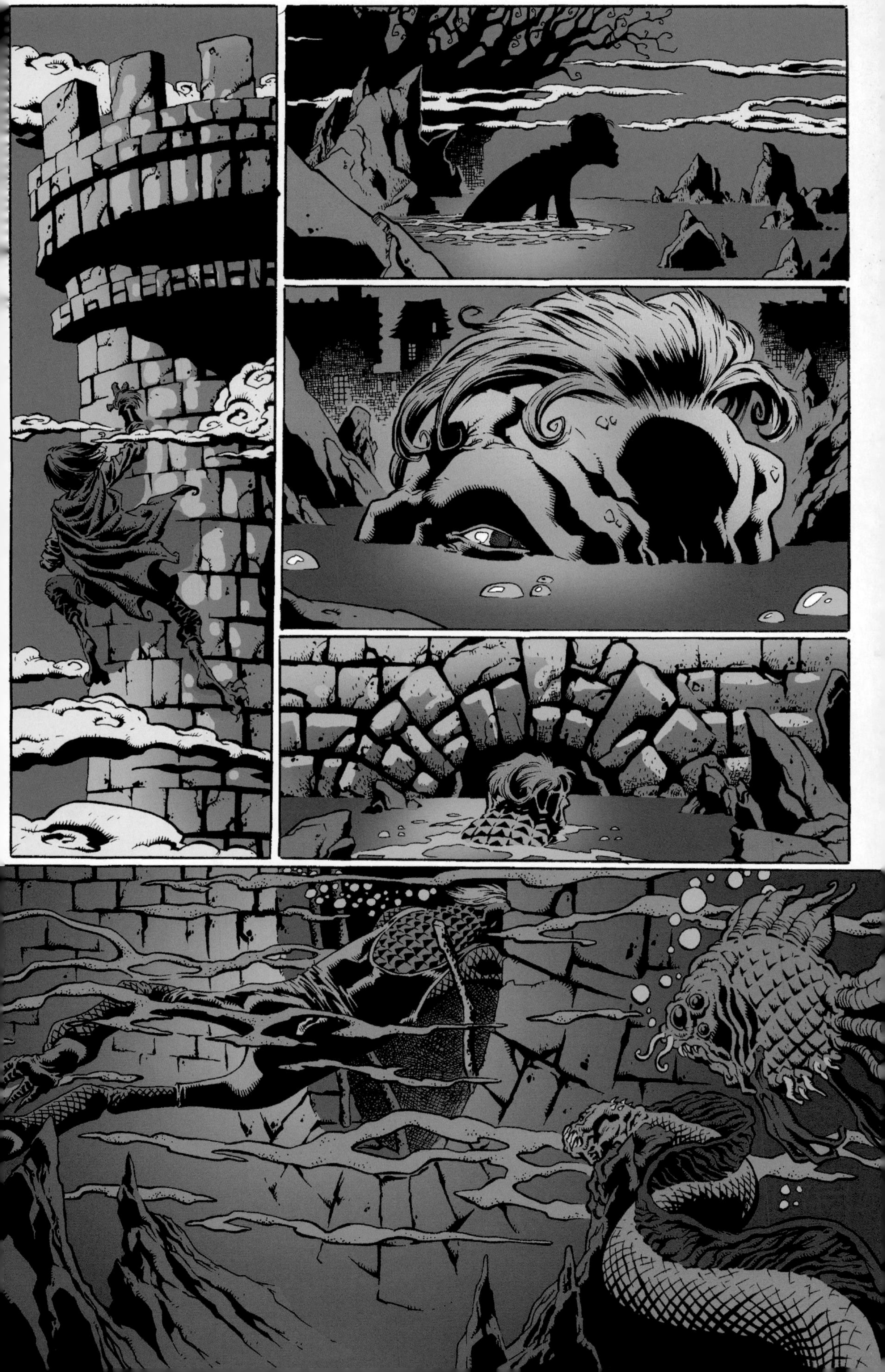

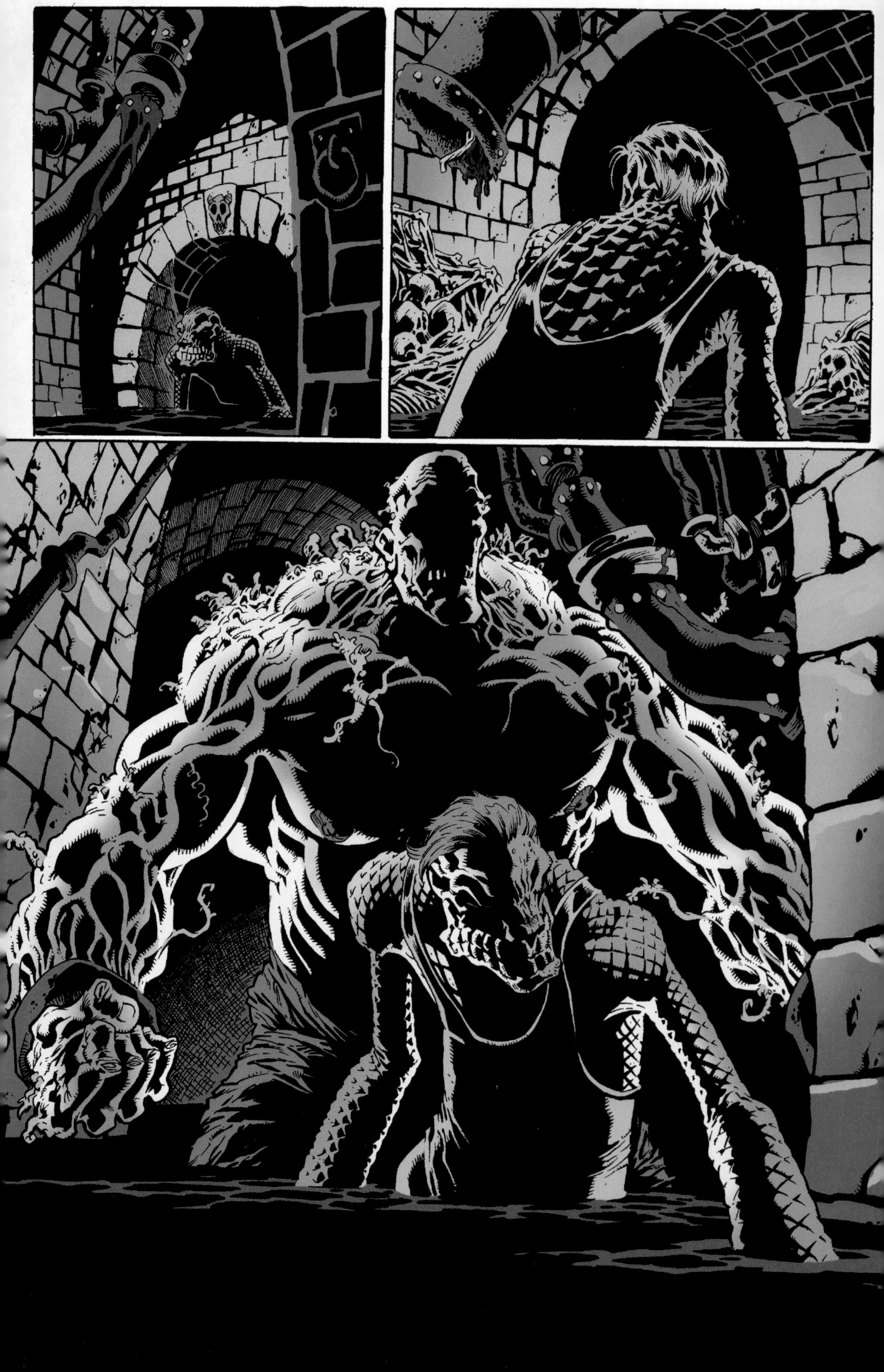

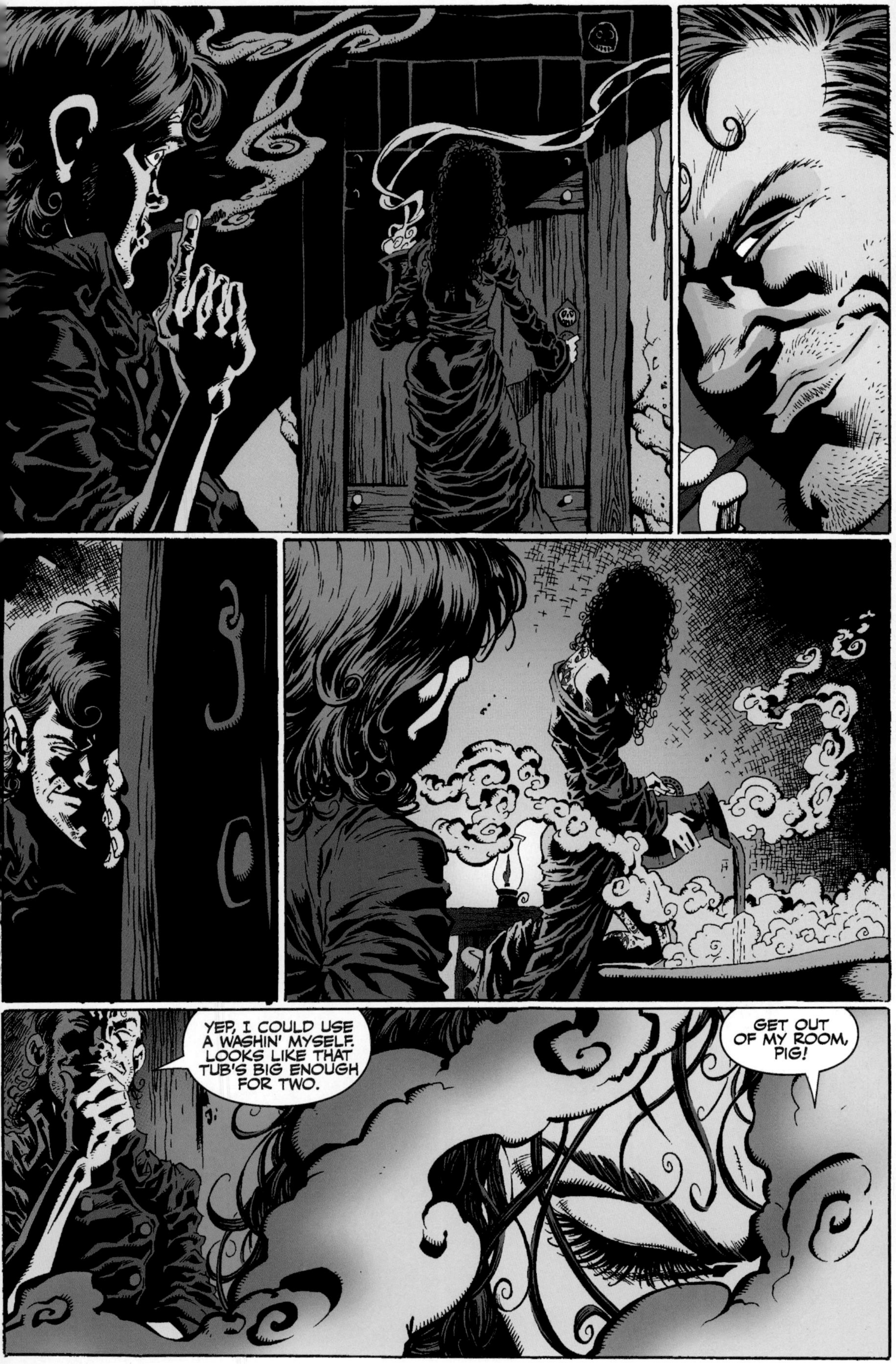
YEP, I COULD USE A WASHIN' MYSELF. LOOKS LIKE THAT TUB'S BIG ENOUGH FOR TWO.
GET OUT OF MY ROOM, PIG!

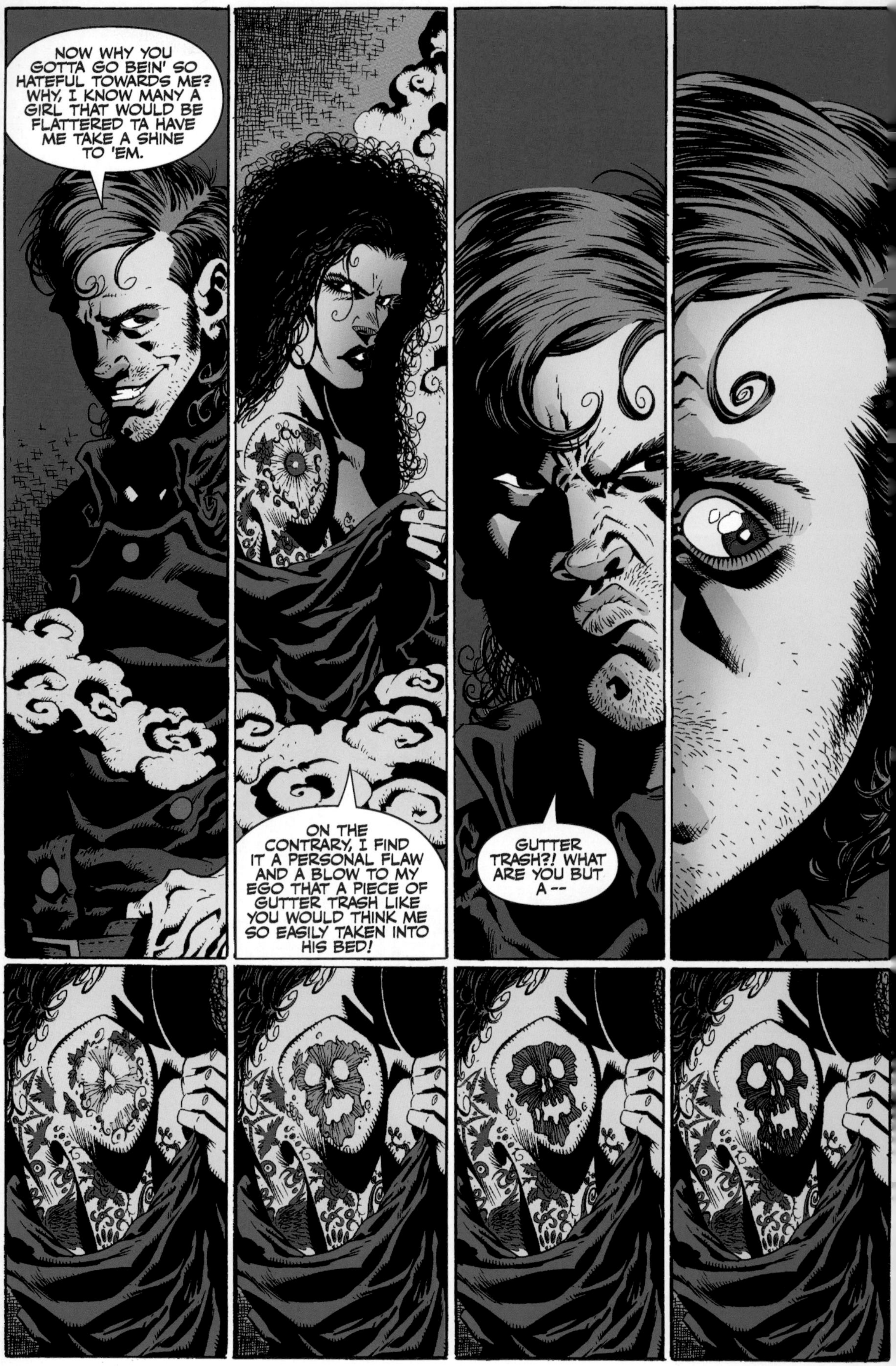
NOW WHY YOU GOTTA GO BEIN' SO HATEFUL TOWARDS ME? WHY, I KNOW MANY A GIRL THAT WOULD BE FLATTERED TA HAVE ME TAKE A SHINE TO 'EM.
ON THE CONTRARY, I FIND IT A PERSONAL FLAW AND A BLOW TO MY EGO THAT A PIECE OF GUTTER TRASH LIKE YOU WOULD THINK ME SO EASILY TAKEN INTO HIS BED!
GUTTER TRASH?! WHAT ARE YOU BUT A --

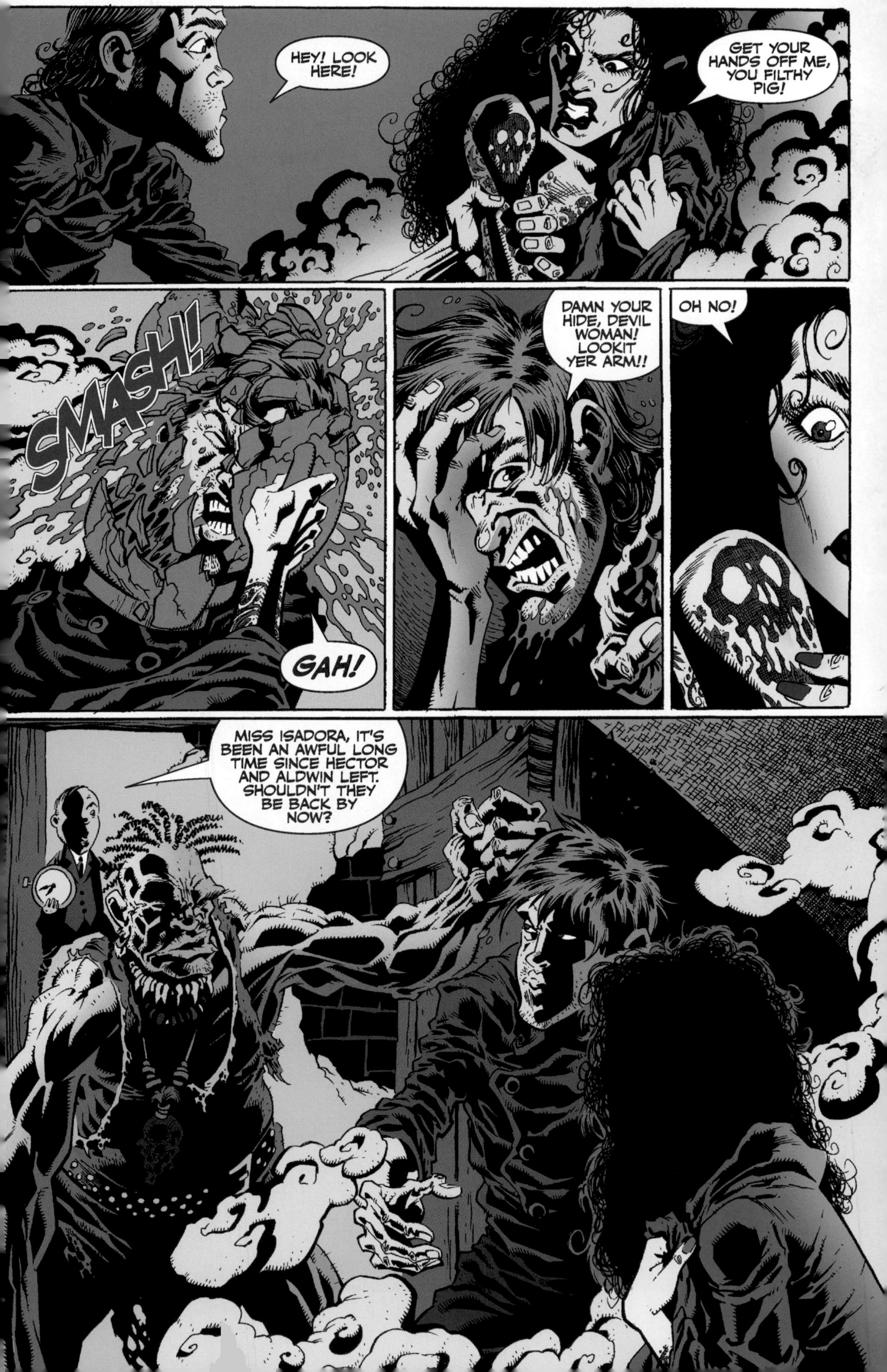
HEY! LOOK HERE!
GET YOUR HANDS OFF ME, YOU FILTHY PIG!
SMASH!
GAH!
DAMN YOUR HIDE, DEVIL WOMAN! LOOKIT YER ARM!!
OH NO!
MISS ISADORA, IT'S BEEN AN AWFUL LONG TIME SINCE HECTOR AND ALDWIN LEFT. SHOULDN'T THEY BE BACK BY NOW?

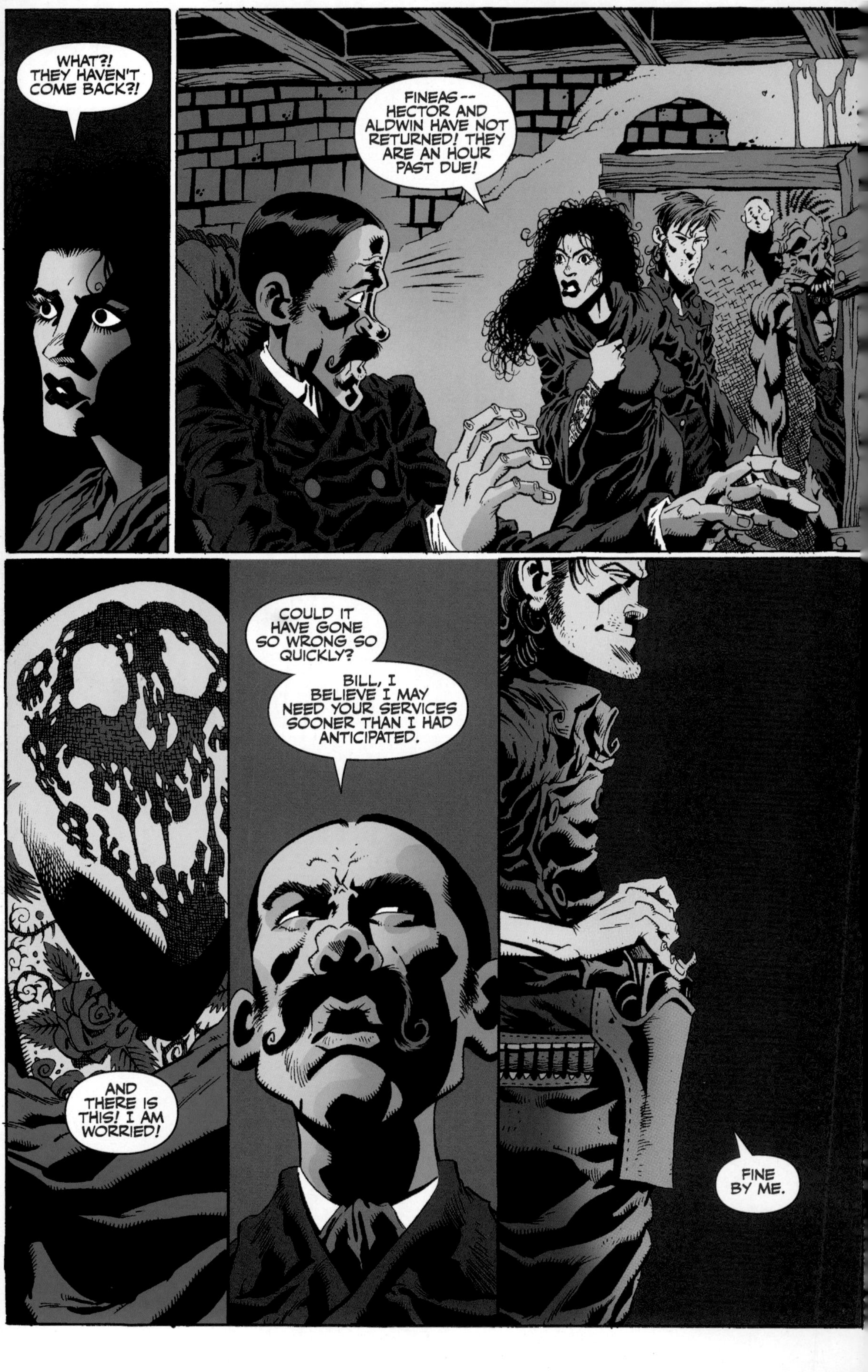
WHAT?! THEY HAVEN'T COME BACK?!
FINEAS-- HECTOR AND ALDWIN HAVE NOT RETURNED! THEY ARE AN HOUR PAST DUE!
AND THERE IS THIS! I AM WORRIED!
COULD IT HAVE GONE SO WRONG SO QUICKLY?
BILL, I BELIEVE I MAY NEED YOUR SERVICES SOONER THAN I HAD ANTICIPATED.
FINE BY ME.

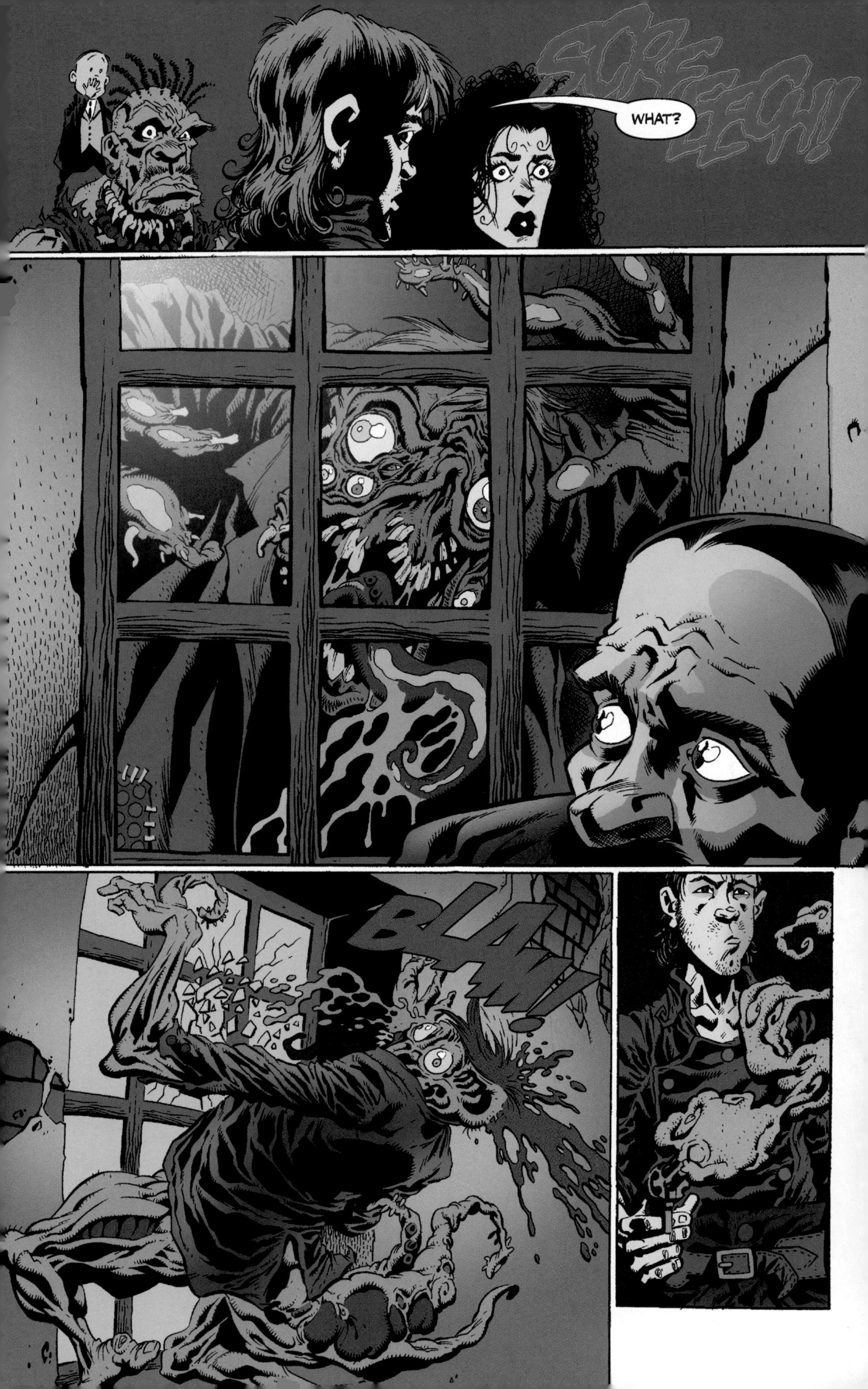
SCREEECH!
WHAT?
BLAM!

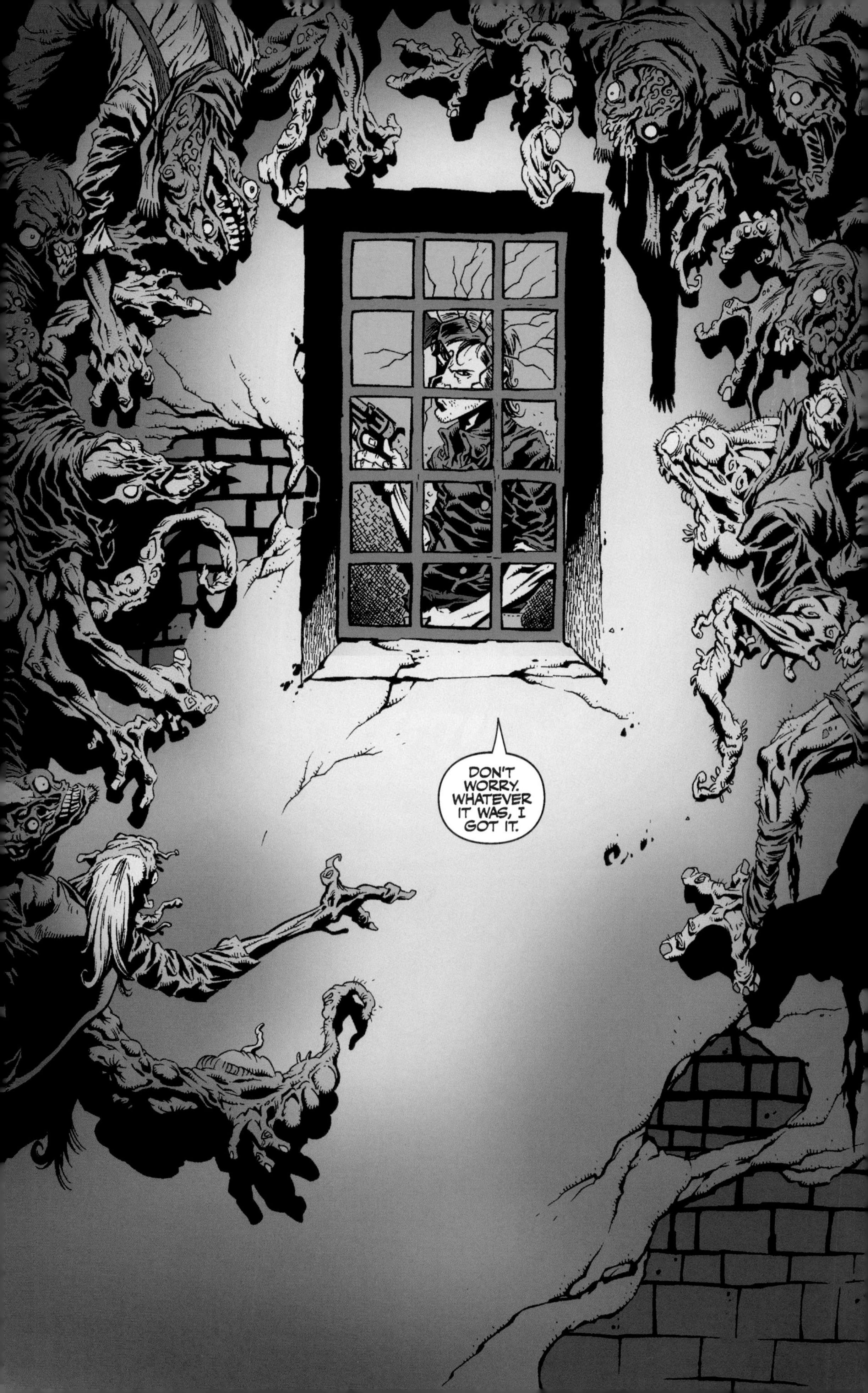
DON'T WORRY. WHATEVER IT WAS, I GOT IT.

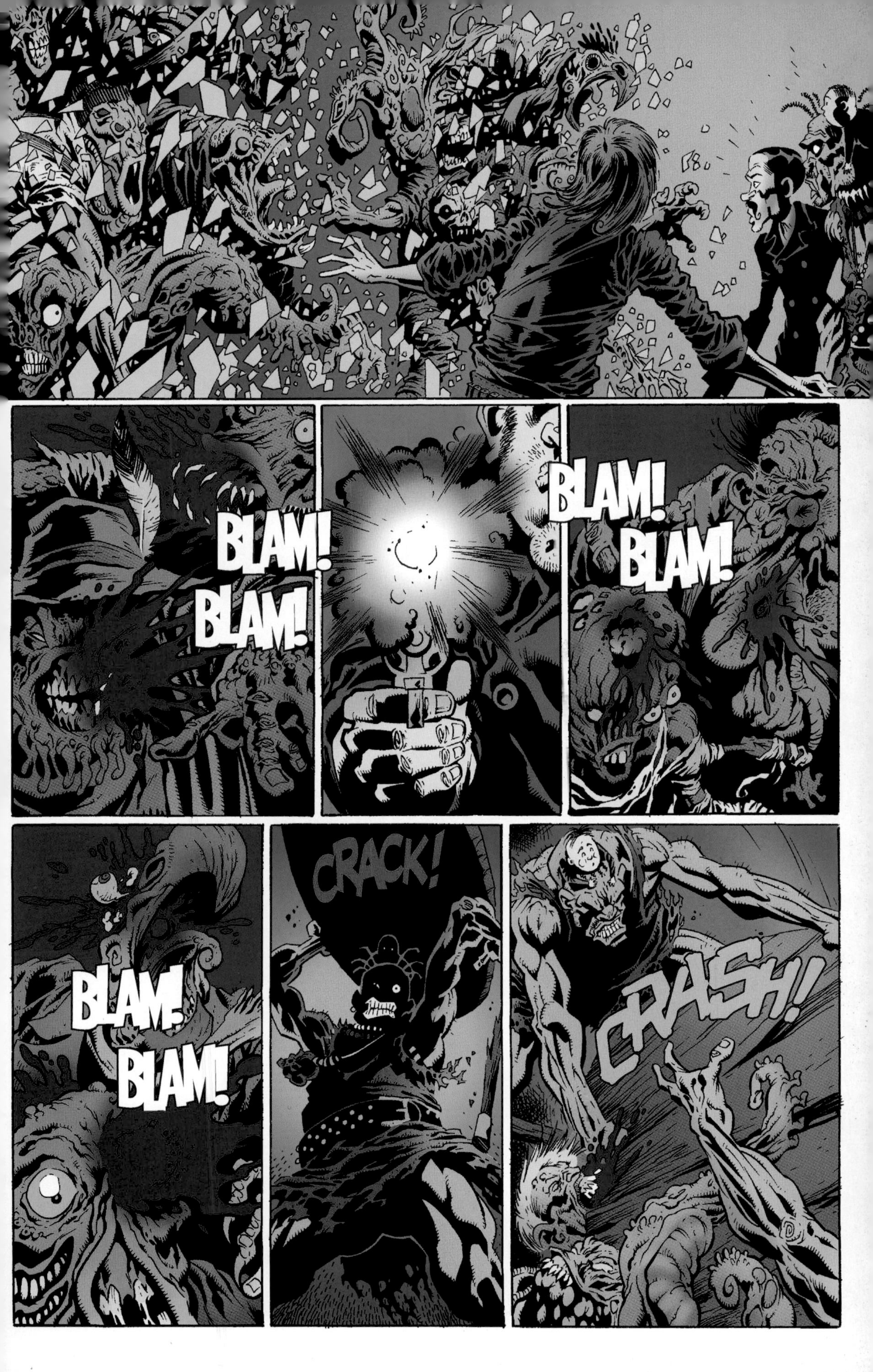
BLAM!
BLAM!
BLAM!
BLAM!
BLAM!
BLAM!
CRACK!
CRASH!

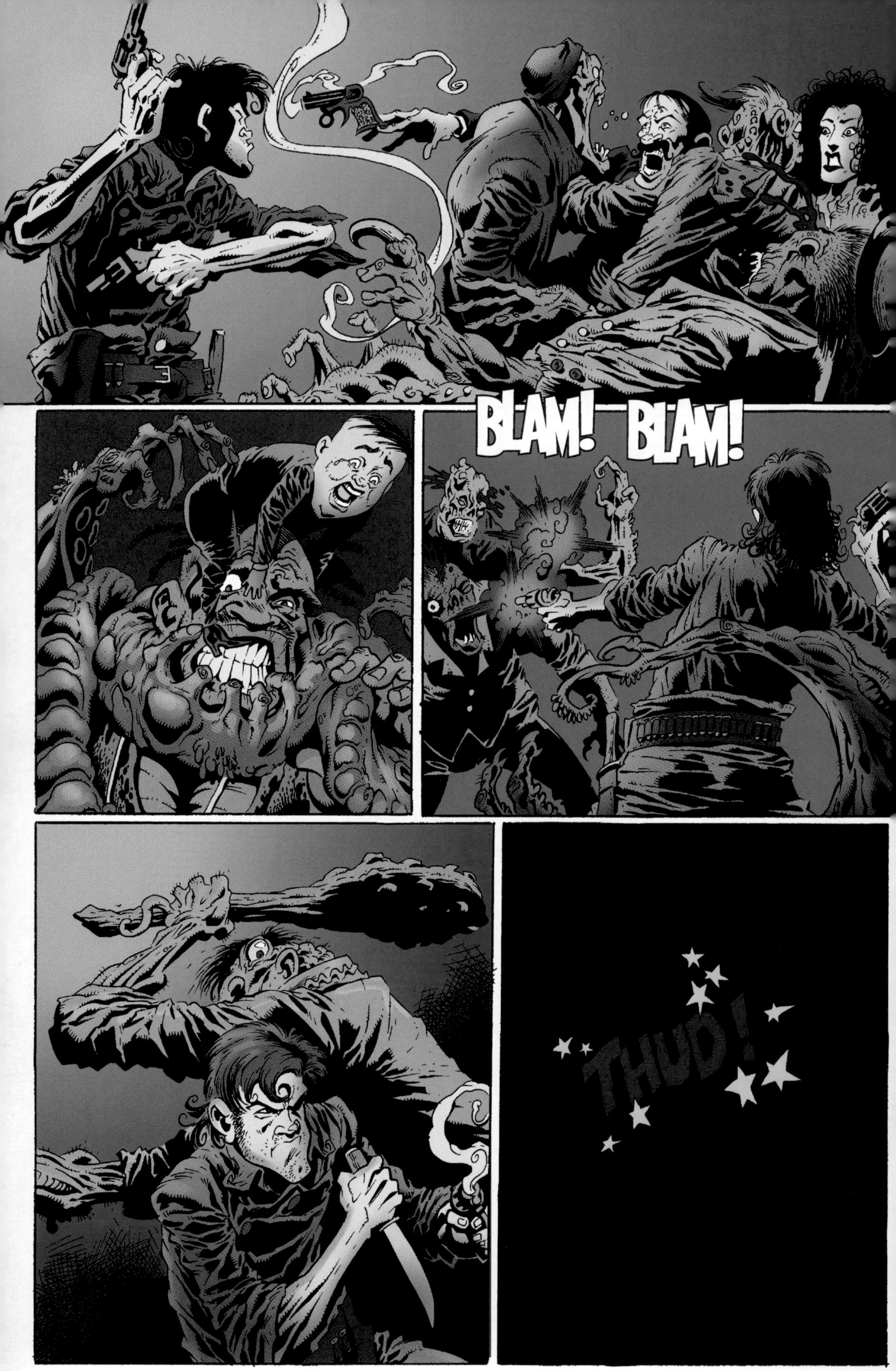
BLAM! BLAM!
THUD!

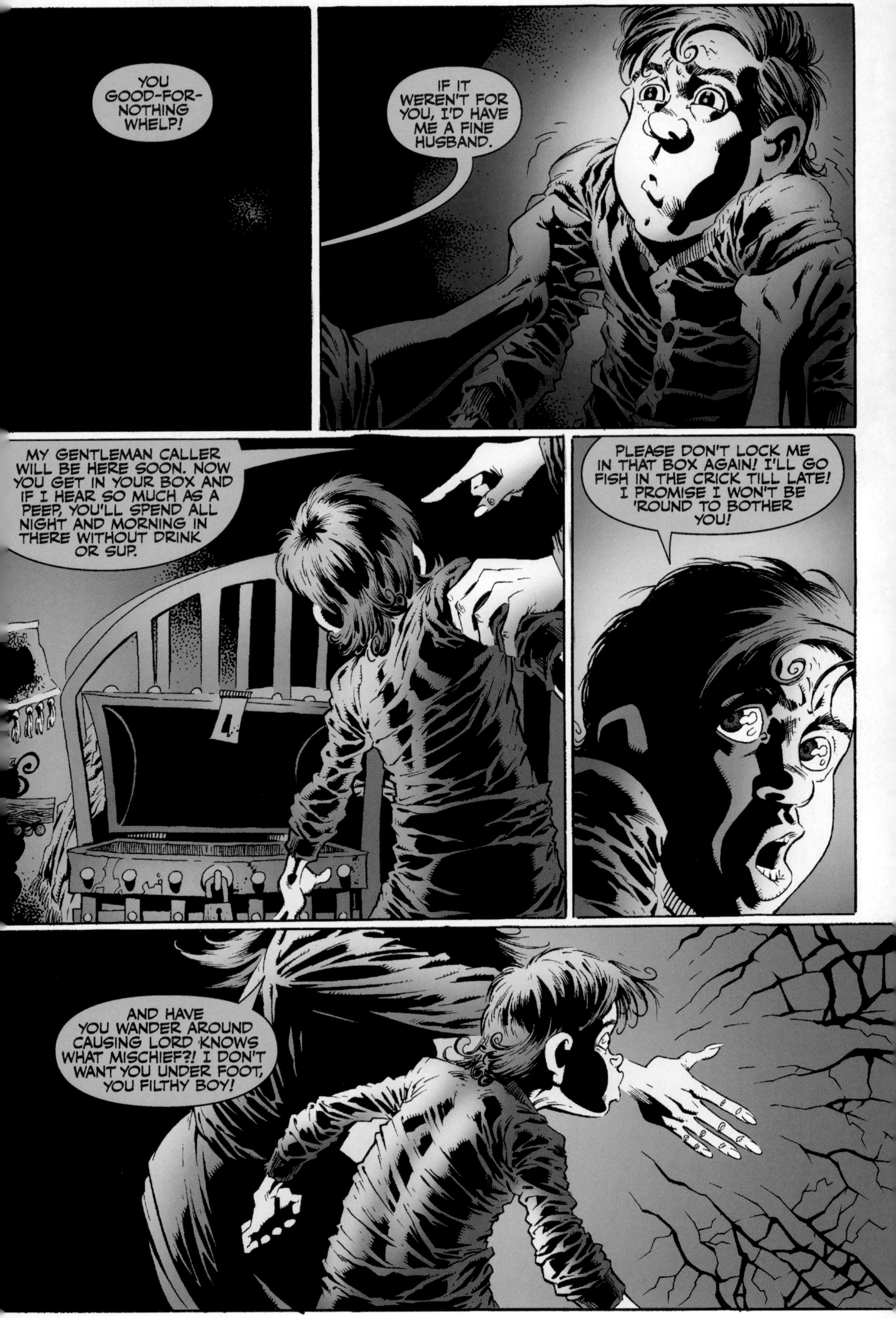
YOU GOOD-FOR-NOTHING WHELP!
IF IT WEREN'T FOR YOU, I'D HAVE ME A FINE HUSBAND.
MY GENTLEMAN CALLER WILL BE HERE SOON. NOW YOU GET IN YOUR BOX AND IF I HEAR SO MUCH AS A PEEP, YOU'LL SPEND ALL NIGHT AND MORNING IN THERE WITHOUT DRINK OR SUP.
PLEASE DON'T LOCK ME IN THAT BOX AGAIN! I'LL GO FISH IN THE CRICK TILL LATE! I PROMISE I WON'T BE 'ROUND TO BOTHER YOU!
AND HAVE YOU WANDER AROUND CAUSING LORD KNOWS WHAT MISCHIEF?! I DON'T WANT YOU UNDER FOOT, YOU FILTHY BOY!

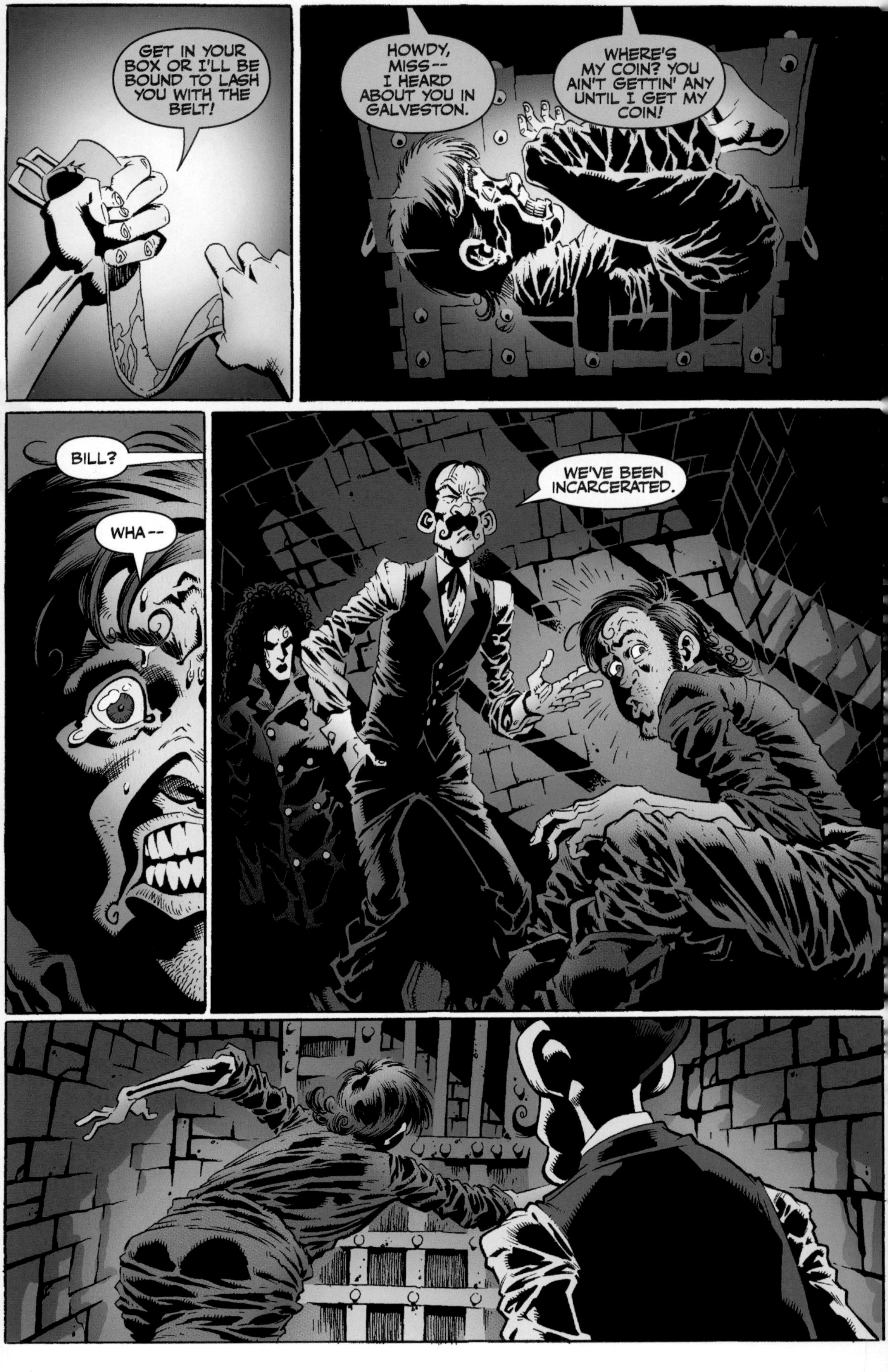
GET IN YOUR BOX OR I'LL BE BOUND TO LASH YOU WITH THE BELT!
HOWDY, MISS-- I HEARD ABOUT YOU IN GALVESTON.
WHERE'S MY COIN? YOU AIN'T GETTIN' ANY UNTIL I GET MY COIN!
BILL?
WHA--
WE'VE BEEN INCARCERATED.

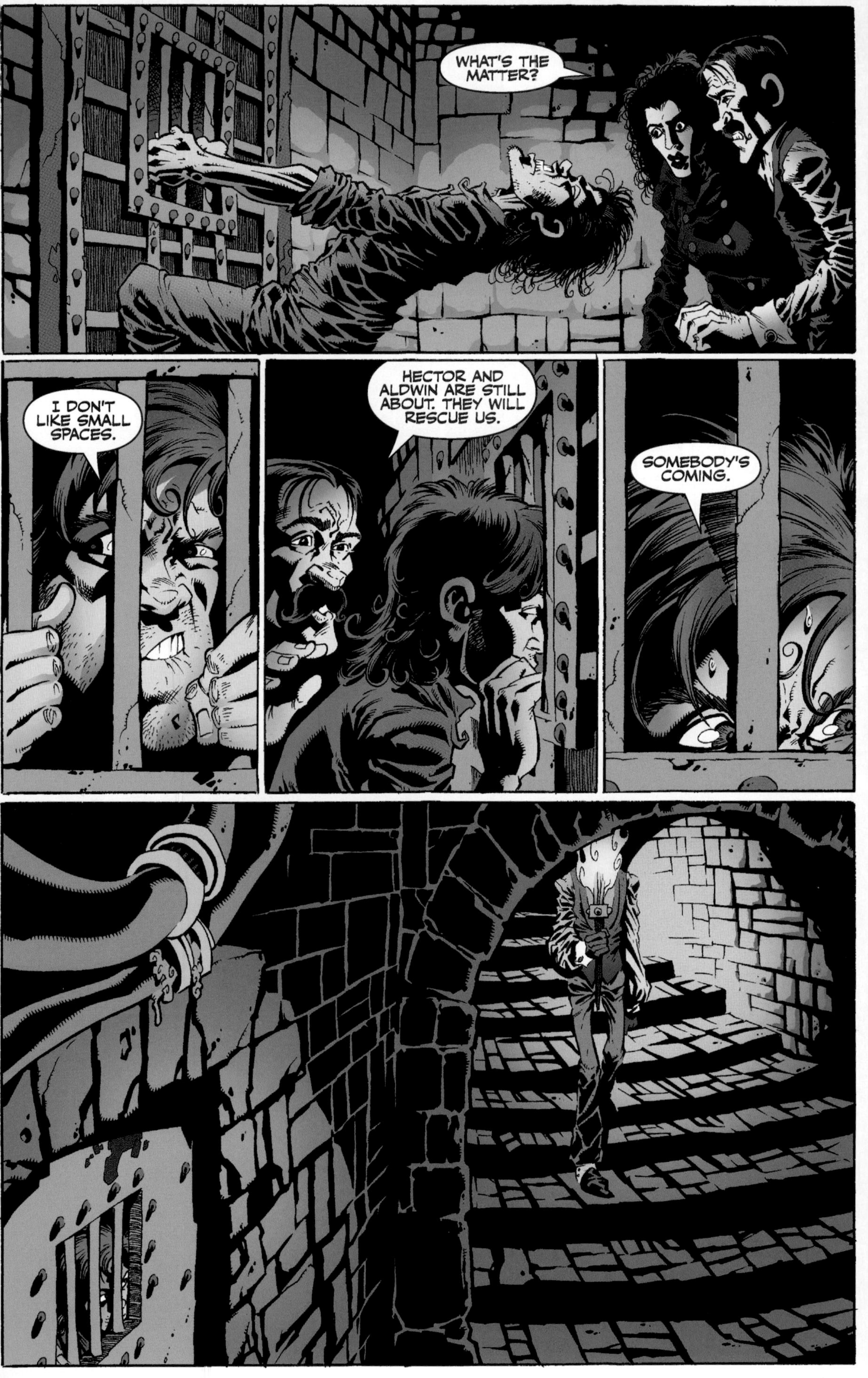
WHAT'S THE MATTER?
I DON'T LIKE SMALL SPACES.
HECTOR AND ALDWIN ARE STILL ABOUT. THEY WILL RESCUE US.
SOMEBODY'S COMING.

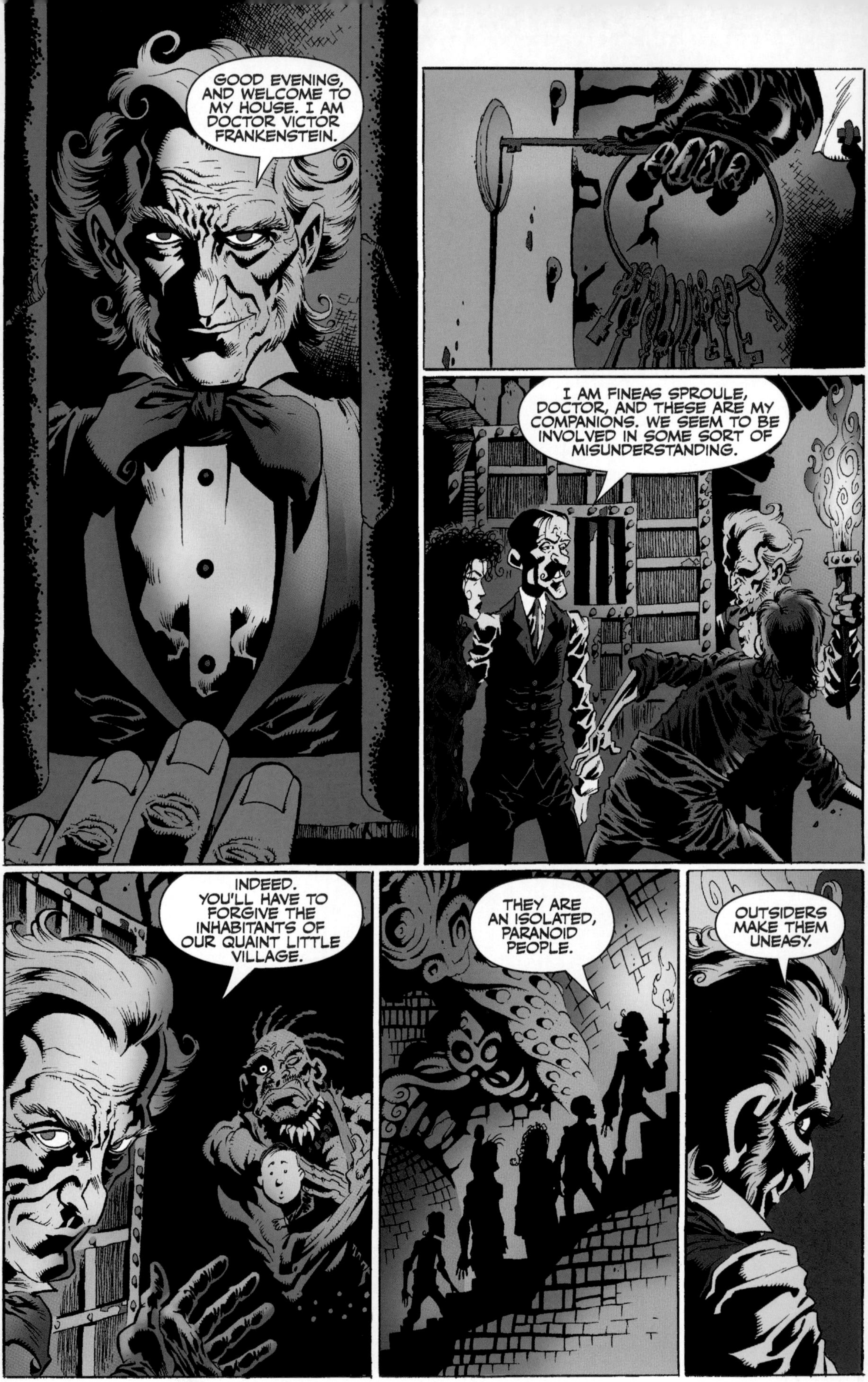

GOOD EVENING, AND WELCOME TO MY HOUSE. I AM DOCTOR VICTOR FRANKENSTEIN.
I AM FINEAS SPROULE, DOCTOR, AND THESE ARE MY COMPANIONS. WE SEEM TO BE INVOLVED IN SOME SORT OF MISUNDERSTANDING.
INDEED. YOU'LL HAVE TO FORGIVE THE INHABITANTS OF OUR QUAINT LITTLE VILLAGE.
THEY ARE AN ISOLATED, PARANOID PEOPLE.
OUTSIDERS MAKE THEM UNEASY.

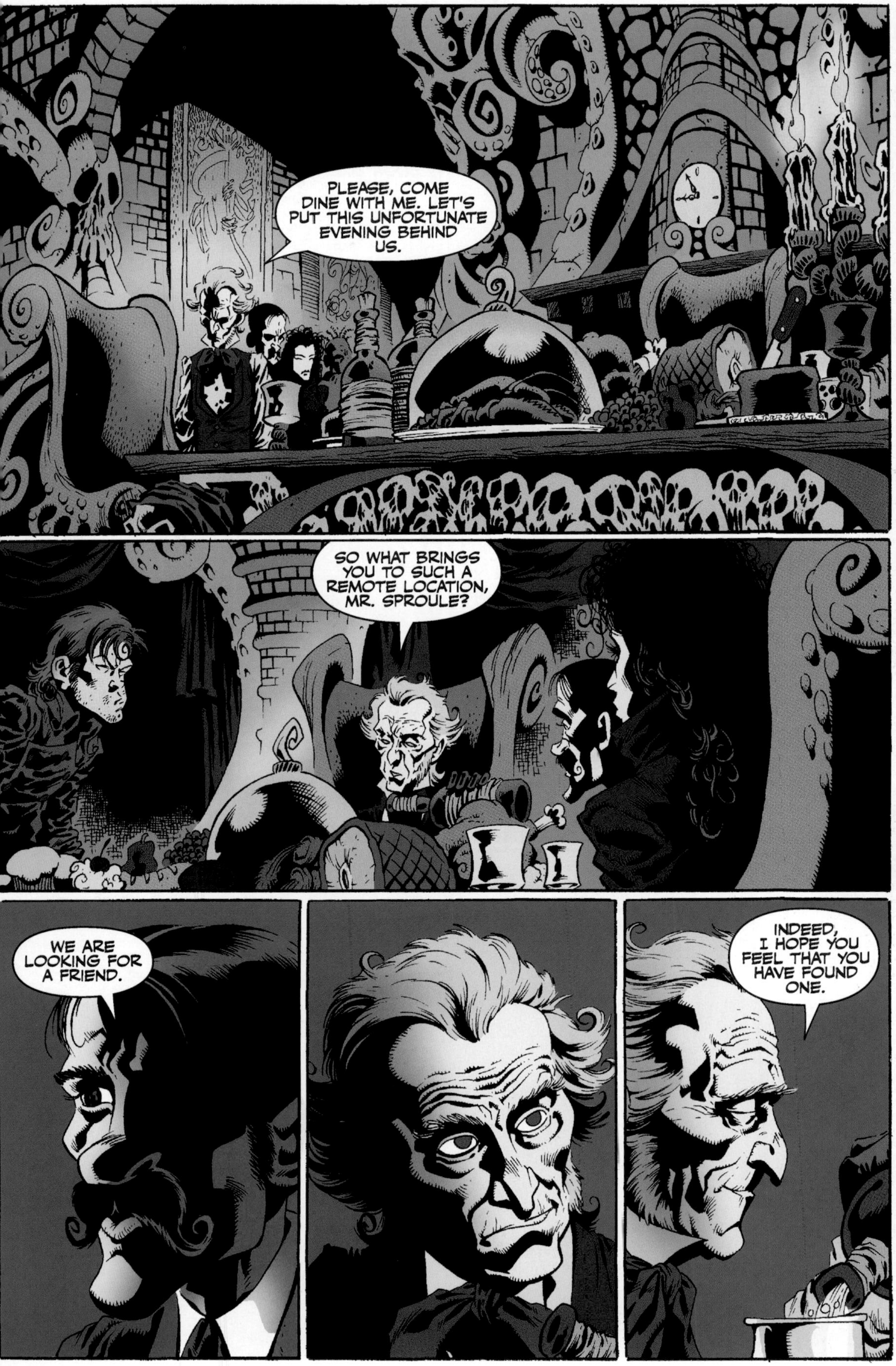
PLEASE, COME DINE WITH ME. LET'S PUT THIS UNFORTUNATE EVENING BEHIND US.
SO WHAT BRINGS YOU TO SUCH A REMOTE LOCATION, MR. SPROULE?
WE ARE LOOKING FOR A FRIEND.
INDEED, I HOPE YOU FEEL THAT YOU HAVE FOUND ONE.

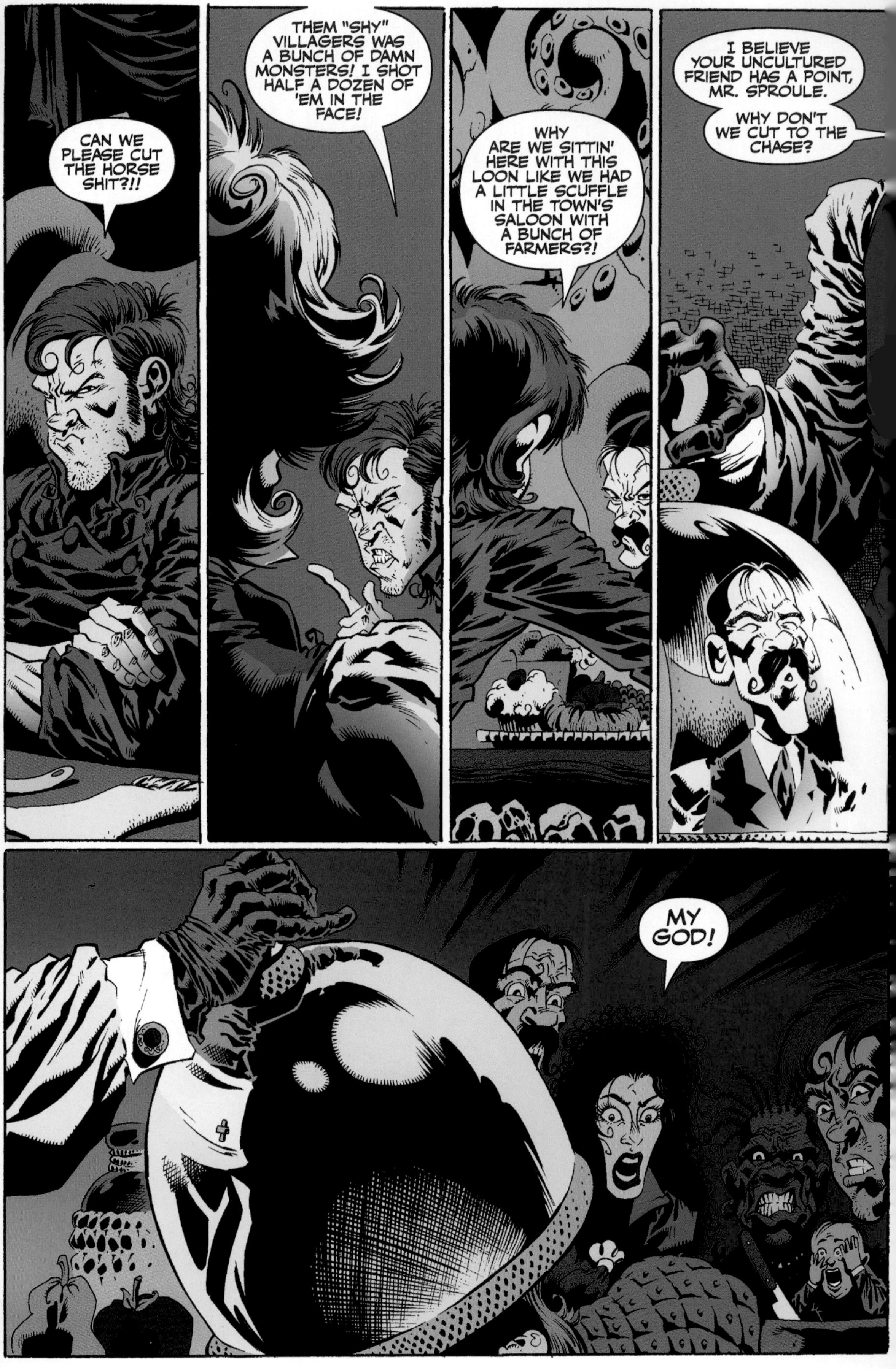
CAN WE PLEASE CUT THE HORSE SHIT?!!
THEM "SHY" VILLAGERS WAS A BUNCH OF DAMN MONSTERS! I SHOT HALF A DOZEN OF 'EM IN THE FACE!
WHY ARE WE SITTIN' HERE WITH THIS LOON LIKE WE HAD A LITTLE SCUFFLE IN THE TOWN'S SALOON WITH A BUNCH OF FARMERS?!
I BELIEVE YOUR UNCULTURED FRIEND HAS A POINT, MR. SPROULE.
WHY DON'T WE CUT TO THE CHASE?
MY GOD!

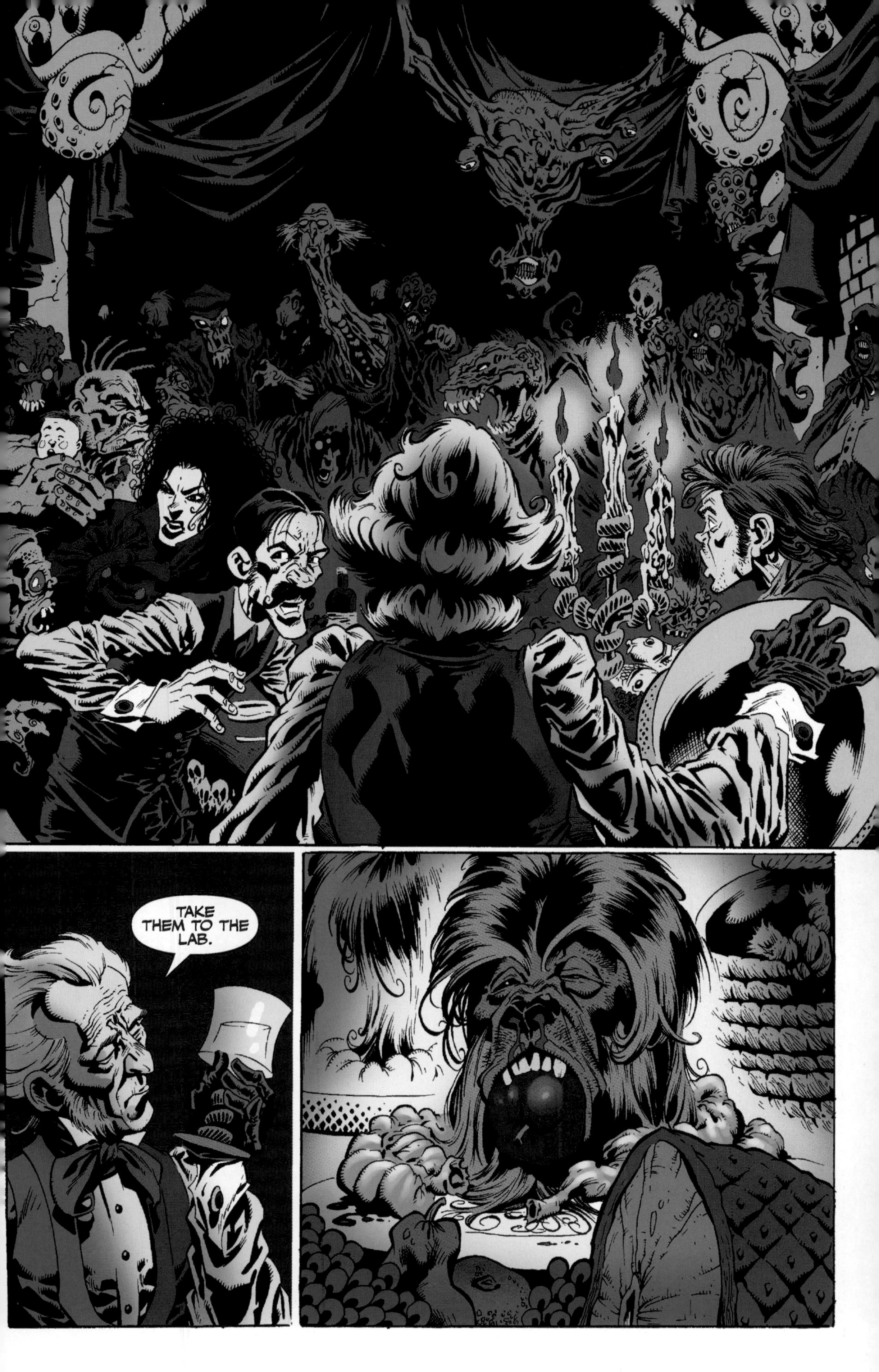
TAKE THEM TO THE LAB.

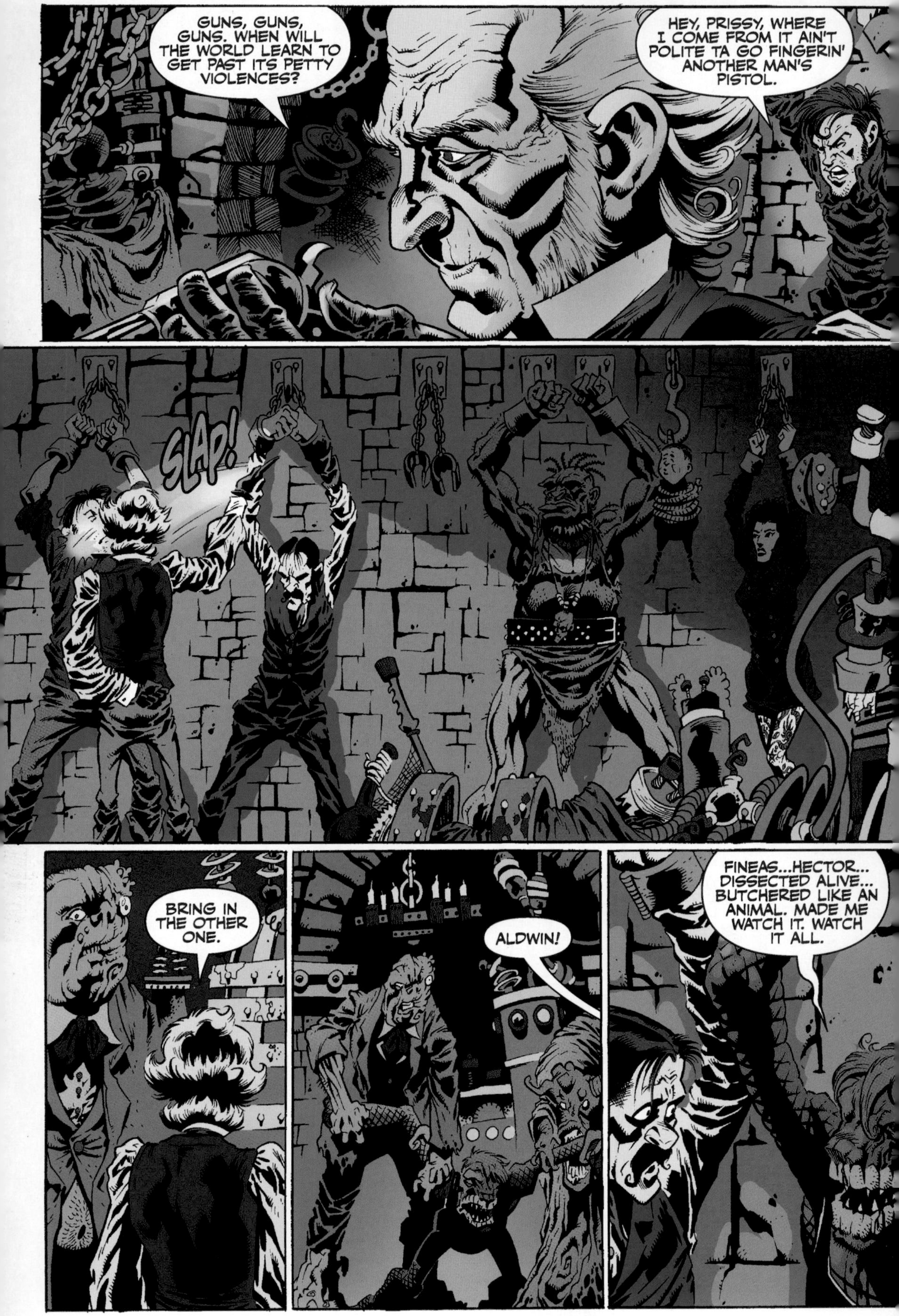
GUNS, GUNS, GUNS. WHEN WILL THE WORLD LEARN TO GET PAST ITS PETTY VIOLENCES?
HEY, PRISSY, WHERE I COME FROM IT AIN'T POLITE TA GO FINGERIN' ANOTHER MAN'S PISTOL.
SLAP!
BRING IN THE OTHER ONE.
ALDWIN!
FINEAS...HECTOR... DISSECTED ALIVE... BUTCHERED LIKE AN ANIMAL. MADE ME WATCH IT. WATCH IT ALL.

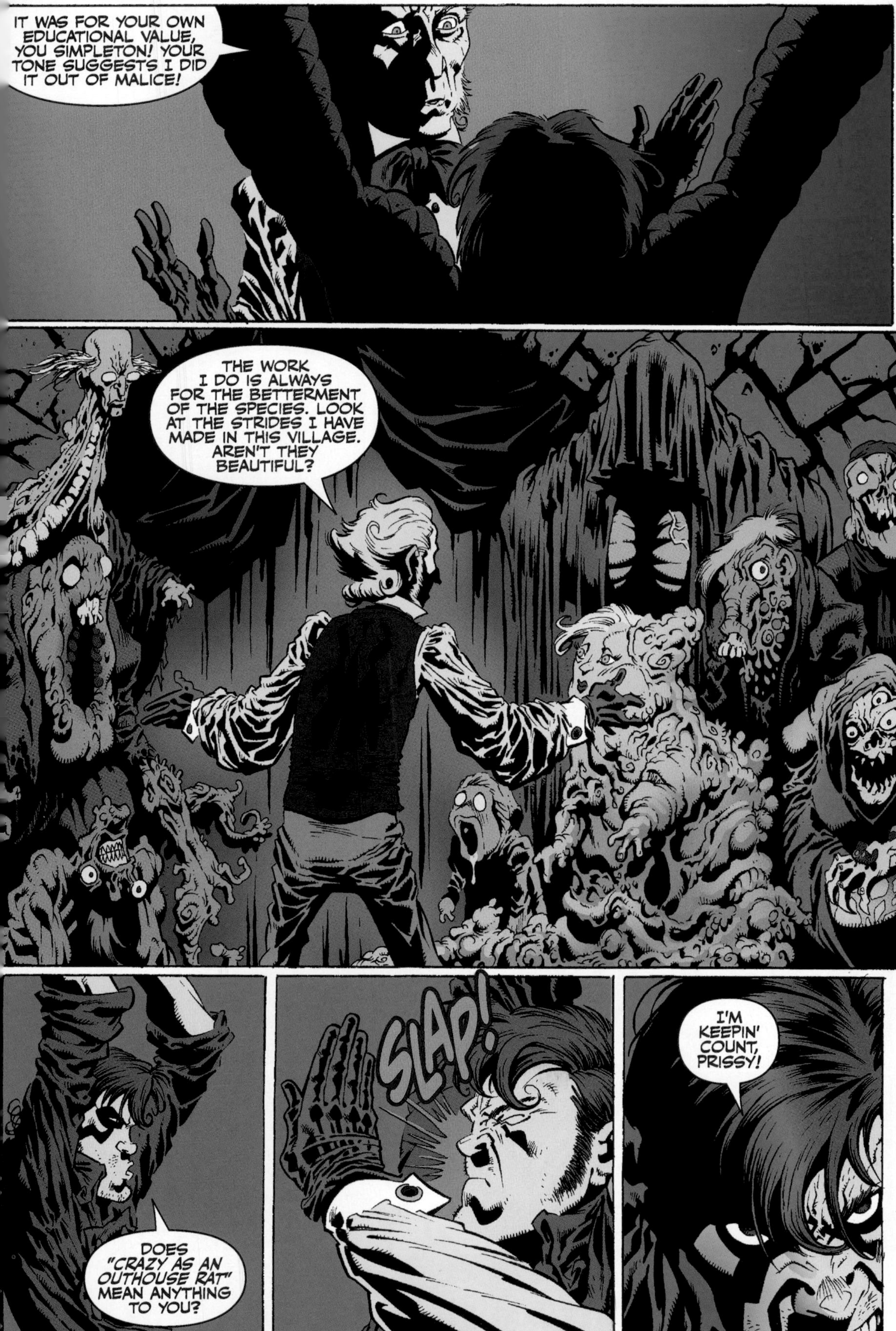
IT WAS FOR YOUR OWN EDUCATIONAL VALUE, YOU SIMPLETON! YOUR TONE SUGGESTS I DID IT OUT OF MALICE!
THE WORK I DO IS ALWAYS FOR THE BETTERMENT OF THE SPECIES. LOOK AT THE STRIDES I HAVE MADE IN THIS VILLAGE. AREN'T THEY BEAUTIFUL?
DOES "CRAZY AS AN OUTHOUSE RAT" MEAN ANYTHING TO YOU?
SLAP!
I'M KEEPIN' COUNT, PRISSY!

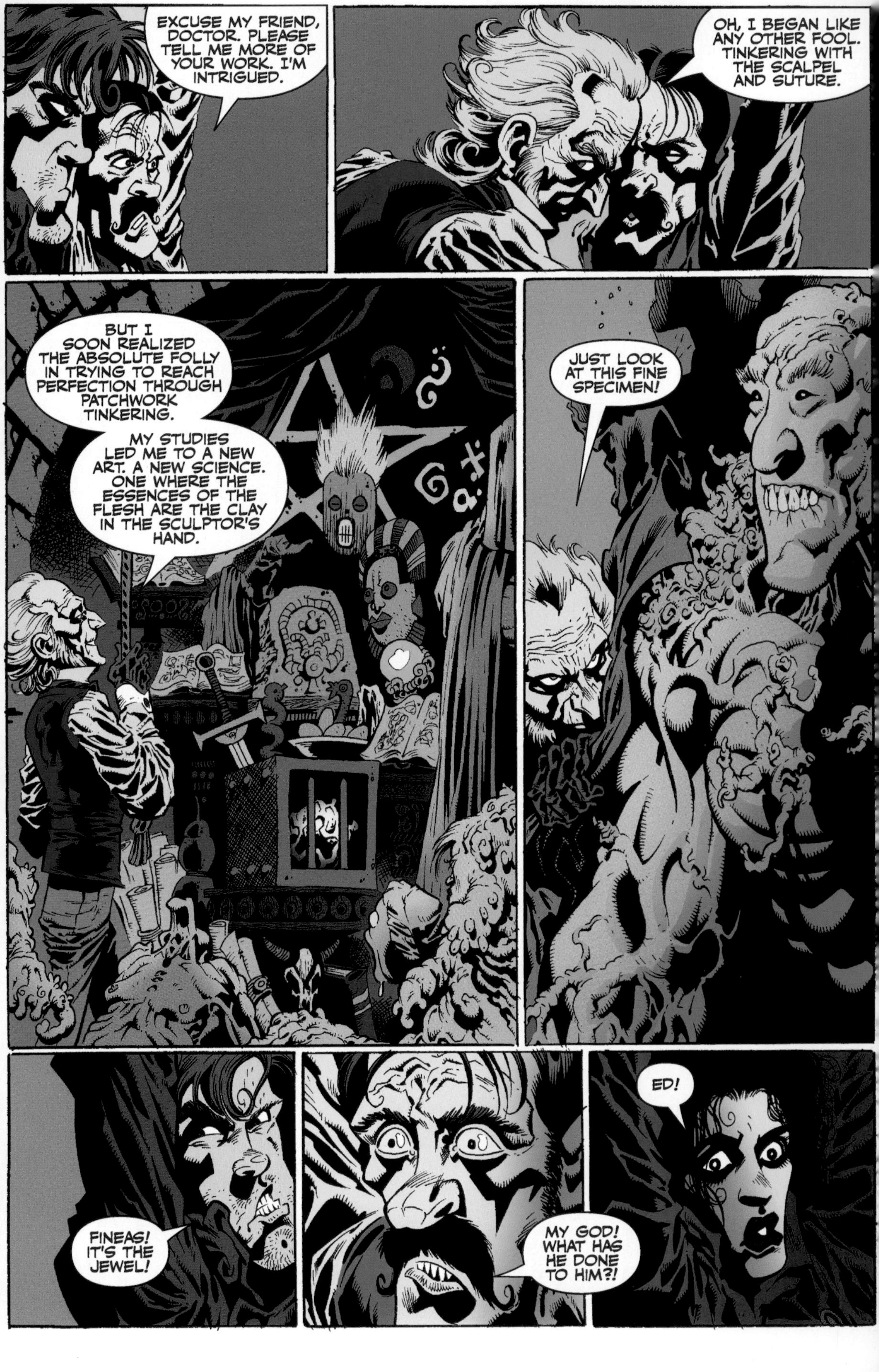
EXCUSE MY FRIEND, DOCTOR. PLEASE TELL ME MORE OF YOUR WORK. I'M INTRIGUED.
OH, I BEGAN LIKE ANY OTHER FOOL. TINKERING WITH THE SCALPEL AND SUTURE.
BUT I SOON REALIZED THE ABSOLUTE FOLLY IN TRYING TO REACH PERFECTION THROUGH PATCHWORK TINKERING.
MY STUDIES LED ME TO A NEW ART. A NEW SCIENCE. ONE WHERE THE ESSENCES OF THE FLESH ARE THE CLAY IN THE SCULPTOR'S HAND.
JUST LOOK AT THIS FINE SPECIMEN!
FINEAS! IT'S THE JEWEL!
MY GOD! WHAT HAS HE DONE TO HIM?!
ED!

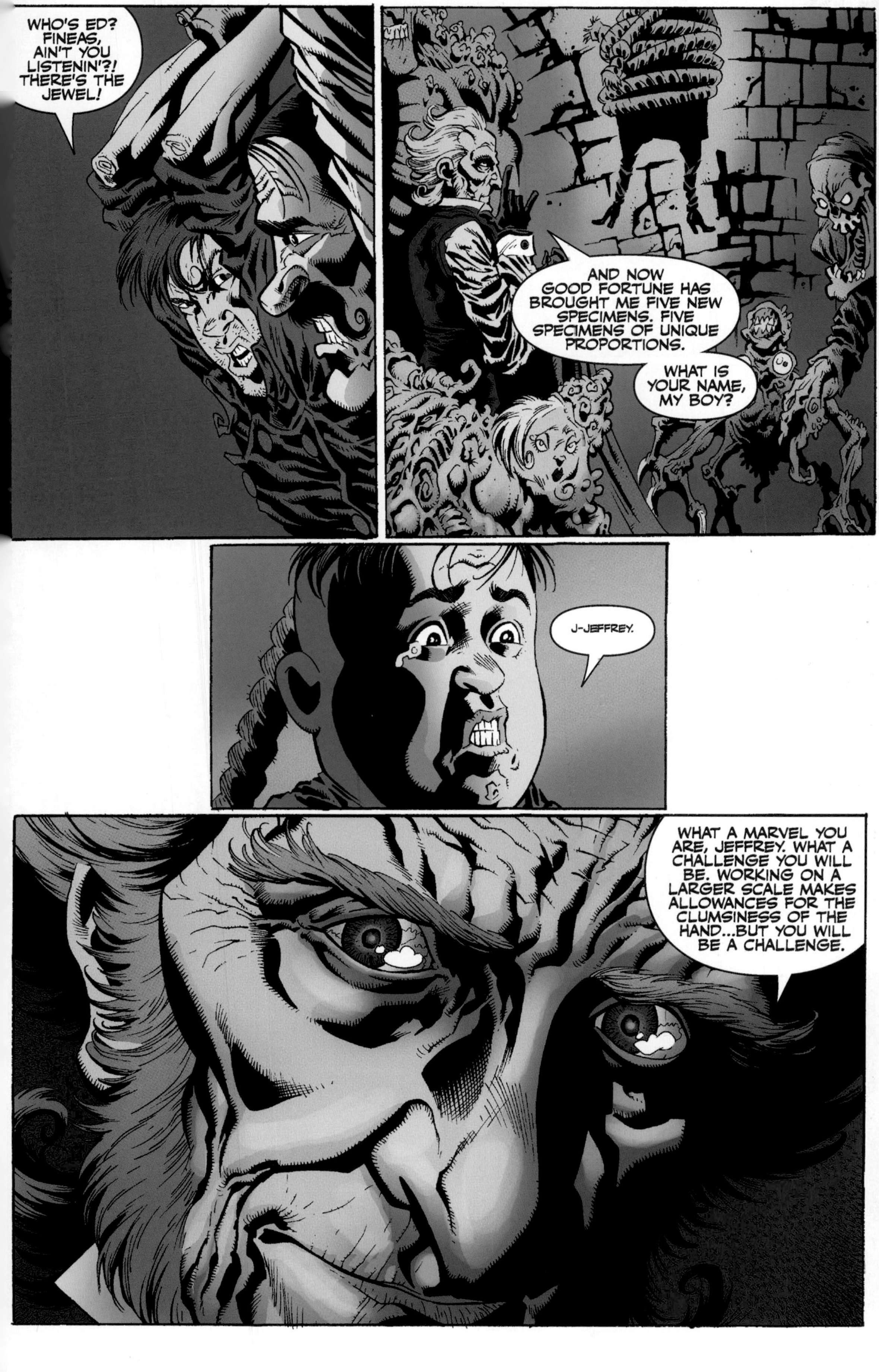
WHO'S ED? FINEAS, AIN'T YOU LISTENIN'?! THERE'S THE JEWEL!
AND NOW GOOD FORTUNE HAS BROUGHT ME FIVE NEW SPECIMENS. FIVE SPECIMENS OF UNIQUE PROPORTIONS.
WHAT IS YOUR NAME, MY BOY?
J-JEFFREY.
WHAT A MARVEL YOU ARE, JEFFREY. WHAT A CHALLENGE YOU WILL BE. WORKING ON A LARGER SCALE MAKES ALLOWANCES FOR THE CLUMSINESS OF THE HAND...BUT YOU WILL BE A CHALLENGE.

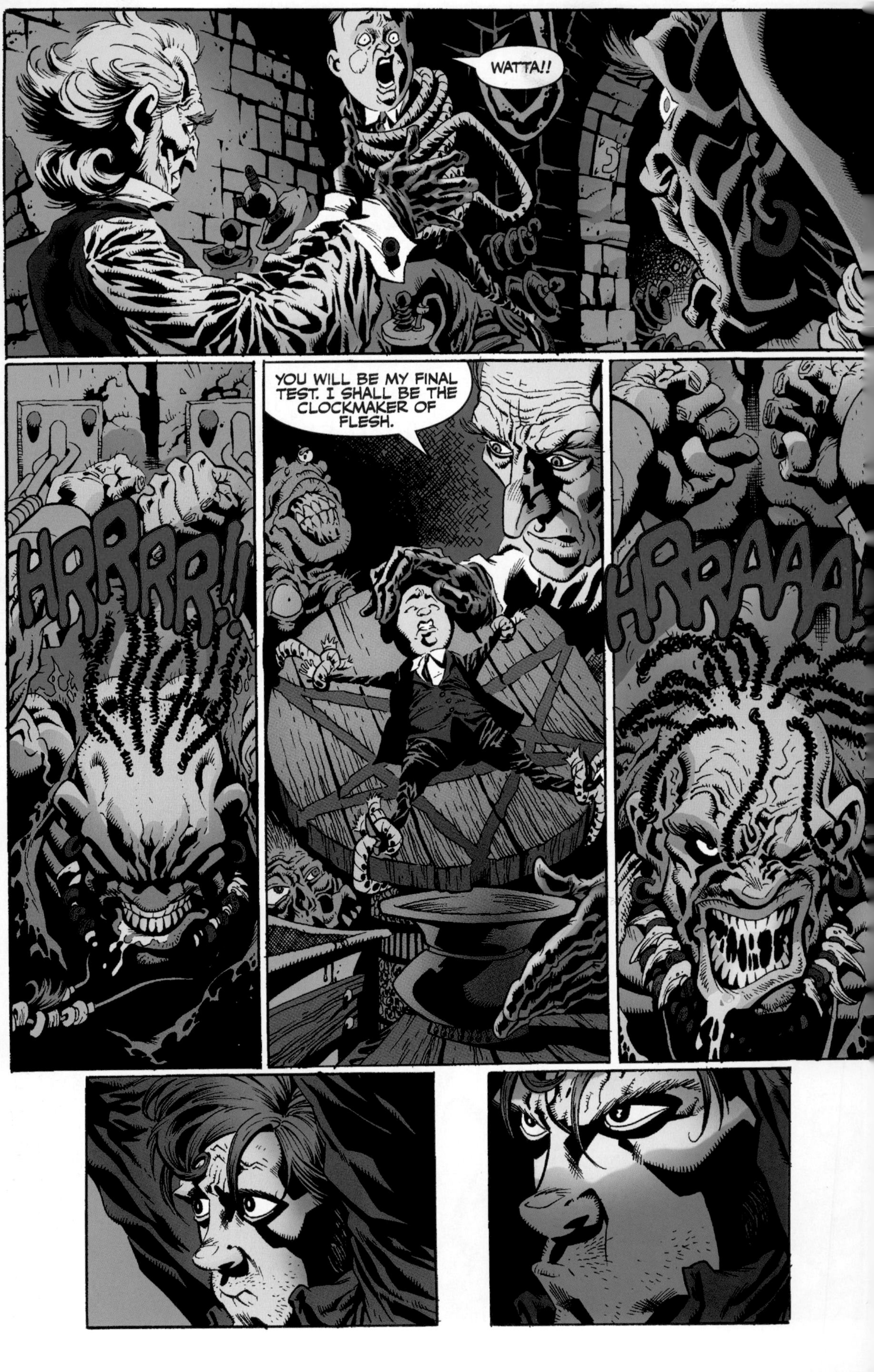
WATTA!!
HRRRR!!
YOU WILL BE MY FINAL TEST. I SHALL BE THE CLOCKMAKER OF FLESH.
HRRAAA!

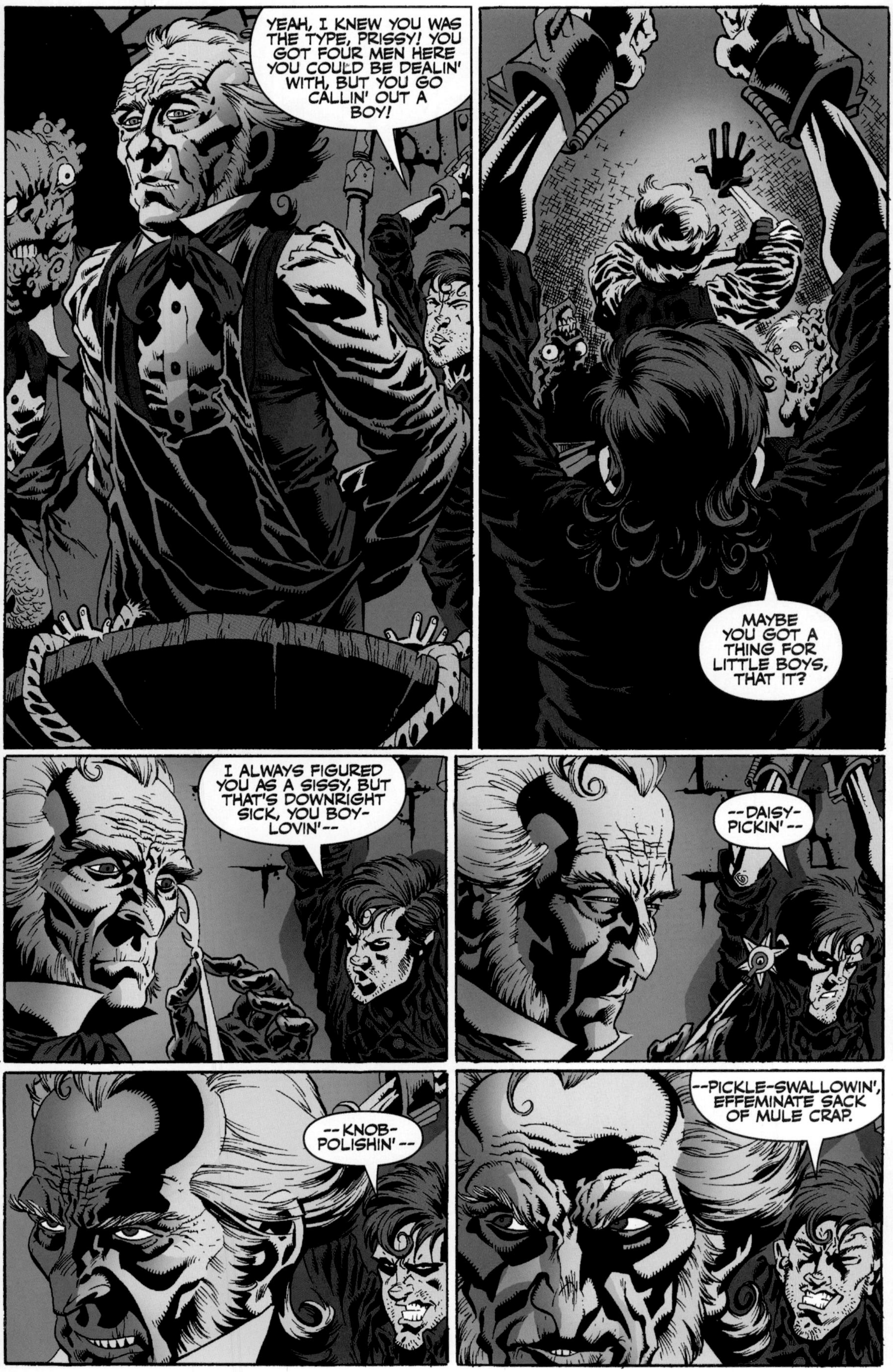
YEAH, I KNEW YOU WAS THE TYPE, PRISSY! YOU GOT FOUR MEN HERE YOU COULD BE DEALIN' WITH, BUT YOU GO CALLIN' OUT A BOY!
MAYBE YOU GOT A THING FOR LITTLE BOYS, THAT IT?
I ALWAYS FIGURED YOU AS A SISSY, BUT THAT'S DOWNRIGHT SICK, YOU BOY-LOVIN'--
--DAISY-PICKIN'--
--KNOB-POLISHIN'--
--PICKLE-SWALLOWIN', EFFEMINATE SACK OF MULE CRAP.

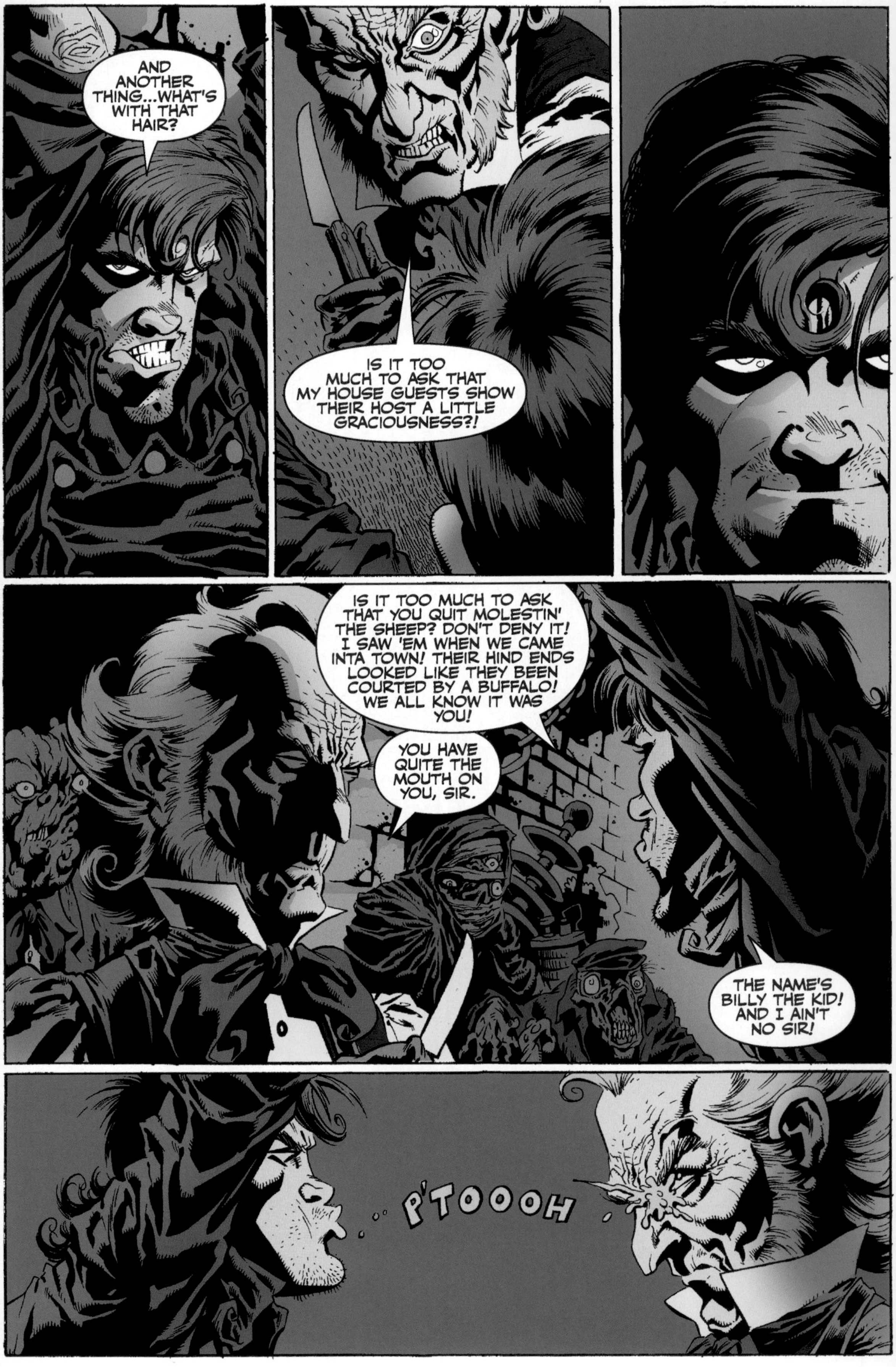
AND ANOTHER THING...WHAT'S WITH THAT HAIR?
IS IT TOO MUCH TO ASK THAT MY HOUSE GUESTS SHOW THEIR HOST A LITTLE GRACIOUSNESS?!
IS IT TOO MUCH TO ASK THAT YOU QUIT MOLESTIN' THE SHEEP? DON'T DENY IT! I SAW 'EM WHEN WE CAME INTA TOWN! THEIR HIND ENDS LOOKED LIKE THEY BEEN COURTED BY A BUFFALO! WE ALL KNOW IT WAS YOU!
YOU HAVE QUITE THE MOUTH ON YOU, SIR.
THE NAME'S BILLY THE KID! AND I AIN'T NO SIR!
P'TOOOH

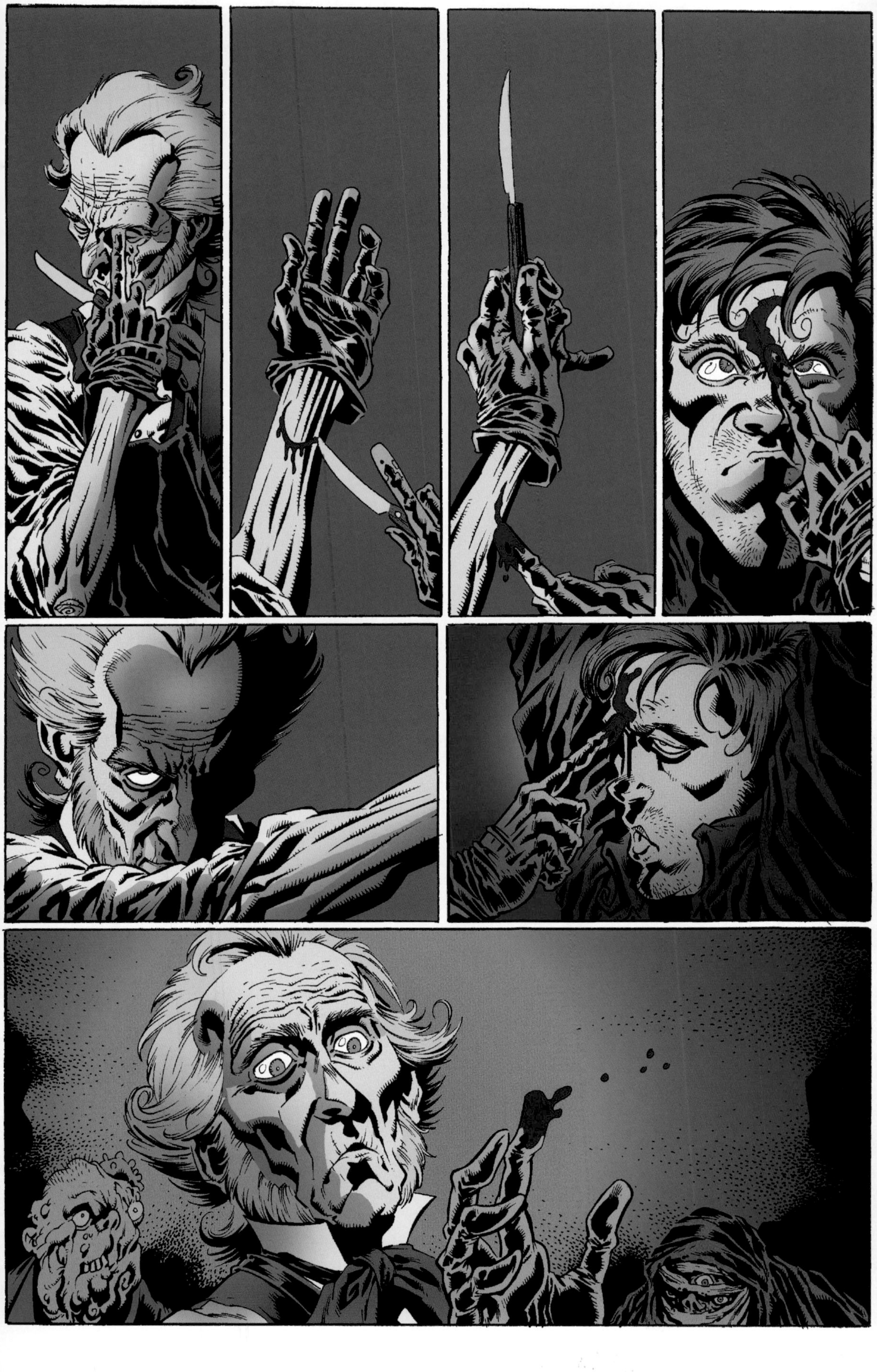

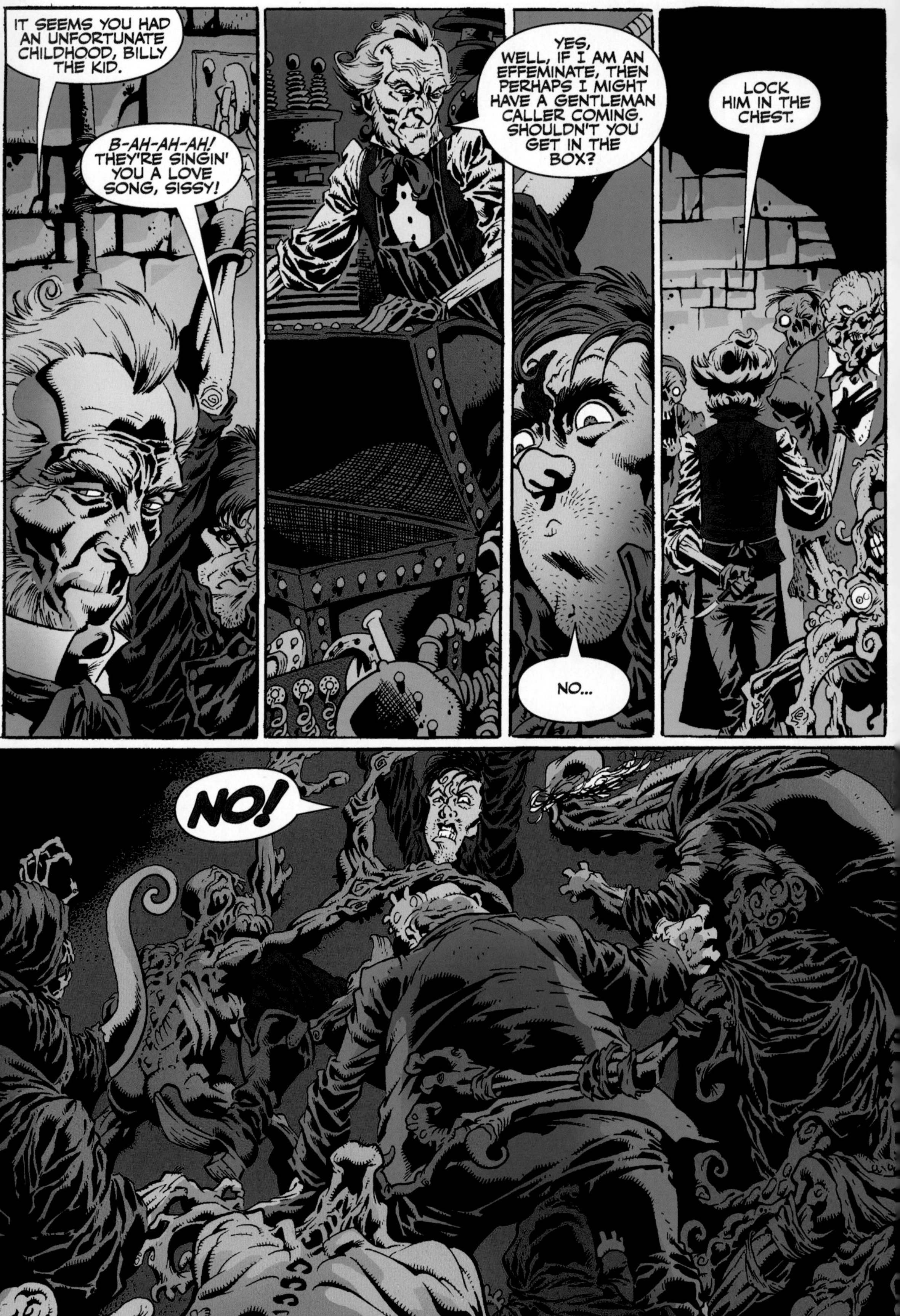
IT SEEMS YOU HAD AN UNFORTUNATE CHILDHOOD, BILLY THE KID.
B-AH-AH-AH! THEY'RE SINGIN' YOU A LOVE SONG, SISSY!
YES, WELL, IF I AM AN EFFEMINATE, THEN PERHAPS I MIGHT HAVE A GENTLEMAN CALLER COMING. SHOULDN'T YOU GET IN THE BOX?
NO...
LOCK HIM IN THE CHEST.
NO!

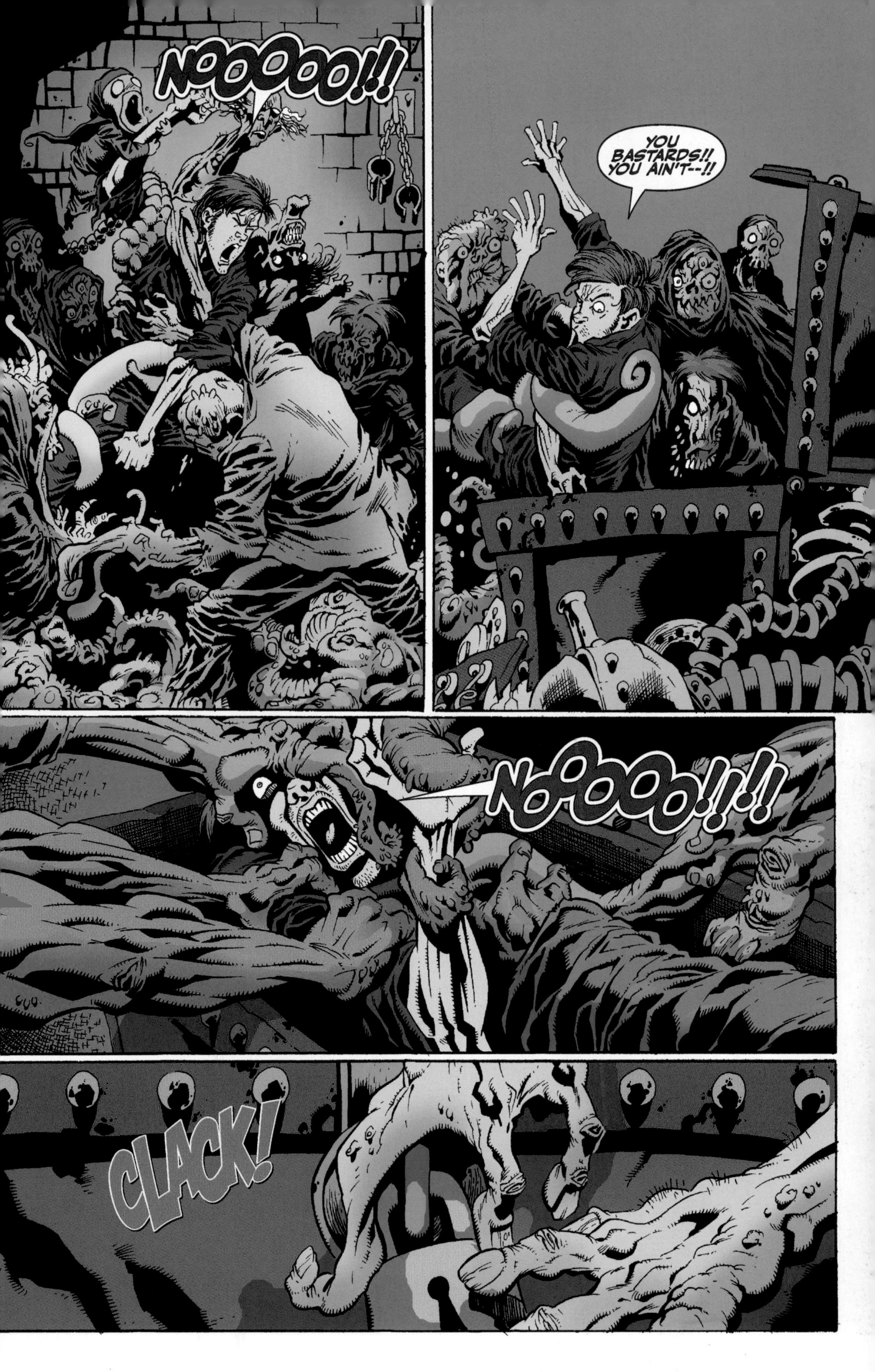
NOOOOO!!
YOU BASTARDS!! YOU AIN'T--!!
NOOOOO!!!!
CLACK!

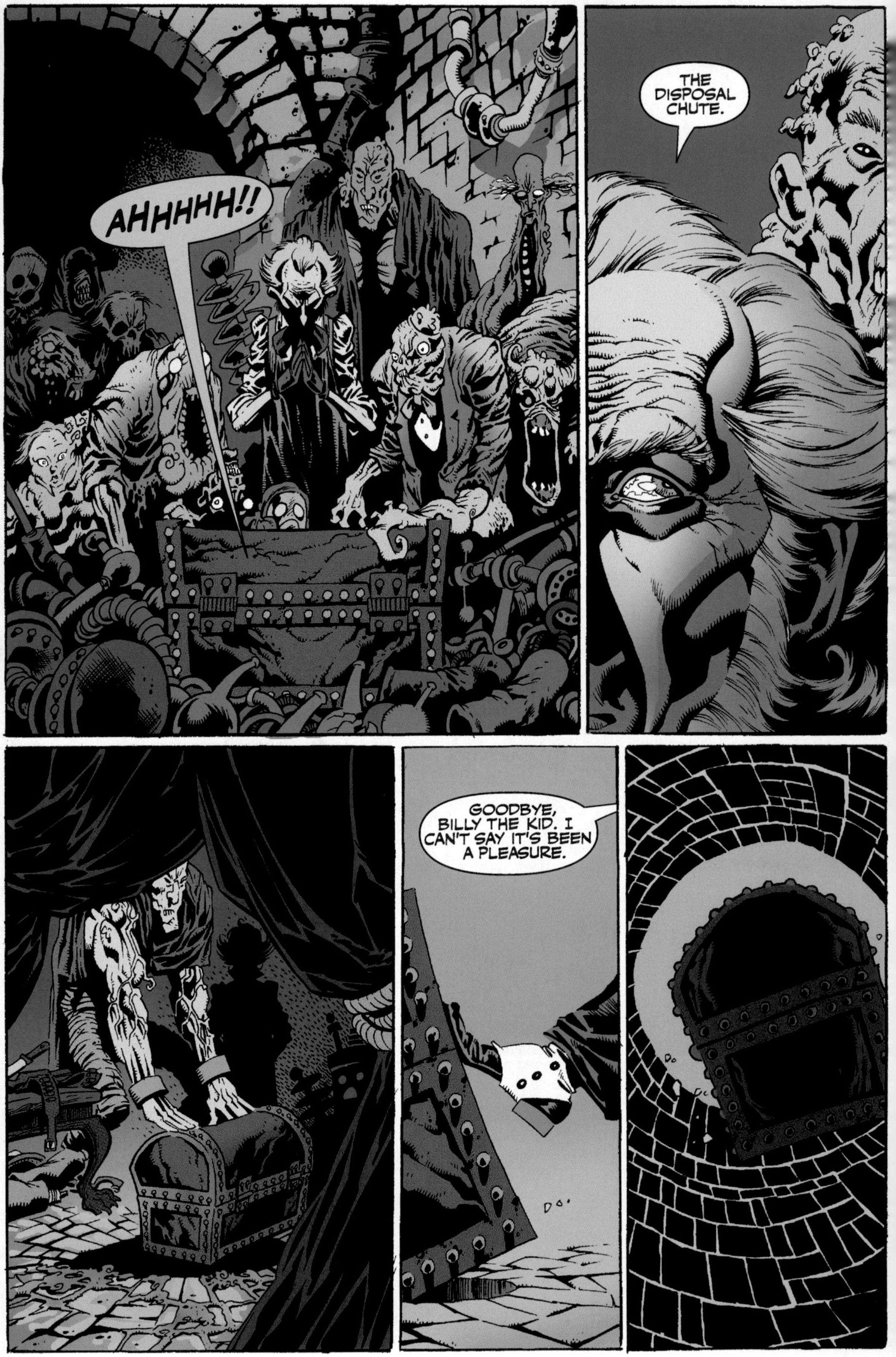
AHHHHH!!
THE DISPOSAL CHUTE.
GOODBYE, BILLY THE KID. I CAN'T SAY IT'S BEEN A PLEASURE.

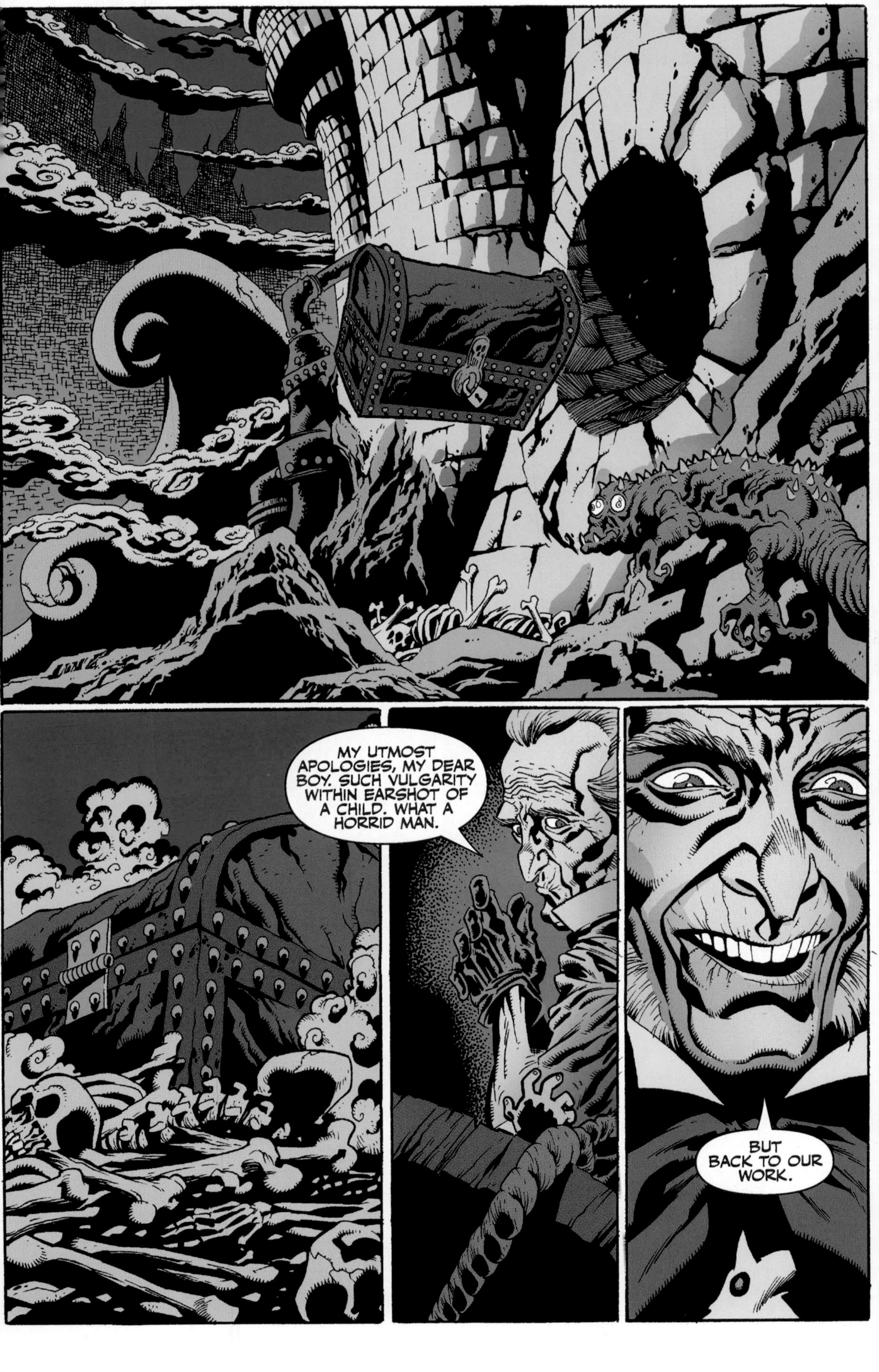
MY UTMOST APOLOGIES, MY DEAR BOY. SUCH VULGARITY WITHIN EARSHOT OF A CHILD. WHAT A HORRID MAN.
BUT BACK TO OUR WORK.

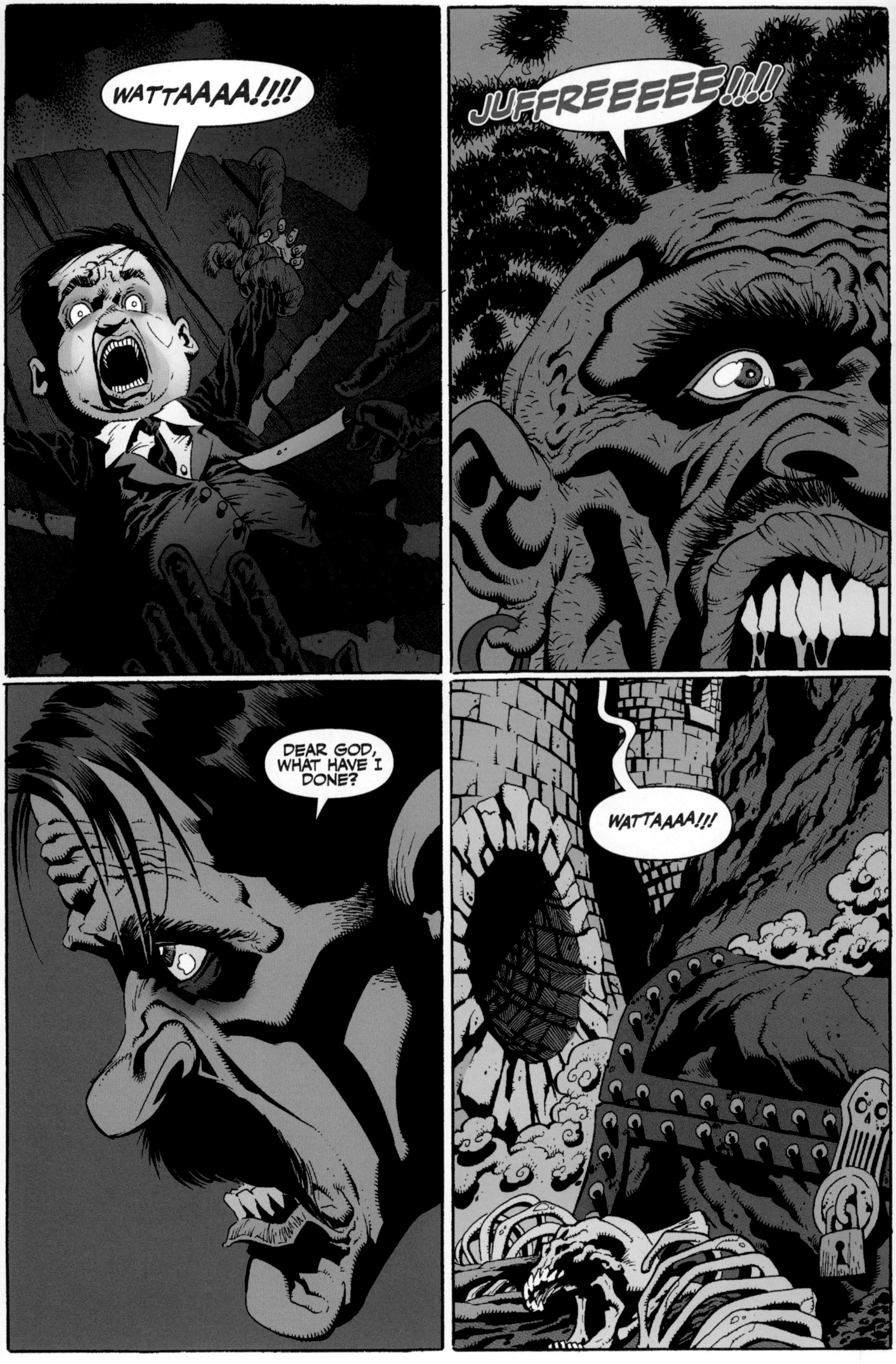
WATTAAAA!!!!
JUFFREEEEEE!!!!!
DEAR GOD, WHAT HAVE I DONE?
WATTAAAA!!!

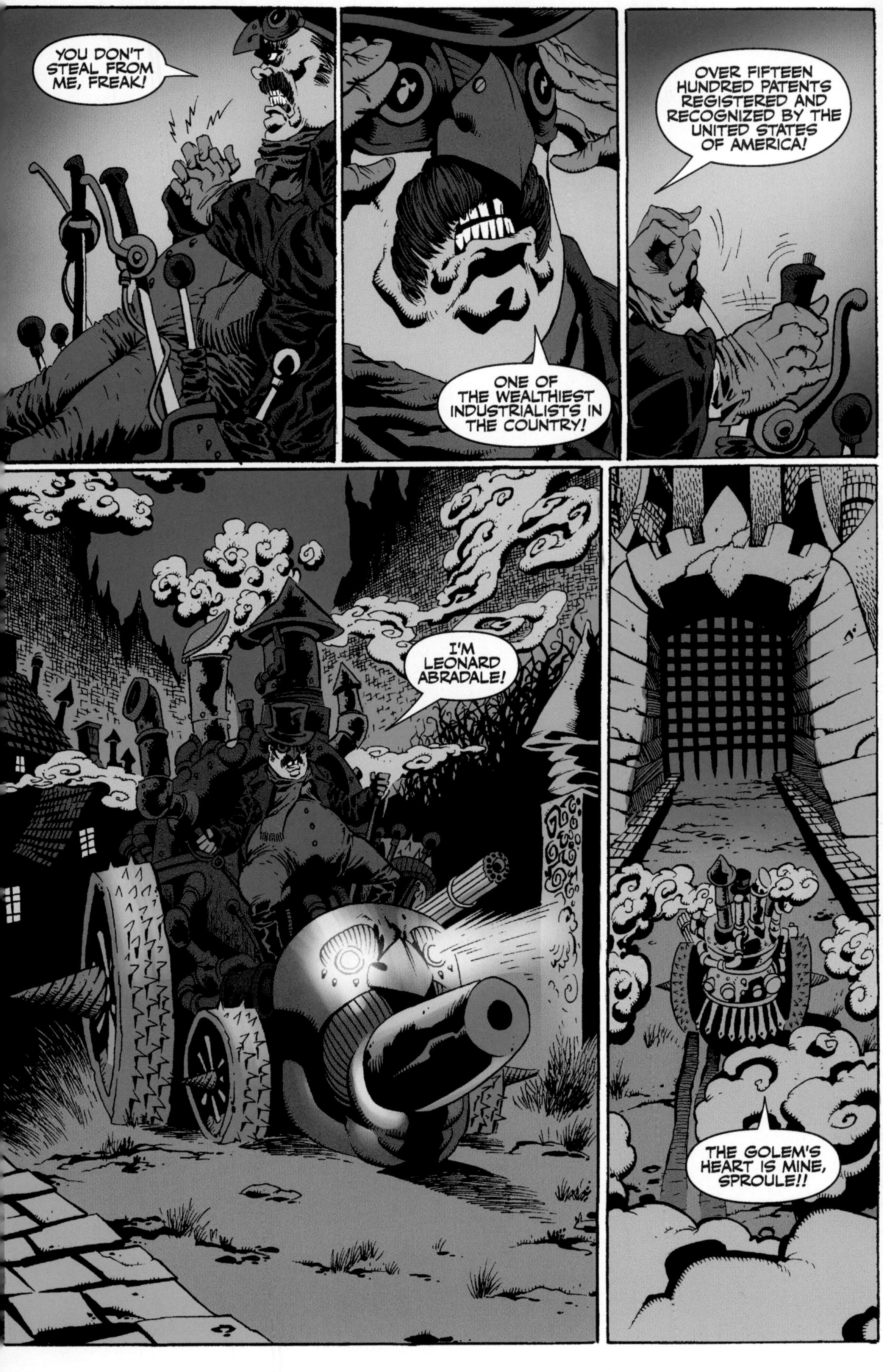
YOU DON'T STEAL FROM ME, FREAK!
ONE OF THE WEALTHIEST INDUSTRIALISTS IN THE COUNTRY!
OVER FIFTEEN HUNDRED PATENTS REGISTERED AND RECOGNIZED BY THE UNITED STATES OF AMERICA!
I'M LEONARD ABRADALE!
THE GOLEM'S HEART IS MINE, SPROULE!!

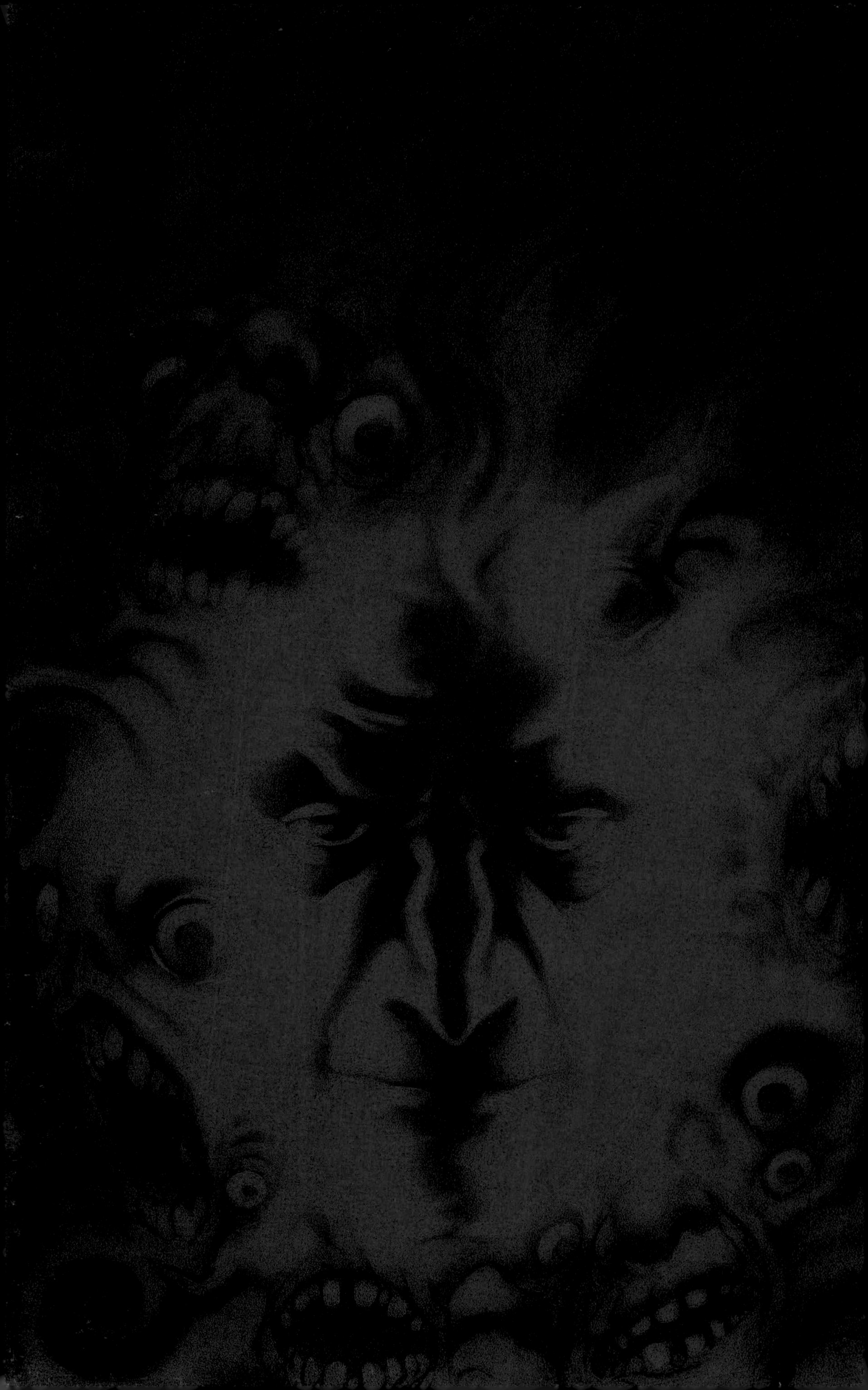

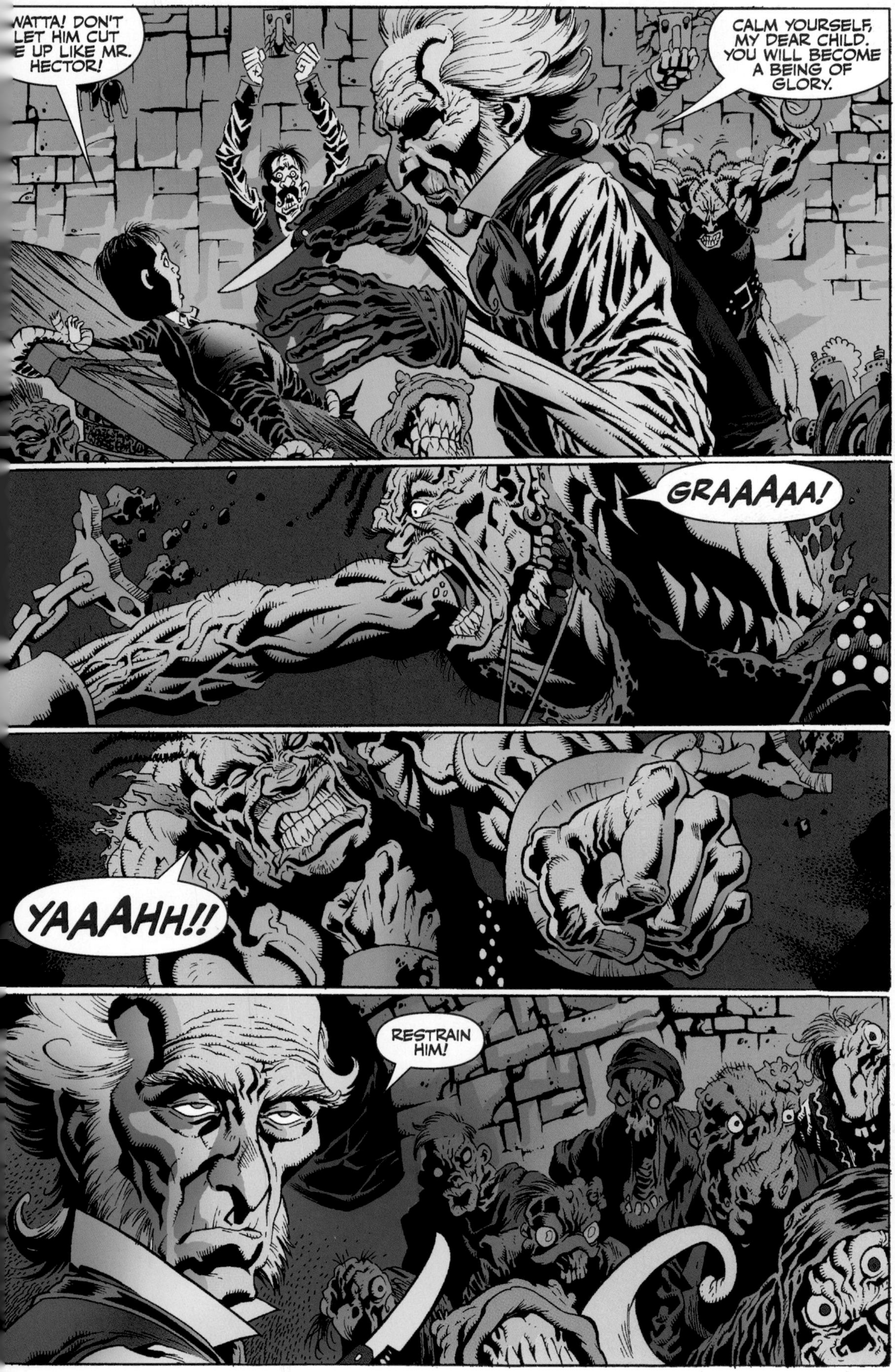
WATTA! DON'T LET HIM CUT E UP LIKE MR. HECTOR!
CALM YOURSELF, MY DEAR CHILD. YOU WILL BECOME A BEING OF GLORY.
GRAAAAA!
YAAAHH!!
RESTRAIN HIM!

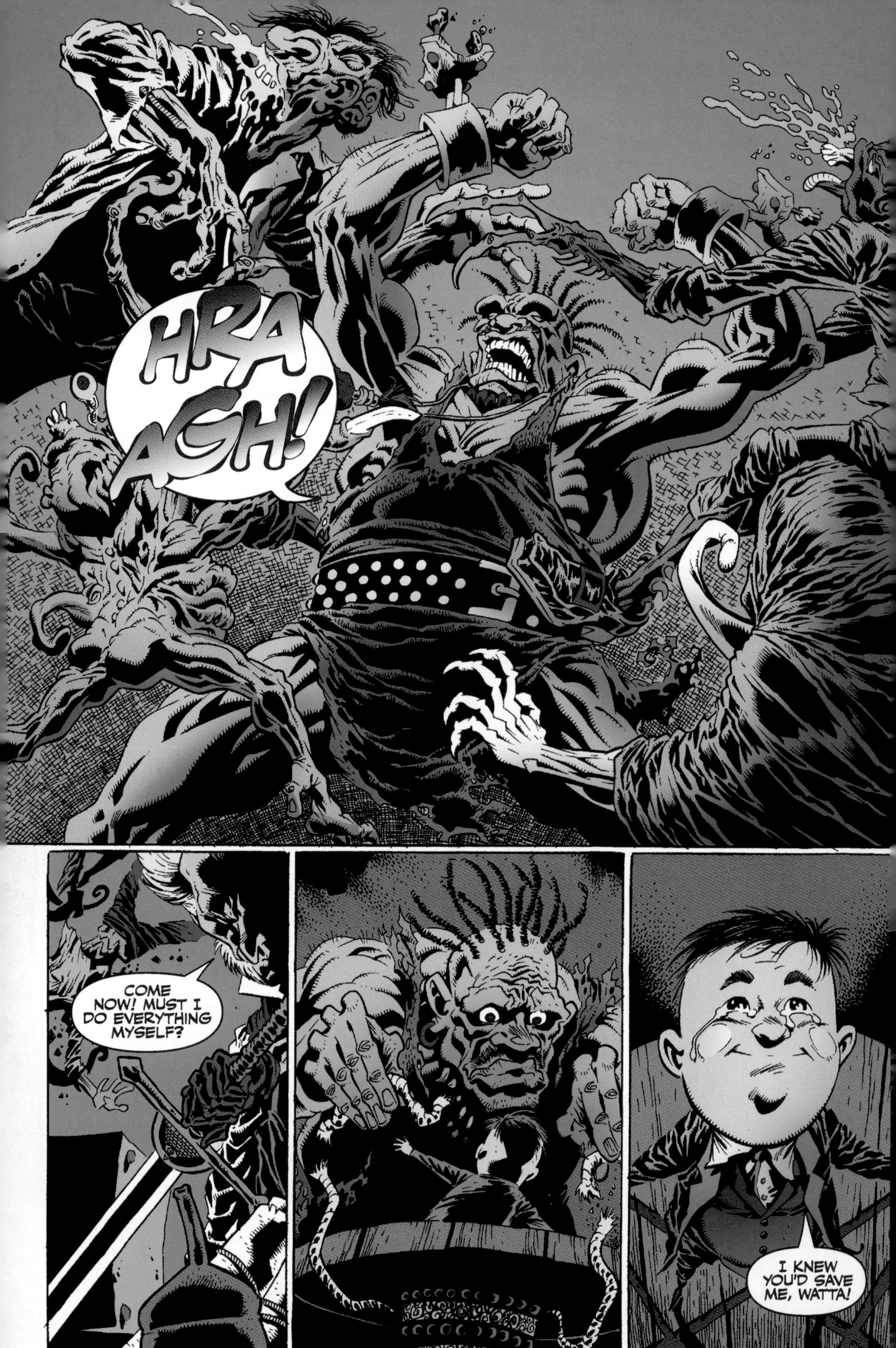
HRAAGH!
COME NOW! MUST I DO EVERYTHING MYSELF?
I KNEW YOU'D SAVE ME, WATTA!

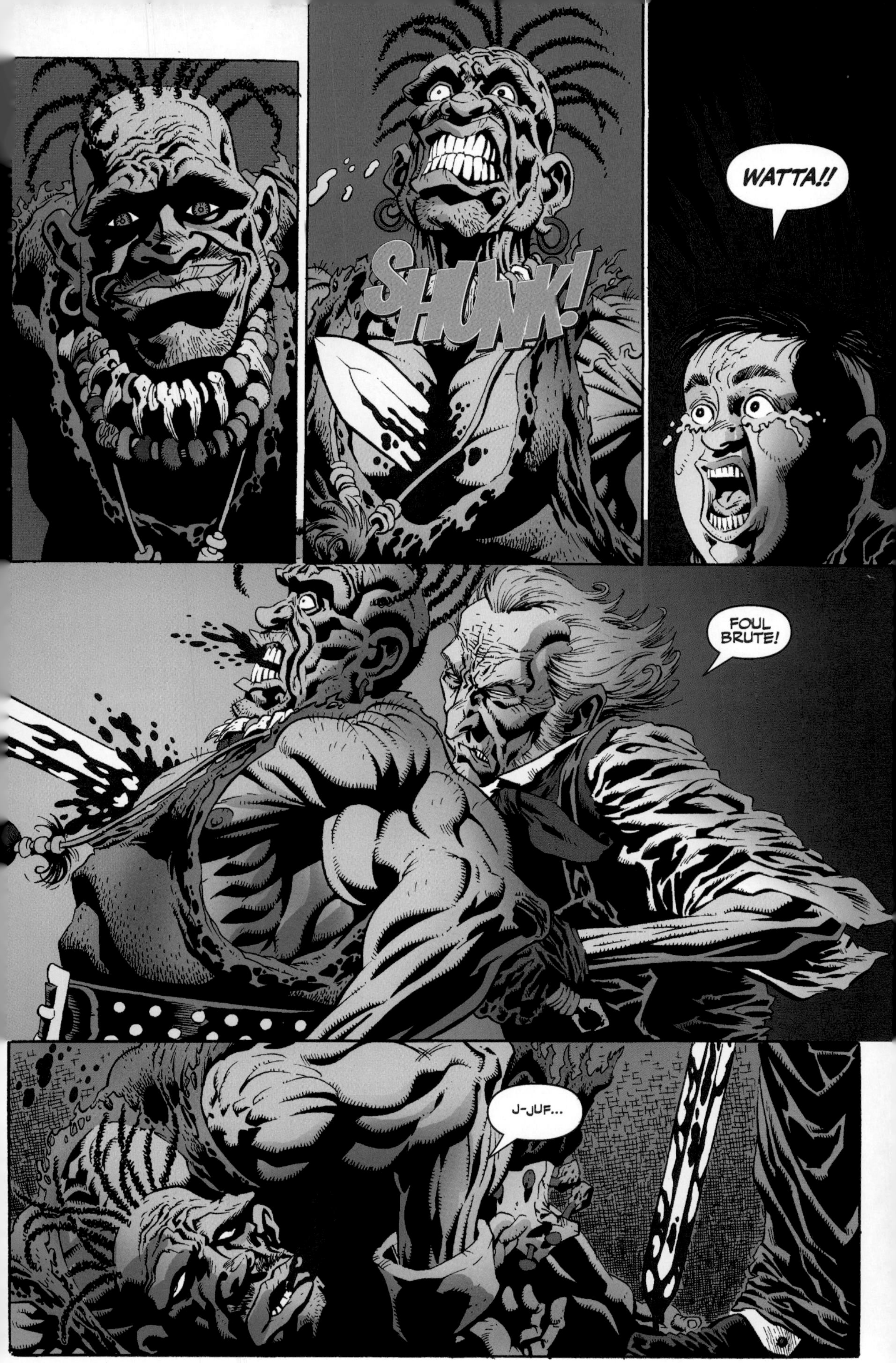
SHUNK!
WATTA!!
FOUL BRUTE!
J-JUF...

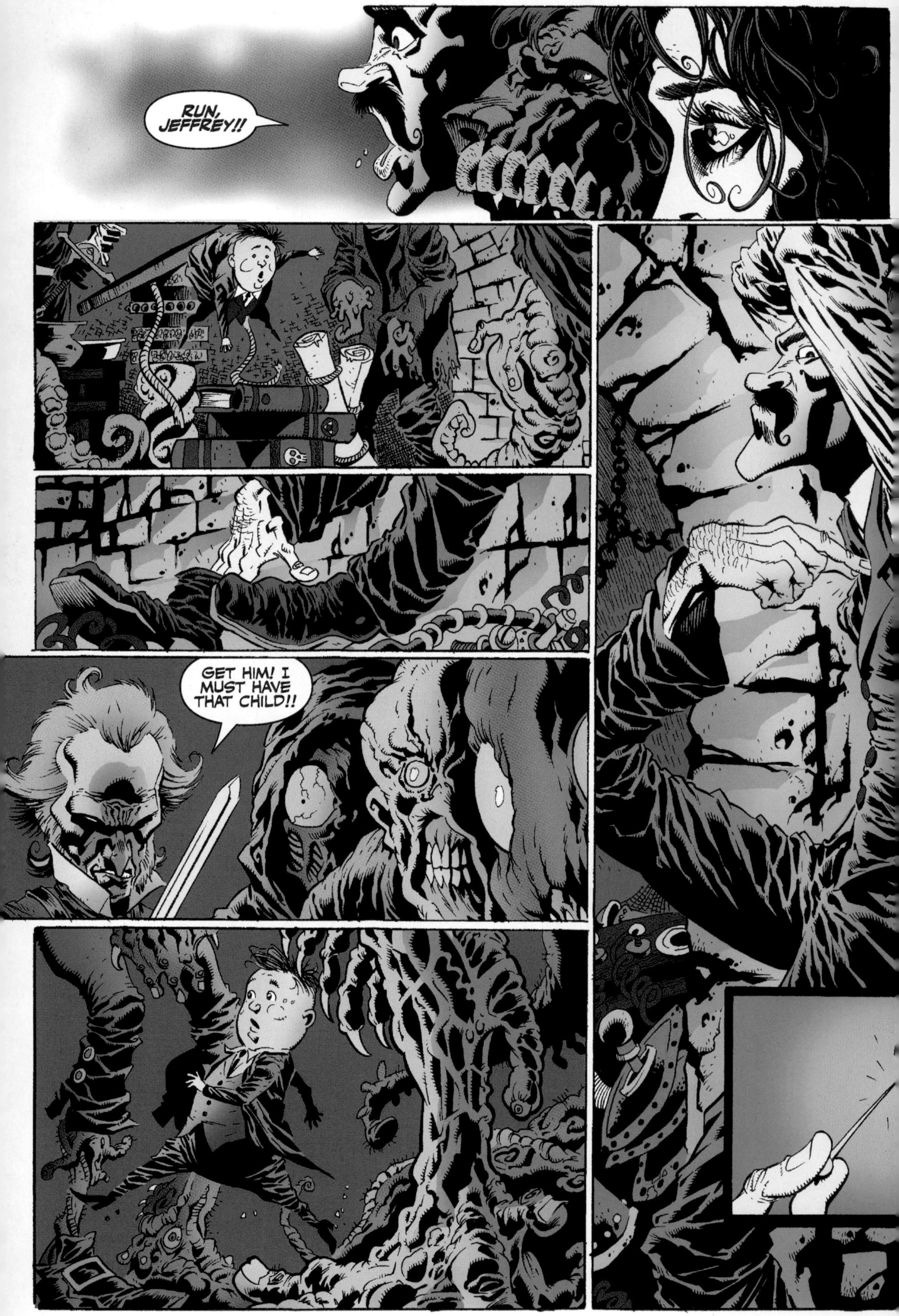
RUN, JEFFREY!!
GET HIM! I MUST HAVE THAT CHILD!!

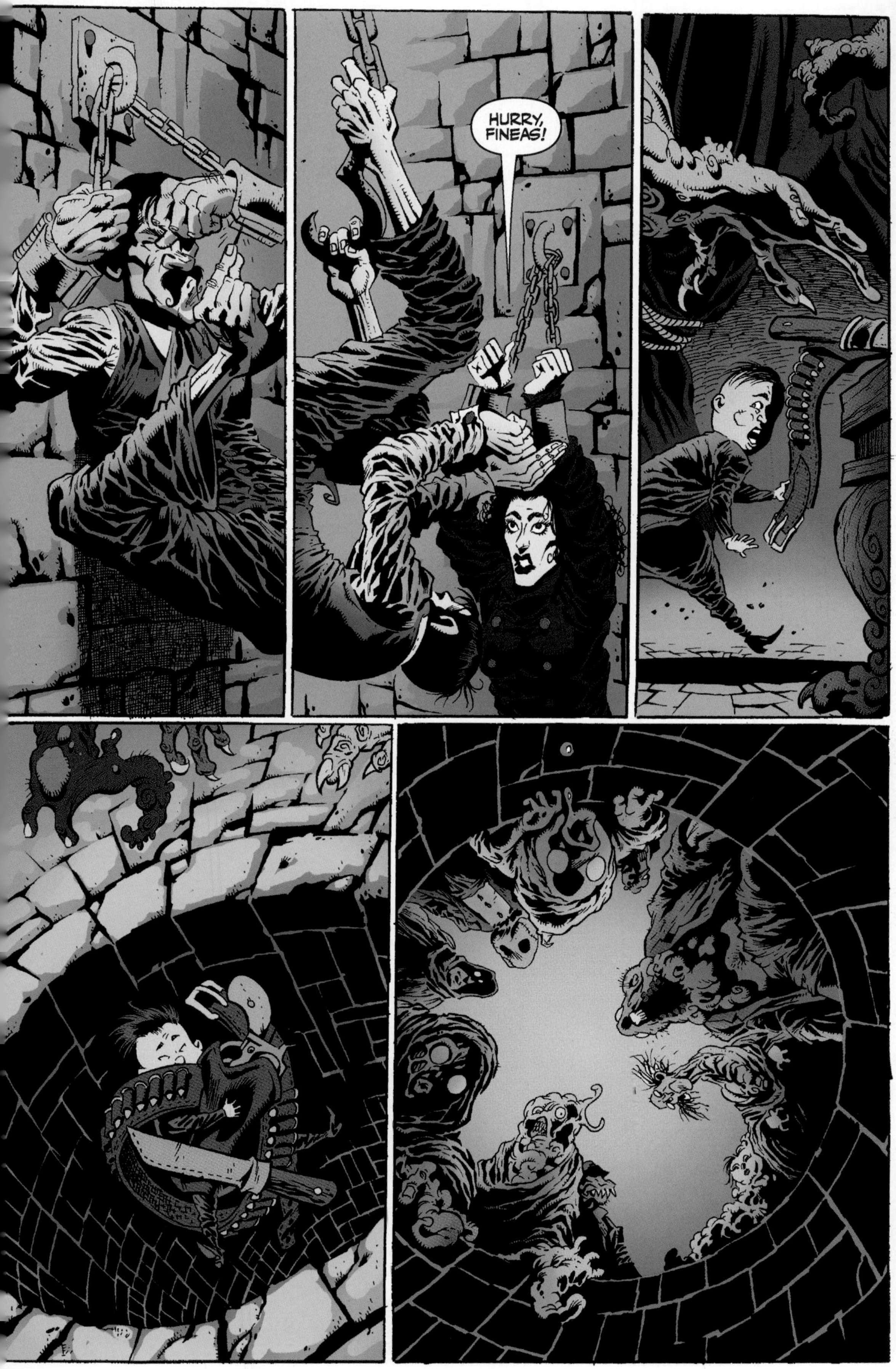
HURRY, FINEAS!

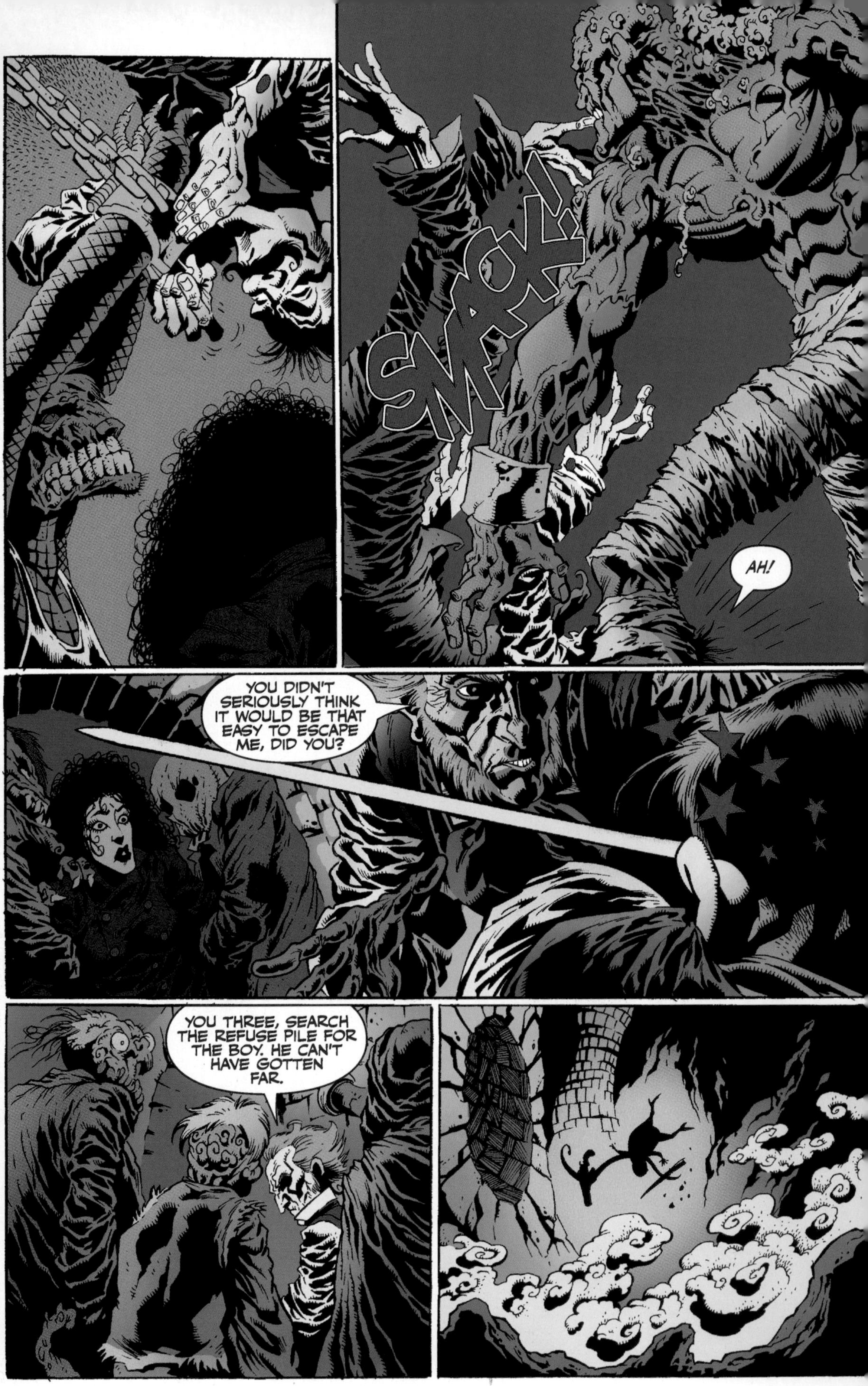
SMACK!
AH!
YOU DIDN'T SERIOUSLY THINK IT WOULD BE THAT EASY TO ESCAPE ME, DID YOU?
YOU THREE, SEARCH THE REFUSE PILE FOR THE BOY. HE CAN'T HAVE GOTTEN FAR.

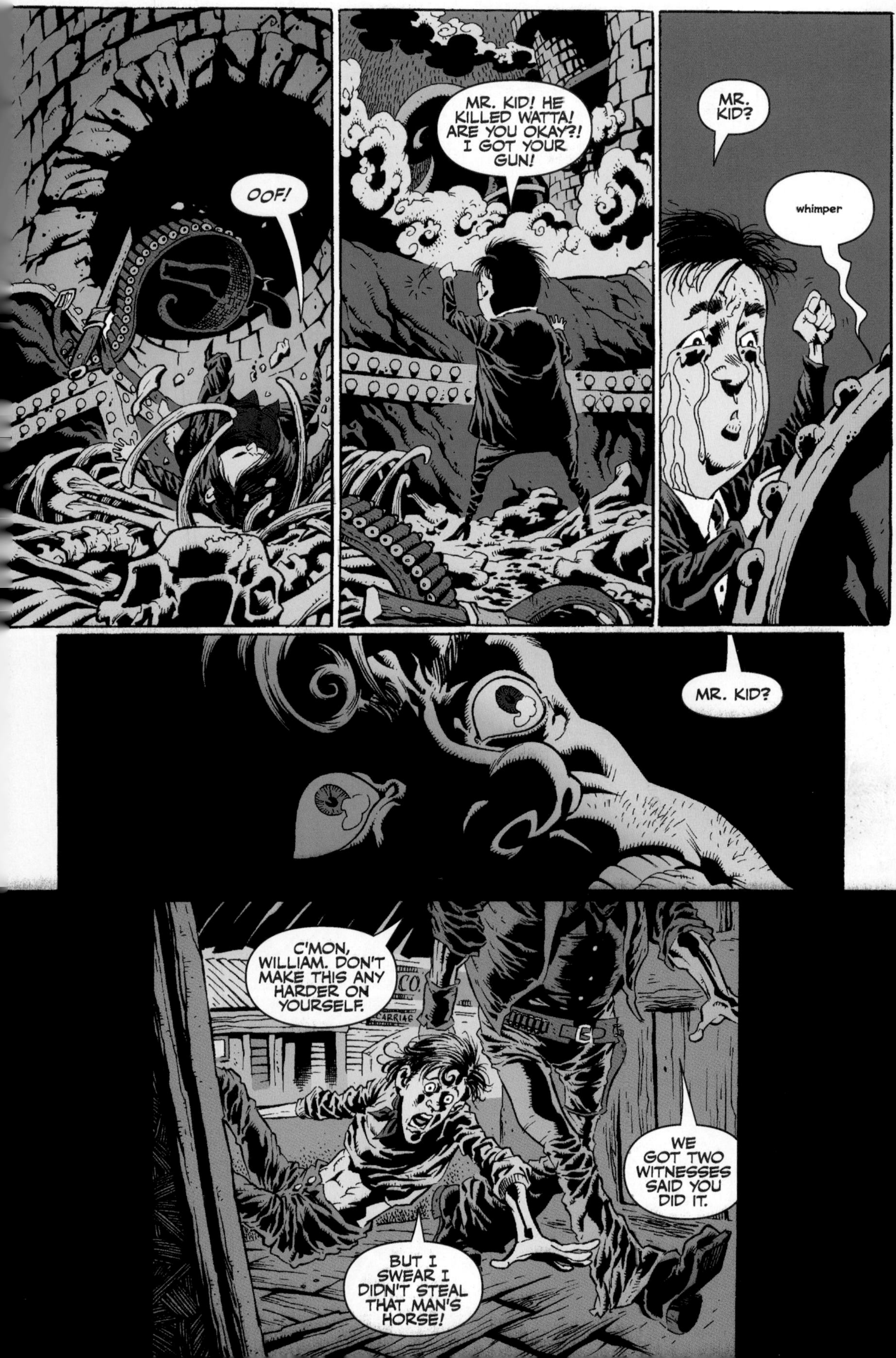
OOF!
MR. KID! HE KILLED WATTA! ARE YOU OKAY?! I GOT YOUR GUN!
MR. KID?
whimper
MR. KID?
C'MON, WILLIAM. DON'T MAKE THIS ANY HARDER ON YOURSELF.
WE GOT TWO WITNESSES SAID YOU DID IT.
BUT I SWEAR I DIDN'T STEAL THAT MAN'S HORSE!

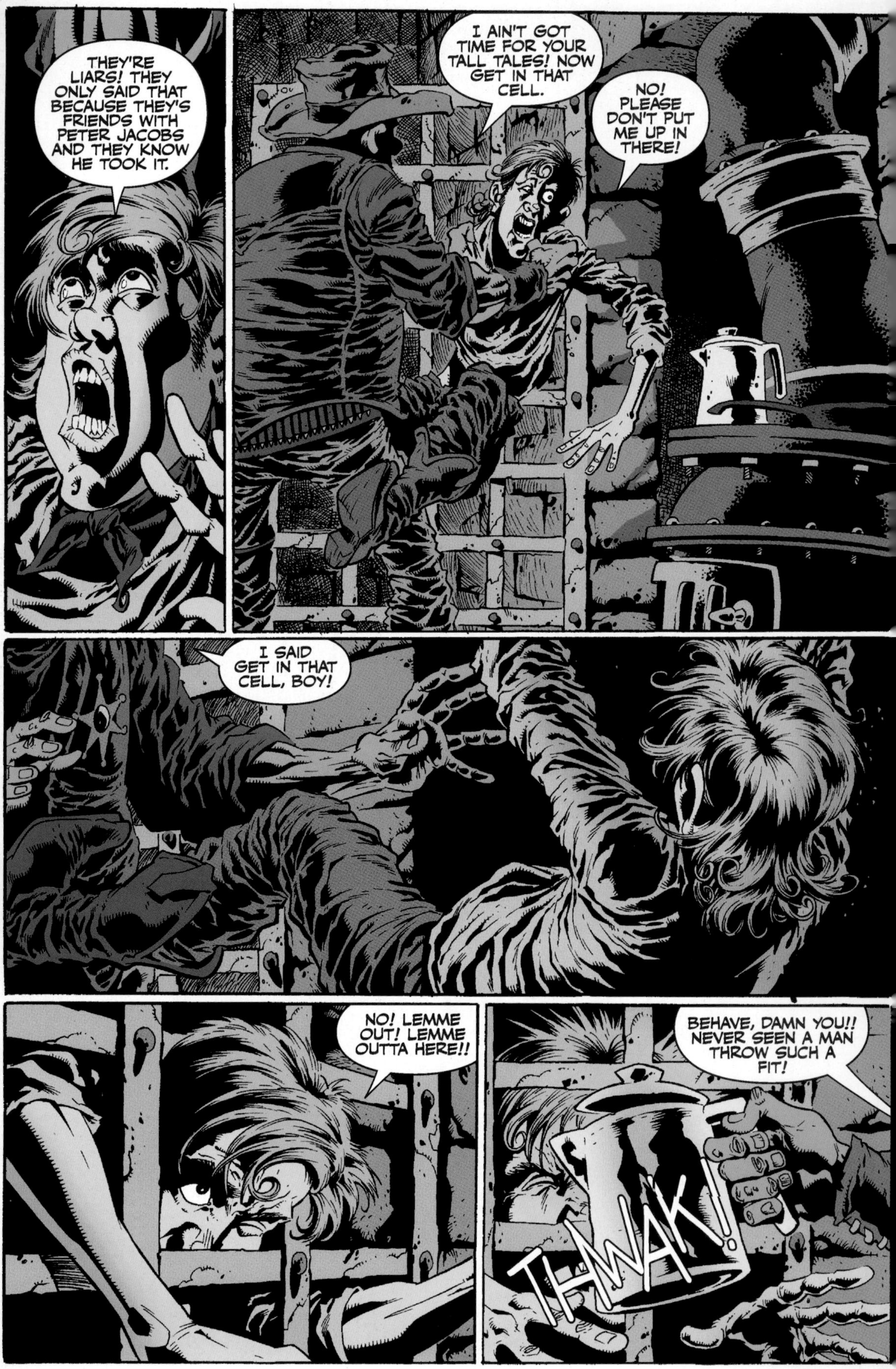
THEY'RE LIARS! THEY ONLY SAID THAT BECAUSE THEY'S FRIENDS WITH PETER JACOBS AND THEY KNOW HE TOOK IT.
I AIN'T GOT TIME FOR YOUR TALL TALES! NOW GET IN THAT CELL.
NO! PLEASE DON'T PUT ME UP IN THERE!
I SAID GET IN THAT CELL, BOY!
NO! LEMME OUT! LEMME OUTTA HERE!!
BEHAVE, DAMN YOU!! NEVER SEEN A MAN THROW SUCH A FIT!
THWAK!

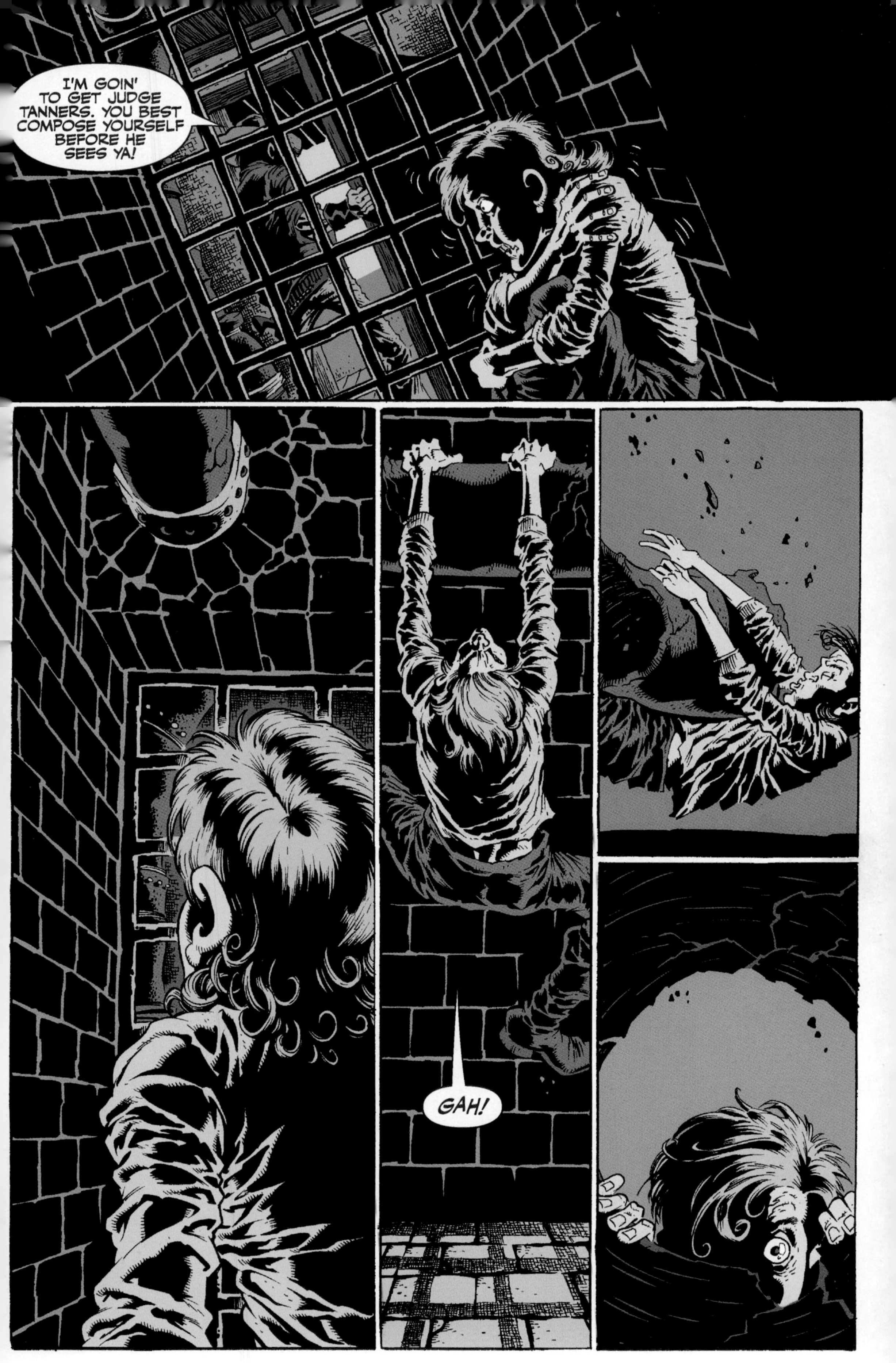
I'M GOIN' TO GET JUDGE TANNERS. YOU BEST COMPOSE YOURSELF BEFORE HE SEES YA!
GAH!

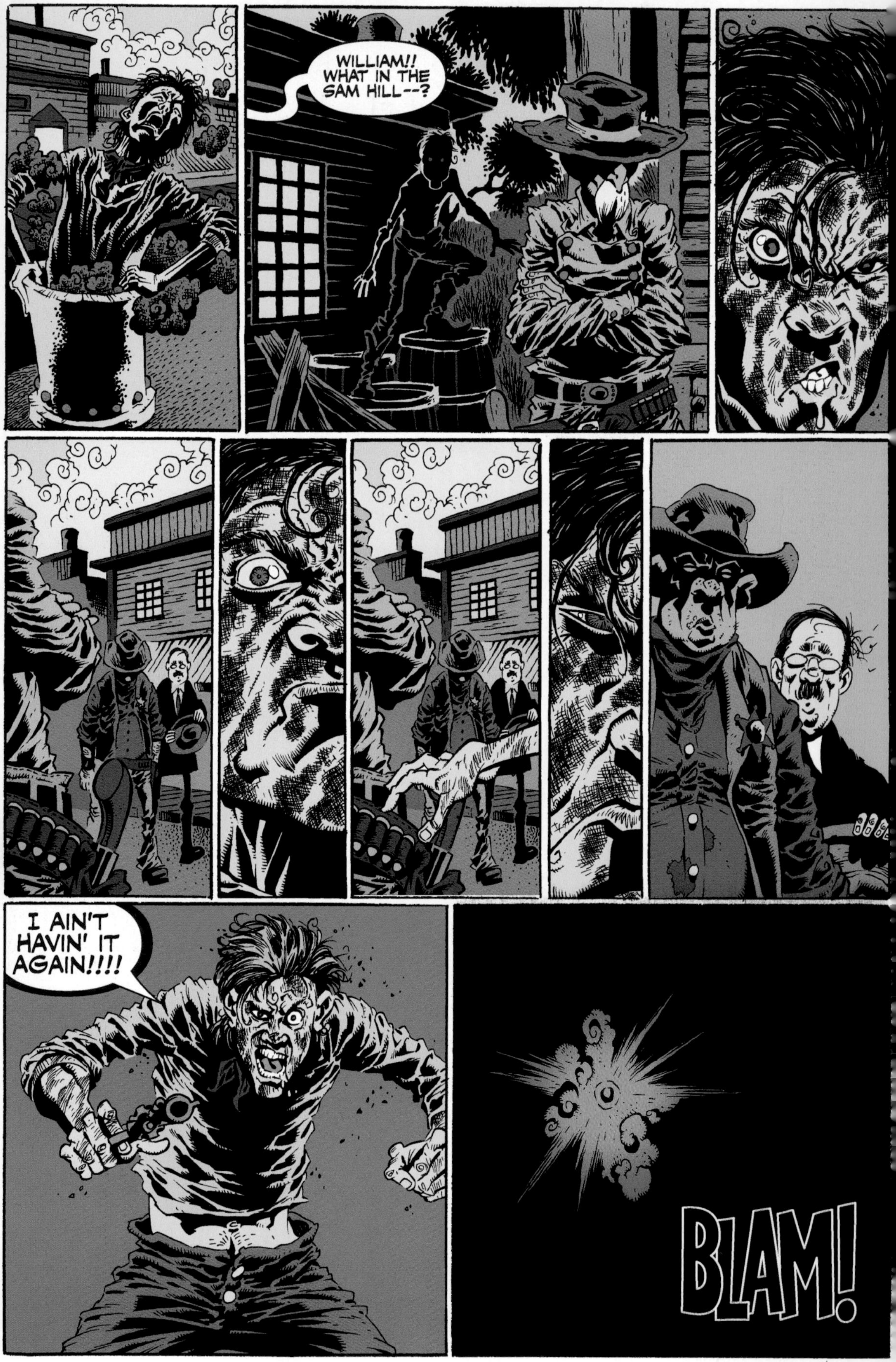
WILLIAM!! WHAT IN THE SAM HILL--?
I AIN'T HAVIN' IT AGAIN!!!!
BLAM!

WHY DID MY MOMMA DO THIS TO ME? MY WATTA IS DEAD, MR. HECTOR IS ALL CUT UP INTO PIECES, AND YOU'RE LOCKED IN A BOX.

PLEASE, MR. KID! PLEASE HELP ME! I'M ALL ALONE! THERE'S NO ONE ELSE LEFT!

MR. KID!! MONSTERS ARE COMING!! HELP ME PLEEEEASE!!

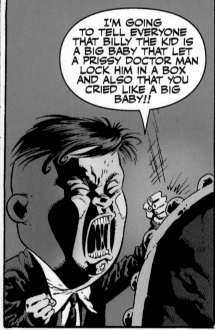

I'M GOING TO TELL EVERYONE THAT BILLY THE KID IS A BIG BABY THAT LET A PRISSY DOCTOR MAN LOCK HIM IN A BOX AND ALSO THAT YOU CRIED LIKE A BIG BABY!!

YOU WERE MY HERO.

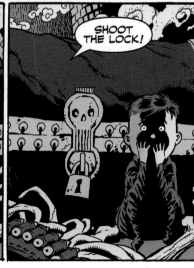

SHOOT THE LOCK!

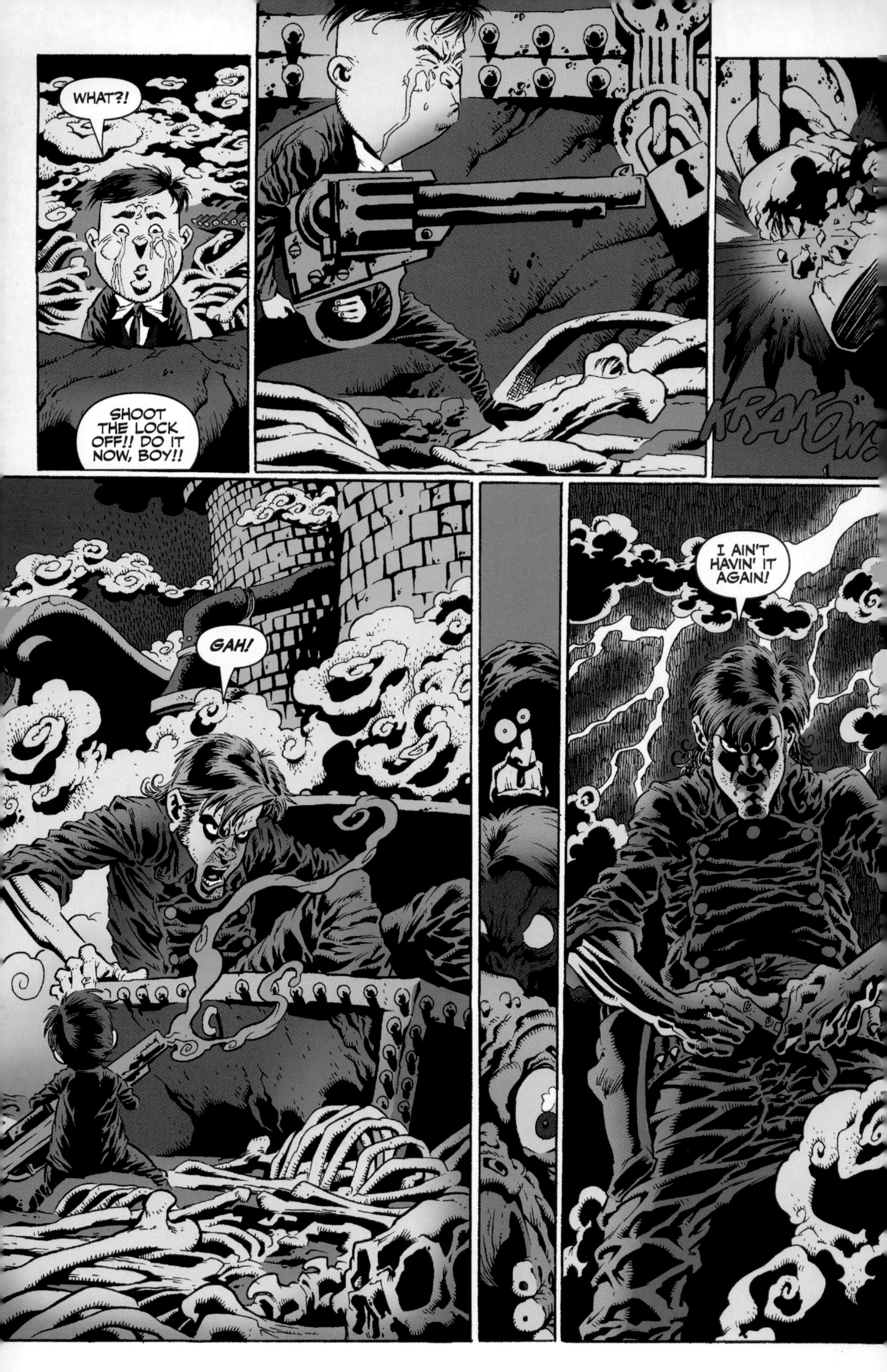
WHAT?!
SHOOT THE LOCK OFF!! DO IT NOW, BOY!!
KRAKOW!
GAH!
I AIN'T HAVIN' IT AGAIN!

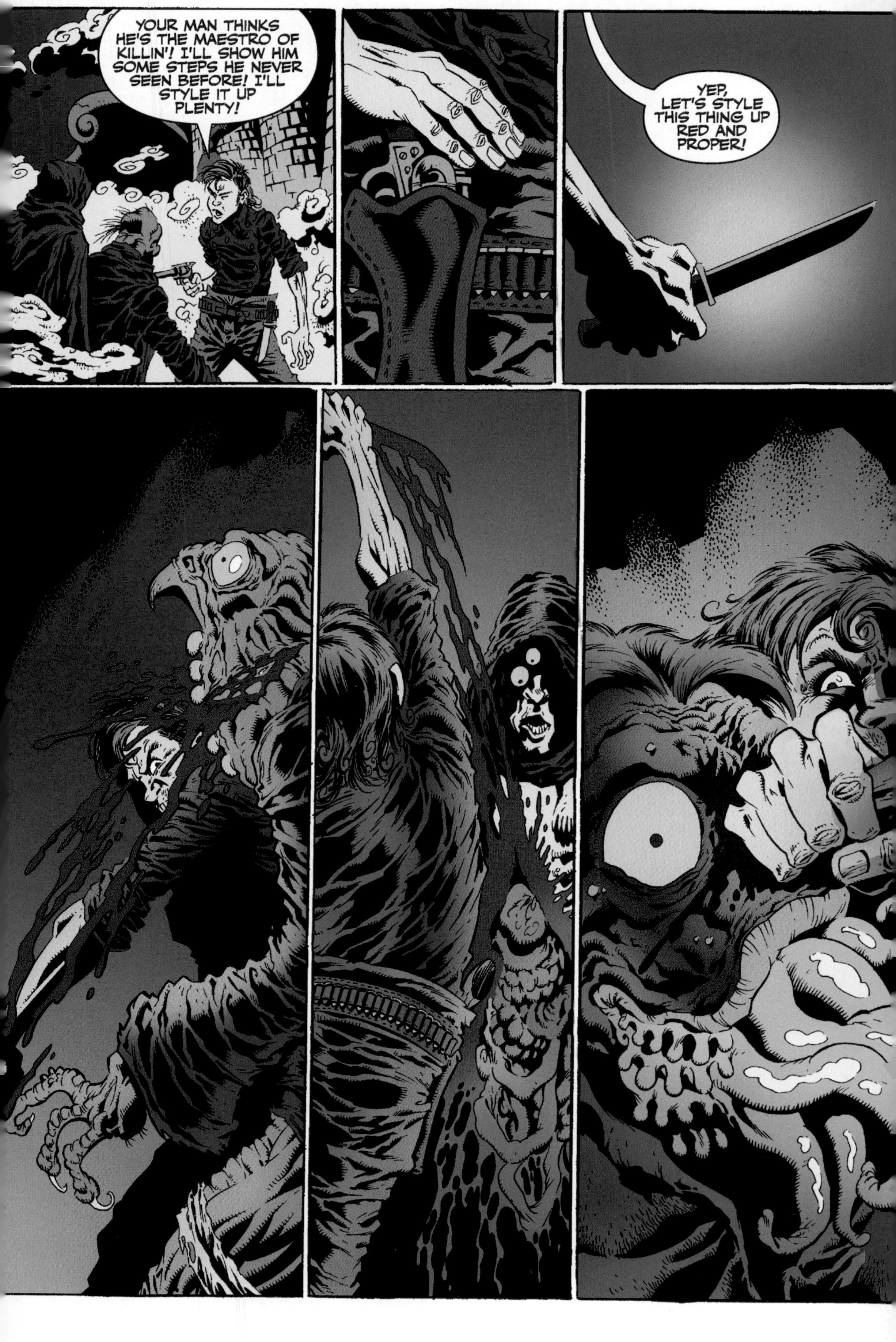

YOUR MAN THINKS HE'S THE MAESTRO OF KILLIN'! I'LL SHOW HIM SOME STEPS HE NEVER SEEN BEFORE! I'LL STYLE IT UP PLENTY!
YEP, LET'S STYLE THIS THING UP RED AND PROPER!

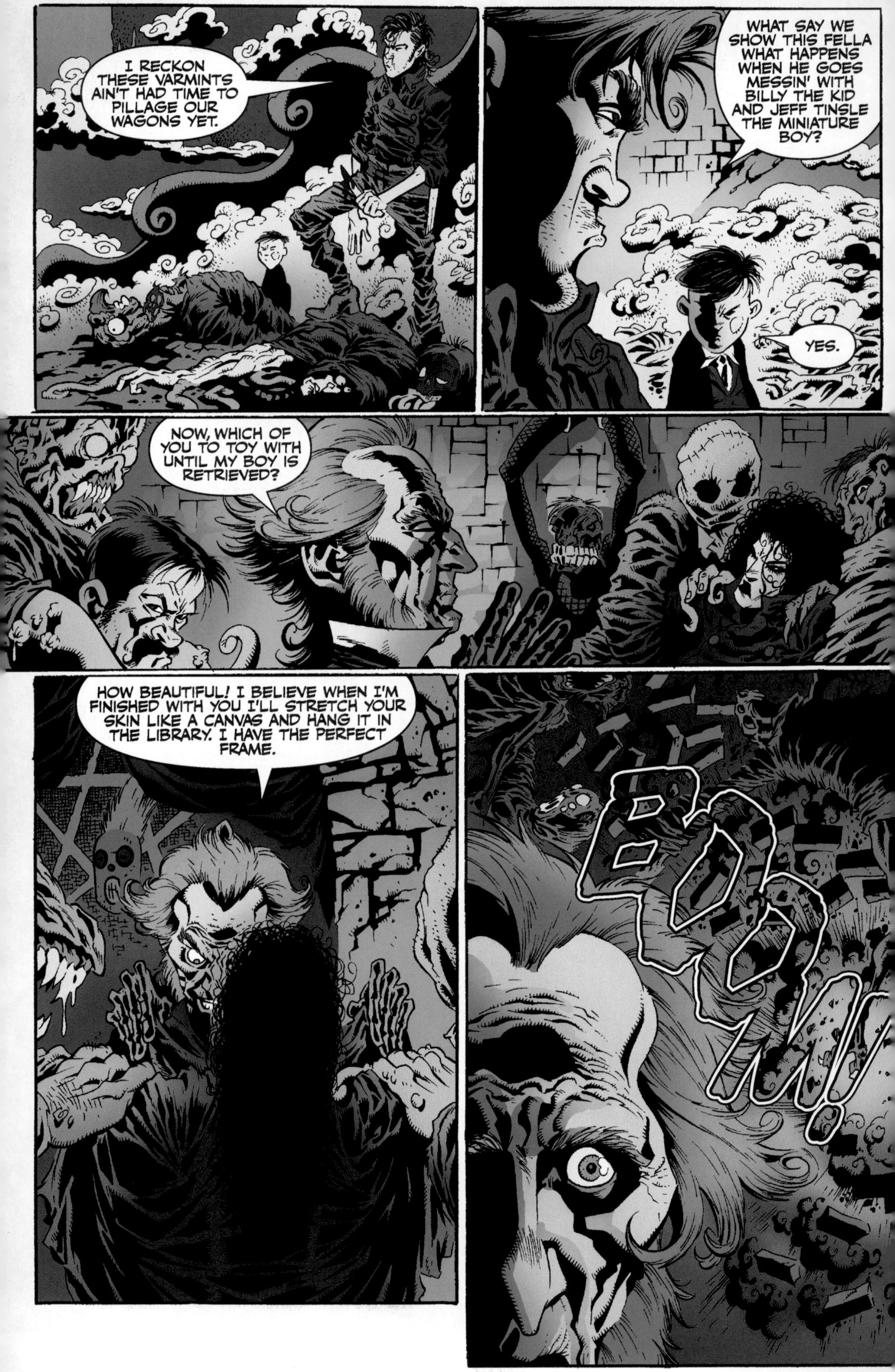
I RECKON THESE VARMINTS AIN'T HAD TIME TO PILLAGE OUR WAGONS YET.
WHAT SAY WE SHOW THIS FELLA WHAT HAPPENS WHEN HE GOES MESSIN' WITH BILLY THE KID AND JEFF TINSLE THE MINIATURE BOY?
YES.
NOW, WHICH OF YOU TO TOY WITH UNTIL MY BOY IS RETRIEVED?
HOW BEAUTIFUL! I BELIEVE WHEN I'M FINISHED WITH YOU I'LL STRETCH YOUR SKIN LIKE A CANVAS AND HANG IT IN THE LIBRARY. I HAVE THE PERFECT FRAME.
BOOM!!

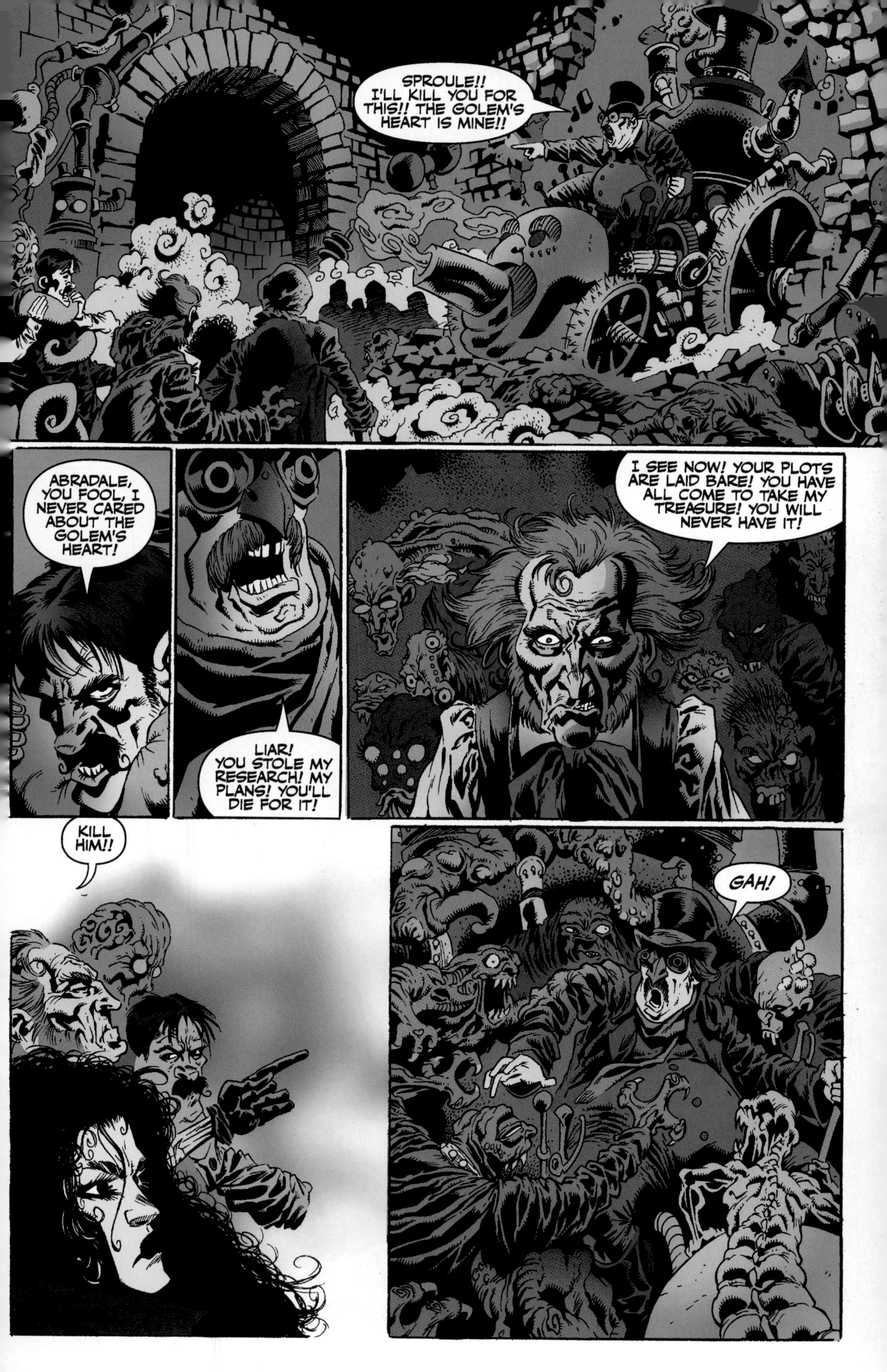
SPROULE!! I'LL KILL YOU FOR THIS!! THE GOLEM'S HEART IS MINE!!
ABRADALE, YOU FOOL, I NEVER CARED ABOUT THE GOLEM'S HEART!
LIAR! YOU STOLE MY RESEARCH! MY PLANS! YOU'LL DIE FOR IT!
I SEE NOW! YOUR PLOTS ARE LAID BARE! YOU HAVE ALL COME TO TAKE MY TREASURE! YOU WILL NEVER HAVE IT!
KILL HIM!!
GAH!

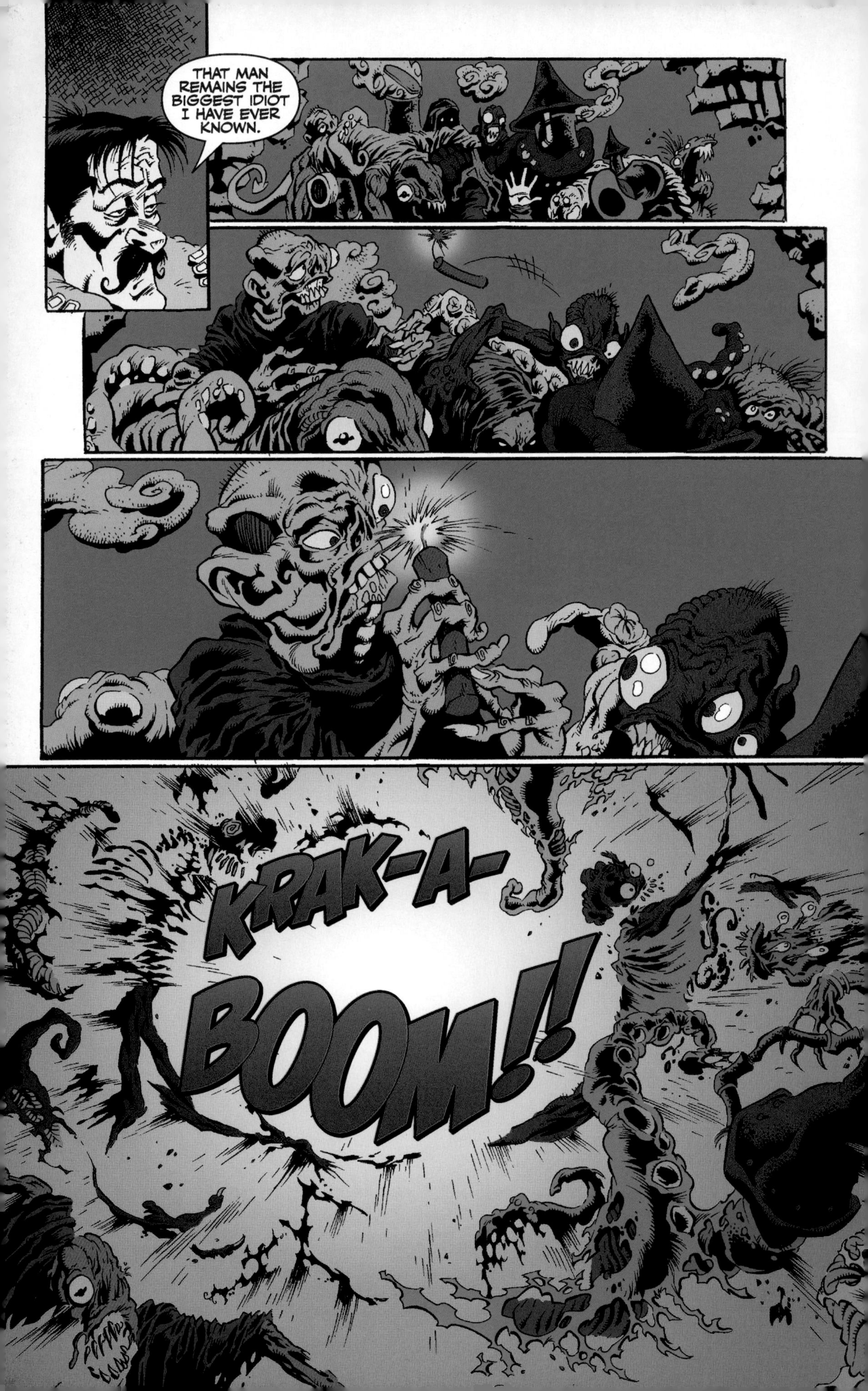
THAT MAN REMAINS THE BIGGEST IDIOT I HAVE EVER KNOWN.
KRAK-A-BOOM!!

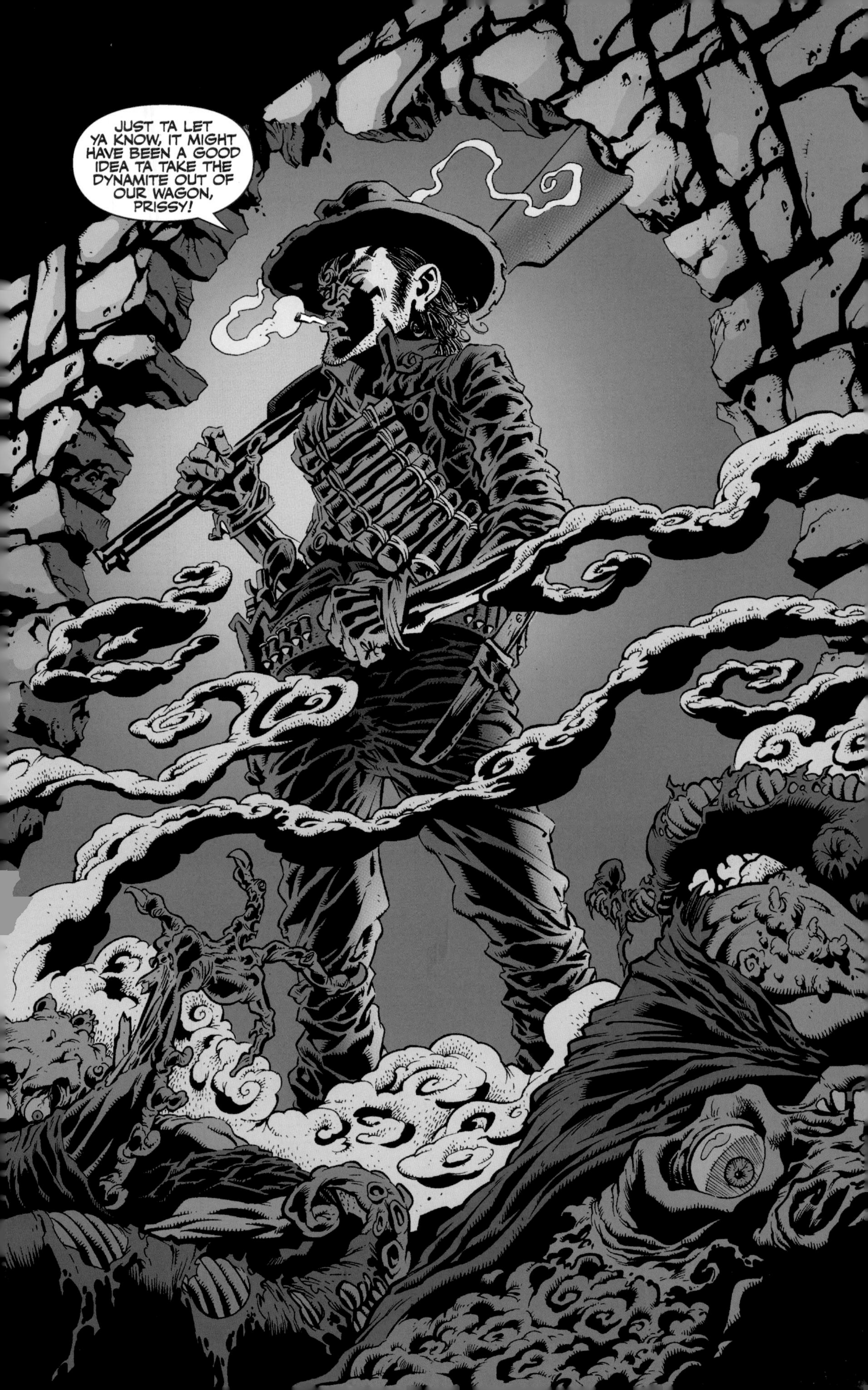
JUST TA LET YA KNOW, IT MIGHT HAVE BEEN A GOOD IDEA TA TAKE THE DYNAMITE OUT OF OUR WAGON, PRISSY!

I'M THROUGH TOYING WITH YOU, WESTERNER! NOW I WILL BUILD YOU ANEW FOR THE SOLE PURPOSE OF TORMENT! THE MOST UNREPENTANT SOUL IN THE BLACKEST CORNER OF HELL WILL HOLD PITY FOR YOUR AGONY!

BLAM! BLAM!

BLAM!

BLAM!

BLAM!

BLAM!

BLAM!

BLAM! BLAM! BLAM!

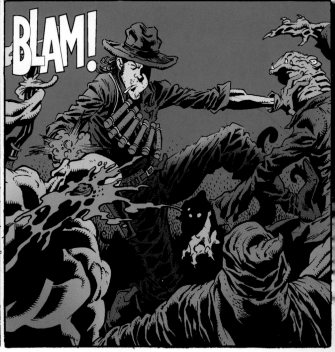

BLAM!

BLAM!

YOU FOOL! YOUR EFFORTS ARE FUTILE! MY ARMY IS VAST! YOU DON'T HAVE AMMUNITION ENOUGH TO KILL THEM ALL!

IT IS MY TREASURE THAT DRIVES THEM! AS LONG AS IT IS IN MY POSSESSION, THEY WILL NEVER FALTER OR DISOBEY!

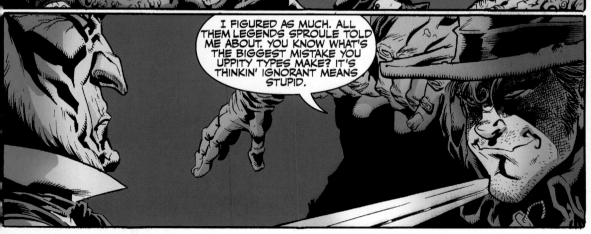

I FIGURED AS MUCH. ALL THEM LEGENDS SPROULE TOLD ME ABOUT. YOU KNOW WHAT'S THE BIGGEST MISTAKE YOU UPPITY TYPES MAKE? IT'S THINKIN' IGNORANT MEANS STUPID.

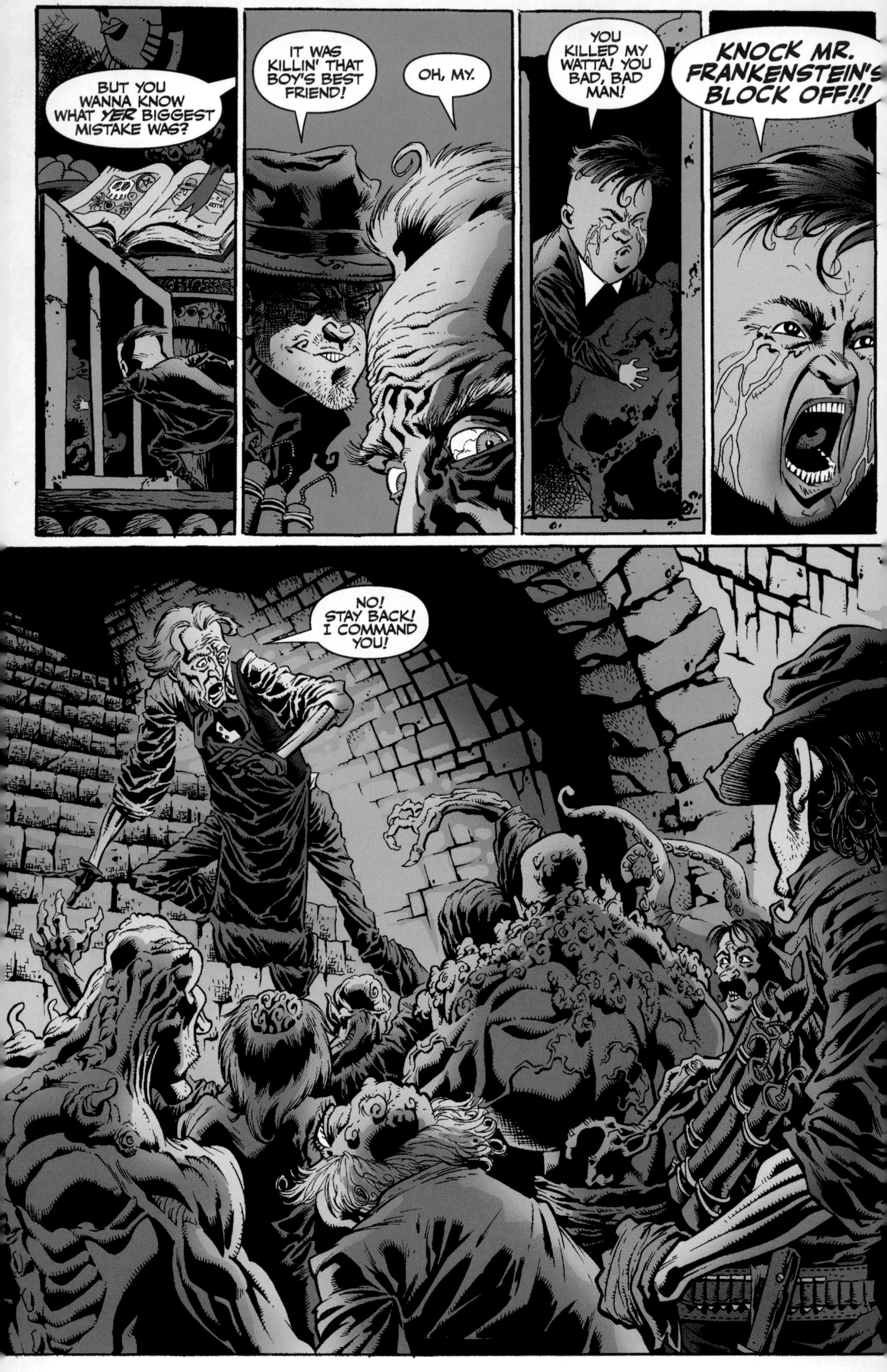
BUT YOU WANNA KNOW WHAT YER BIGGEST MISTAKE WAS?
IT WAS KILLIN' THAT BOY'S BEST FRIEND!
OH, MY.
YOU KILLED MY WATTA! YOU BAD, BAD MAN!
KNOCK MR. FRANKENSTEIN's BLOCK OFF!!!
NO! STAY BACK! I COMMAND YOU!

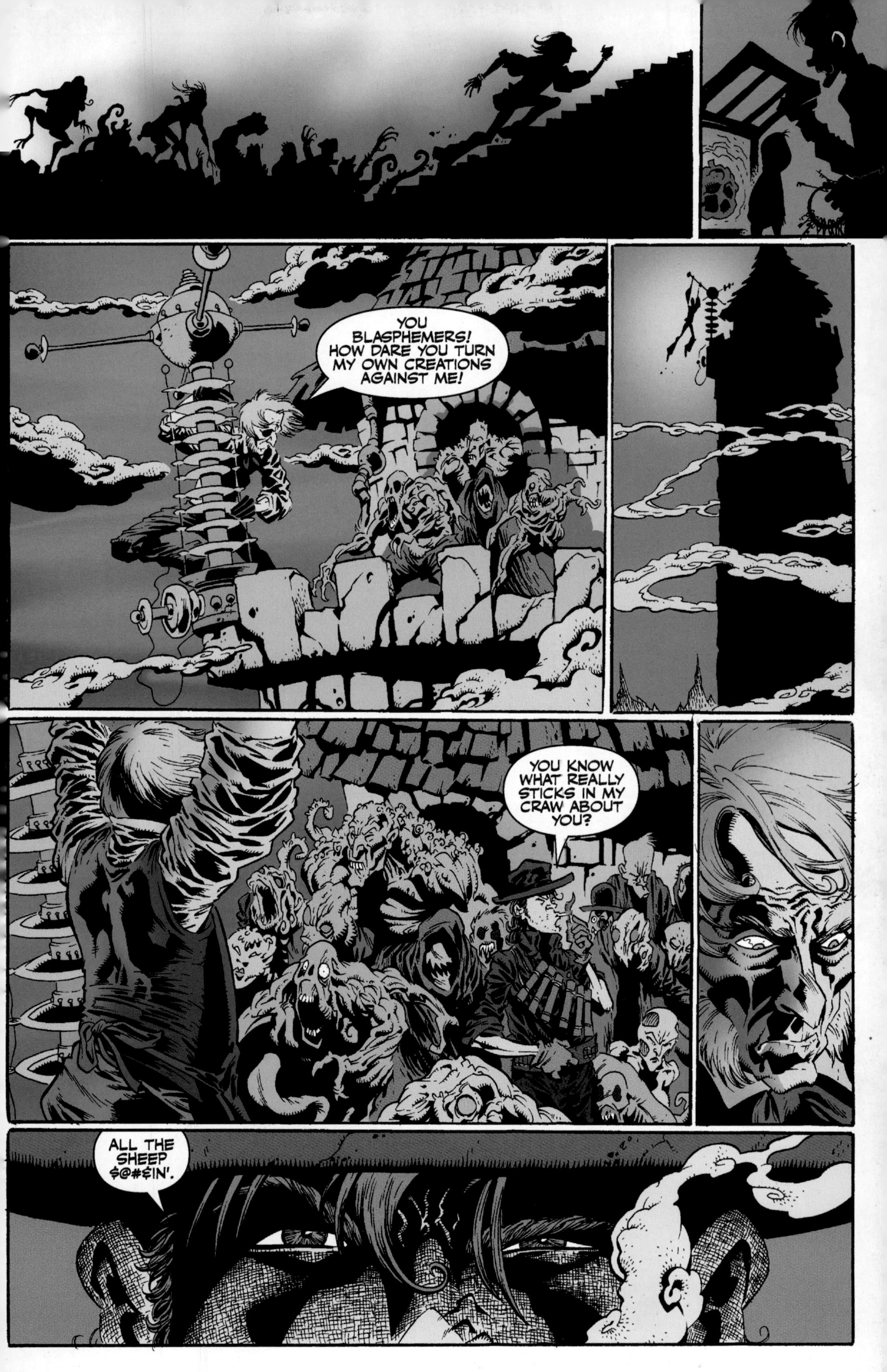
YOU BLASPHEMERS! HOW DARE YOU TURN MY OWN CREATIONS AGAINST ME!
YOU KNOW WHAT REALLY STICKS IN MY CRAW ABOUT YOU?
ALL THE SHEEP $@#&IN'.

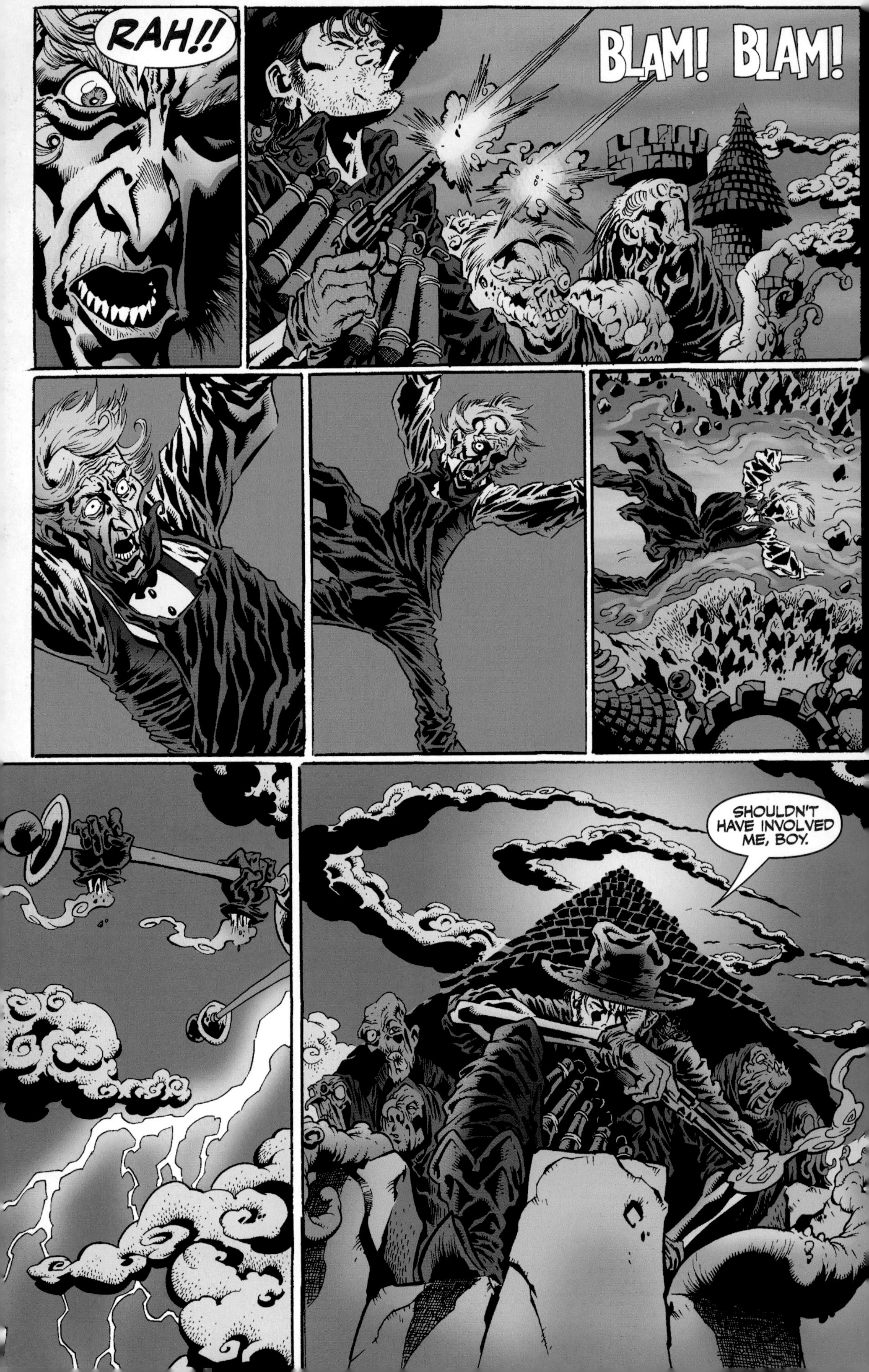
RAH!!
BLAM! BLAM!
SHOULDN'T HAVE INVOLVED ME, BOY.

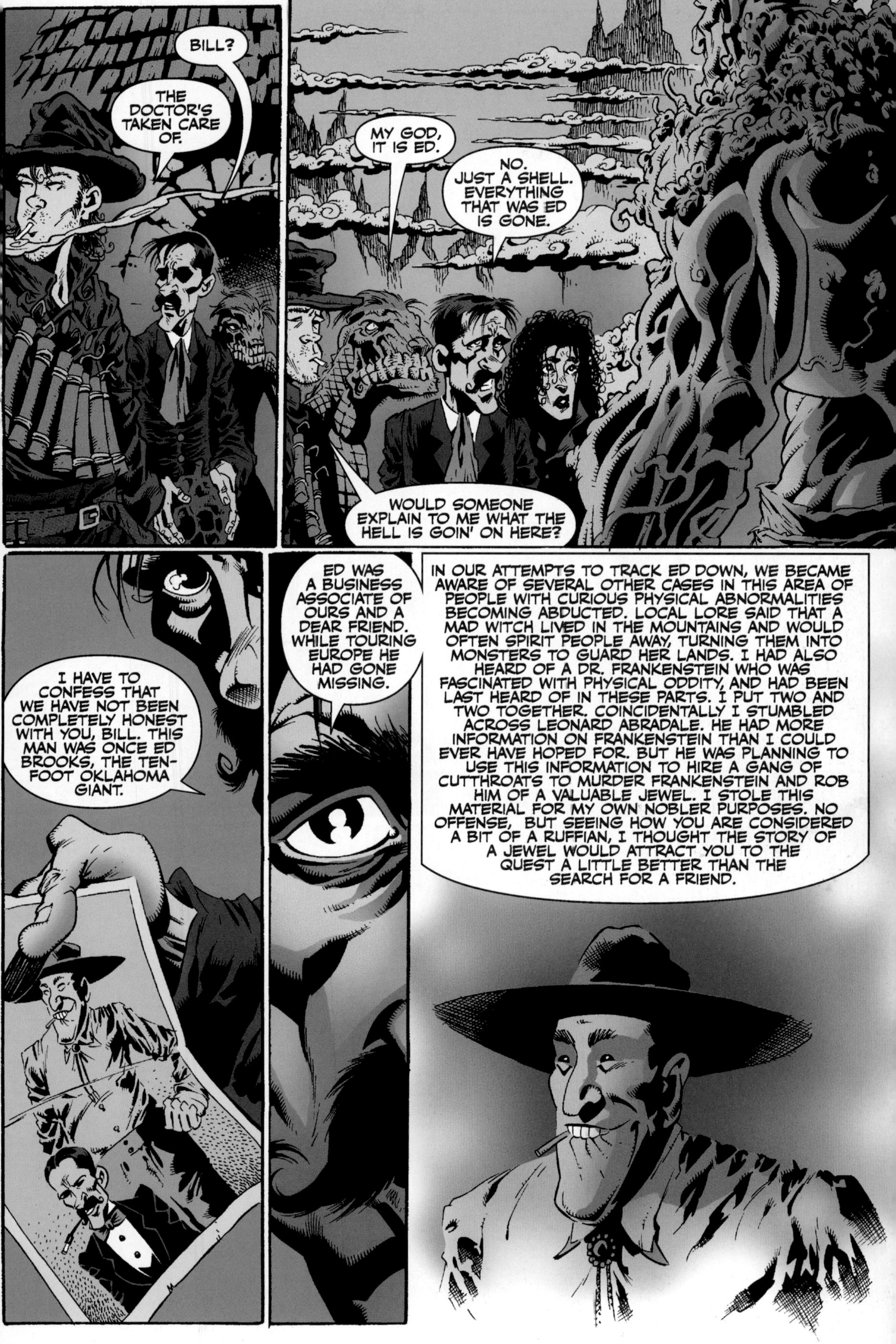
BILL?
THE DOCTOR'S TAKEN CARE OF.
MY GOD, IT IS ED.
NO. JUST A SHELL. EVERYTHING THAT WAS ED IS GONE.
WOULD SOMEONE EXPLAIN TO ME WHAT THE HELL IS GOIN' ON HERE?
I HAVE TO CONFESS THAT WE HAVE NOT BEEN COMPLETELY HONEST WITH YOU, BILL. THIS MAN WAS ONCE ED BROOKS, THE TEN-FOOT OKLAHOMA GIANT.
ED WAS A BUSINESS ASSOCIATE OF OURS AND A DEAR FRIEND. WHILE TOURING EUROPE HE HAD GONE MISSING.
IN OUR ATTEMPTS TO TRACK ED DOWN, WE BECAME AWARE OF SEVERAL OTHER CASES IN THIS AREA OF PEOPLE WITH CURIOUS PHYSICAL ABNORMALITIES BECOMING ABDUCTED. LOCAL LORE SAID THAT A MAD WITCH LIVED IN THE MOUNTAINS AND WOULD OFTEN SPIRIT PEOPLE AWAY, TURNING THEM INTO MONSTERS TO GUARD HER LANDS. I HAD ALSO HEARD OF A DR. FRANKENSTEIN WHO WAS FASCINATED WITH PHYSICAL ODDITY, AND HAD BEEN LAST HEARD OF IN THESE PARTS. I PUT TWO AND TWO TOGETHER. COINCIDENTALLY I STUMBLED ACROSS LEONARD ABRADALE. HE HAD MORE INFORMATION ON FRANKENSTEIN THAN I COULD EVER HAVE HOPED FOR. BUT HE WAS PLANNING TO USE THIS INFORMATION TO HIRE A GANG OF CUTTHROATS TO MURDER FRANKENSTEIN AND ROB HIM OF A VALUABLE JEWEL. I STOLE THIS MATERIAL FOR MY OWN NOBLER PURPOSES. NO OFFENSE, BUT SEEING HOW YOU ARE CONSIDERED A BIT OF A RUFFIAN, I THOUGHT THE STORY OF A JEWEL WOULD ATTRACT YOU TO THE QUEST A LITTLE BETTER THAN THE SEARCH FOR A FRIEND.

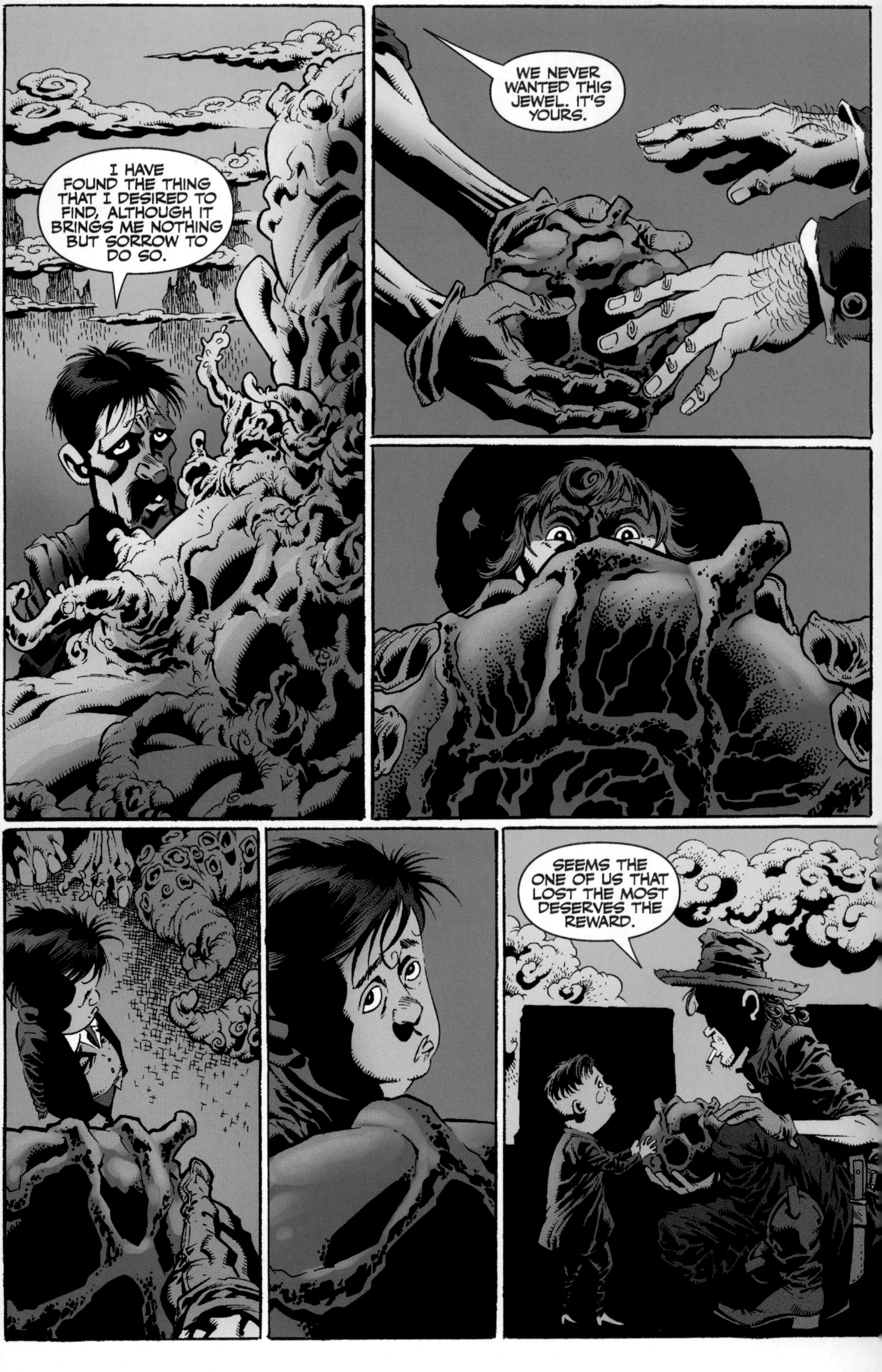
I HAVE FOUND THE THING THAT I DESIRED TO FIND, ALTHOUGH IT BRINGS ME NOTHING BUT SORROW TO DO SO.
WE NEVER WANTED THIS JEWEL. IT'S YOURS.
SEEMS THE ONE OF US THAT LOST THE MOST DESERVES THE REWARD.

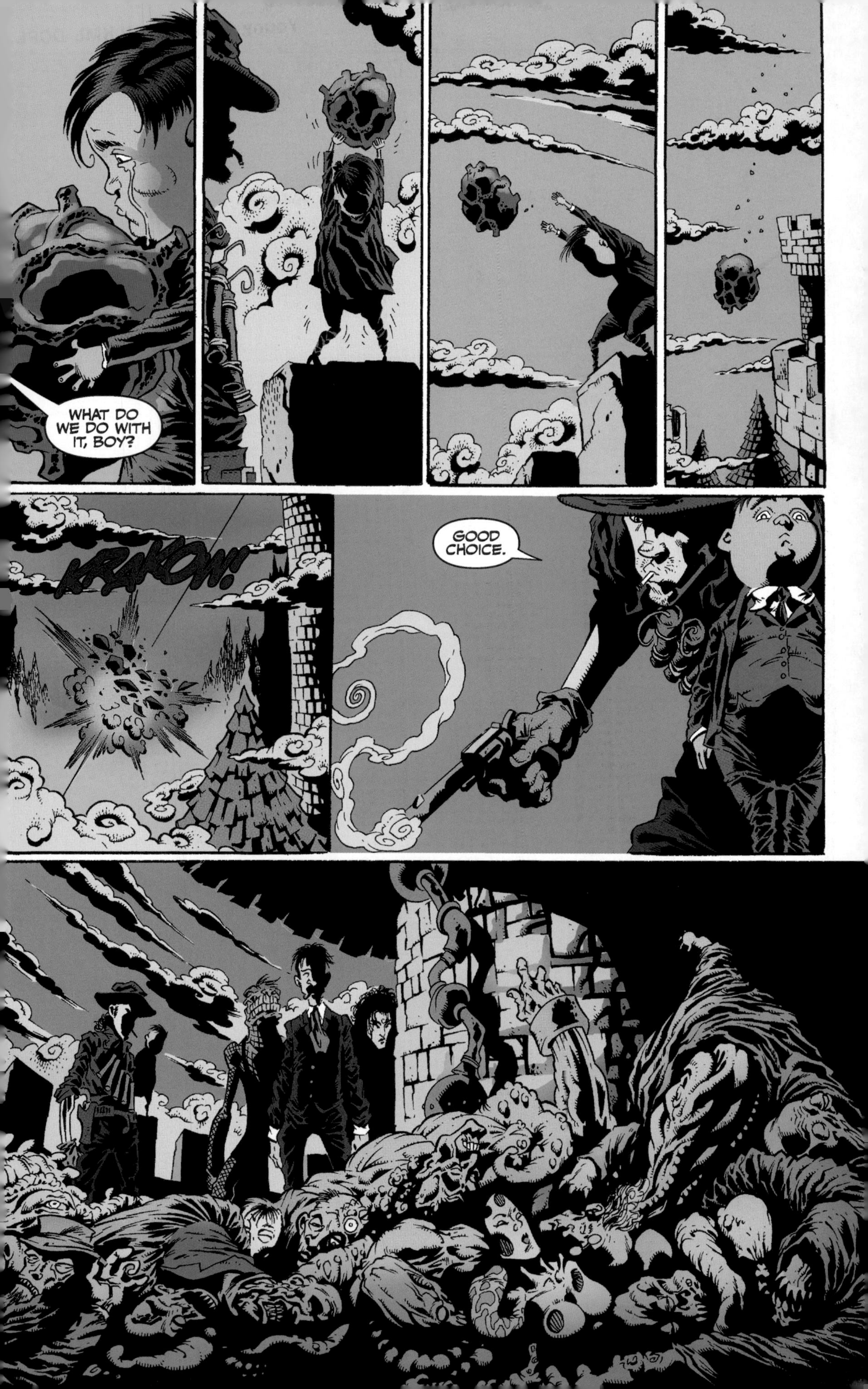
WHAT DO WE DO WITH IT, BOY?
KRAKOW!
GOOD CHOICE.

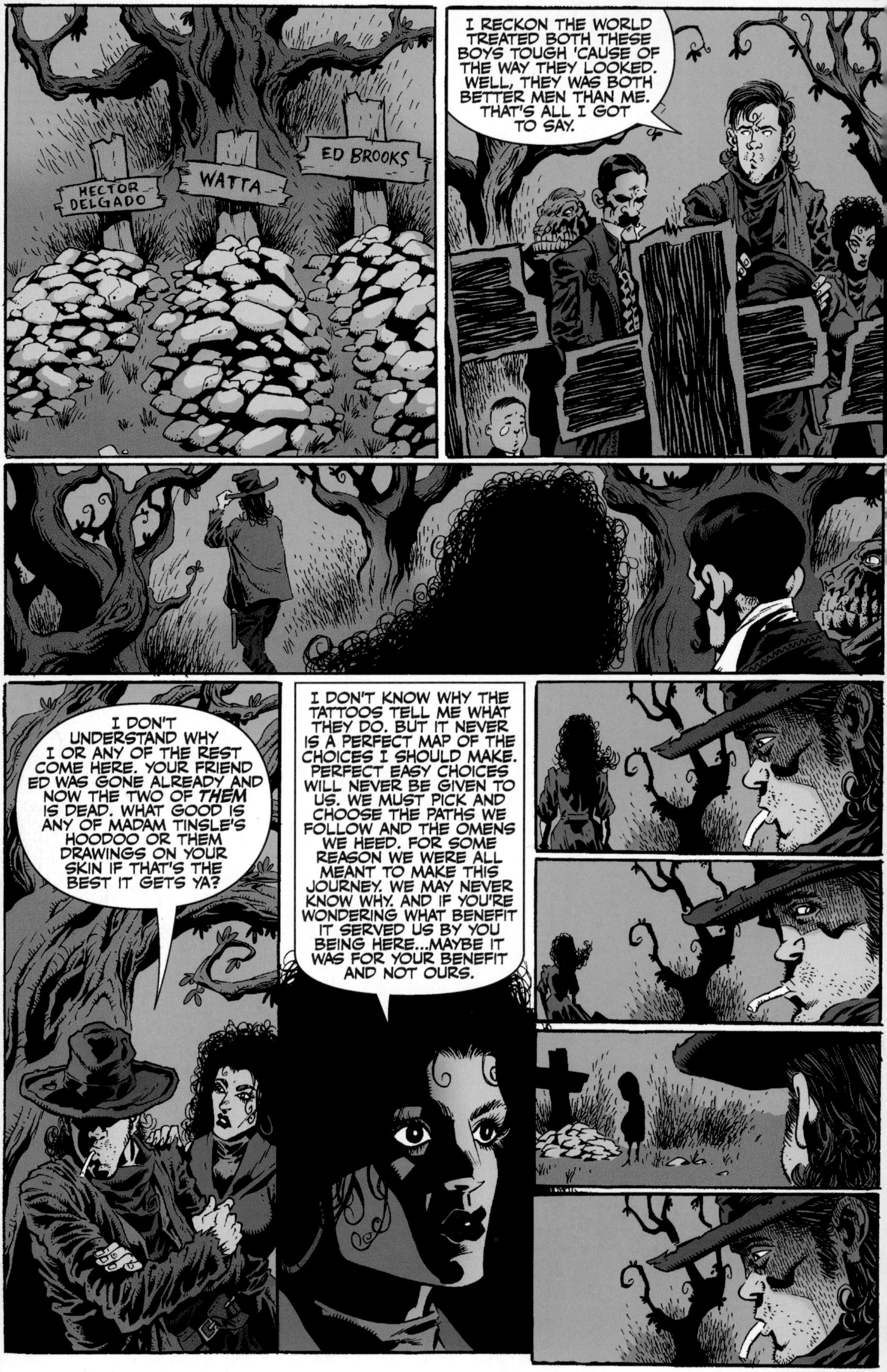
HECTOR DELGADO
WATTA
ED BROOKS
I RECKON THE WORLD TREATED BOTH THESE BOYS TOUGH 'CAUSE OF THE WAY THEY LOOKED. WELL, THEY WAS BOTH BETTER MEN THAN ME. THAT'S ALL I GOT TO SAY.
I DON'T UNDERSTAND WHY I OR ANY OF THE REST COME HERE. YOUR FRIEND ED WAS GONE ALREADY AND NOW THE TWO OF *THEM* IS DEAD. WHAT GOOD IS ANY OF MADAM TINSLE'S HOODOO OR THEM DRAWINGS ON YOUR SKIN IF THAT'S THE BEST IT GETS YA?
I DON'T KNOW WHY THE TATTOOS TELL ME WHAT THEY DO. BUT IT NEVER IS A PERFECT MAP OF THE CHOICES I SHOULD MAKE. PERFECT EASY CHOICES WILL NEVER BE GIVEN TO US. WE MUST PICK AND CHOOSE THE PATHS WE FOLLOW AND THE OMENS WE HEED. FOR SOME REASON WE WERE ALL MEANT TO MAKE THIS JOURNEY. WE MAY NEVER KNOW WHY. AND IF YOU'RE WONDERING WHAT BENEFIT IT SERVED US BY YOU BEING HERE...MAYBE IT WAS FOR YOUR BENEFIT AND NOT OURS.

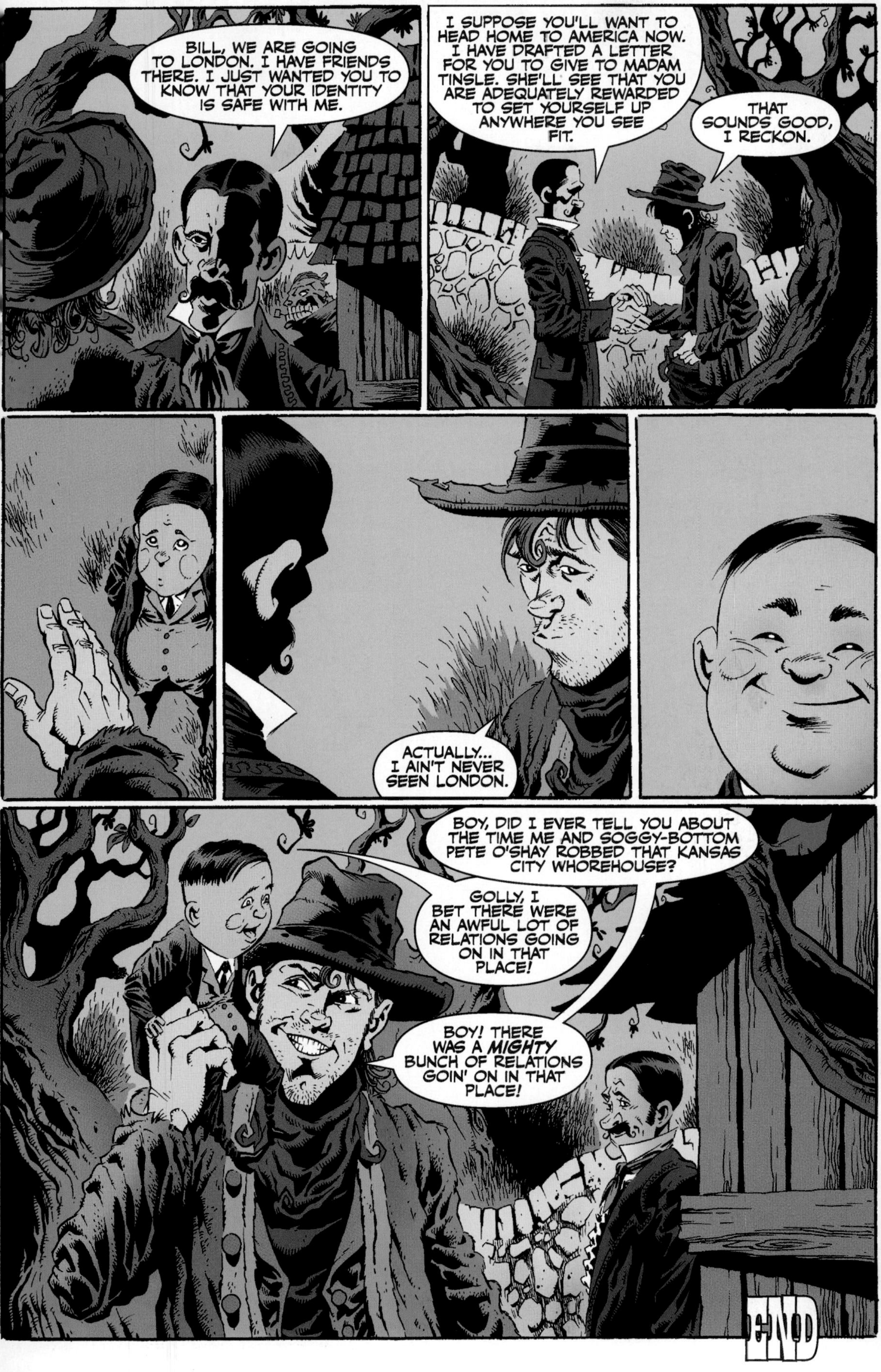
BILL, WE ARE GOING TO LONDON. I HAVE FRIENDS THERE. I JUST WANTED YOU TO KNOW THAT YOUR IDENTITY IS SAFE WITH ME.
I SUPPOSE YOU'LL WANT TO HEAD HOME TO AMERICA NOW. I HAVE DRAFTED A LETTER FOR YOU TO GIVE TO MADAM TINSLE. SHE'LL SEE THAT YOU ARE ADEQUATELY REWARDED TO SET YOURSELF UP ANYWHERE YOU SEE FIT.
THAT SOUNDS GOOD, I RECKON.
ACTUALLY... I AIN'T NEVER SEEN LONDON.
BOY, DID I EVER TELL YOU ABOUT THE TIME ME AND SOGGY-BOTTOM PETE O'SHAY ROBBED THAT KANSAS CITY WHOREHOUSE?
GOLLY, I BET THERE WERE AN AWFUL LOT OF RELATIONS GOING ON IN THAT PLACE!
BOY! THERE WAS A *MIGHTY* BUNCH OF RELATIONS GOIN' ON IN THAT PLACE!
END

ALSO FROM DARK HORSE BOOKS!

THE GOON
NOTHIN' BUT MISERY
by Eric Powell

THE GOON VOLUME 1: NOTHIN' BUT MISERY

by Eric Powell

The Goon is a laugh-out-loud, action-packed romp through the streets of a town infested with zombies. An insane priest is building himself an army of the undead, and there's only one man who can put them in their place: the man they call Goon.

Soft cover, 136 pages, Full color
$15.95 | ISBN: 1-56971-998-5

MIKE MIGNOLA'S
HELLBOY
WEIRD TALES
Volume One

HELLBOY: WEIRD TALES VOLUME ONE

By Joe Casey, John Cassaday, Steve Lieber, Alex Maleev, Eric Powell, Leinil Francis Yu, and many more!
Cover by Mike Mignola

Some of the top writers and artists in today's world of comics provide their take on Hellboy and the B.P.R.D. Old-fashioned pulp fun featuring one of the greatest heroes of modern comics.

Soft cover, 128 pages, Full color
$17.95 | ISBN: 1-56971-622-6

Mike Mignola
Jill Thompson
Evan Dorkin
Kelley Jones
Eric Powell
Gary Gianni
and others
The Dark Horse
BOOK OF THE DEAD

DARK HORSE BOOK OF THE DEAD

by Eric Powell, Mike Mignola, Evan Dorkin, Jill Thompson, Kelley Jones, Gary Gianni, and others

Mike Mignola presents a Hellboy yarn combining Shakespeare and graverobbing in this followup to Dark Horse's Eisner-nominated *Books* of *Hauntings* and *Witchcraft*. New additions for this volume include Goon creator Eric Powell, celebrated B.P.R.D. artist Guy Davis, and Kelley Jones. Plus a rare tale by Conan creator Robert E. Howard.

Hard cover, 96 pages, Full color
$14.95 | ISBN: 1-59307-281-3

MAN WITH THE
SCREAMING BRAIN
BRUCE CAMPBELL DAVID GOODMAN
RICK REMENDER HILARY BARTA

MAN WITH THE SCREAMING BRAIN

by Bruce Campbell, David Goodman, Rick Remender, and Hilary Barta

Based on the film from B-movie mega star Bruce Campbell—an American industrialist determined to exploit the crippled economy of a former Soviet state. But when he hits on the wrong gypsy girl, he soon finds himself in the grip of a mad scientist with a twisted brain-transplant scheme worthy of Dr. Frankenstein.

Soft cover, 104 pages, Full color
$13.95 | ISBN: 1-59307-397-6

DARK HORSE COMICS™ *drawing on your nightmares*
darkhorse.com

AVAILABLE AT YOUR LOCAL COMICS SHOP OR BOOKSTORE

To find a comics shop in your area, call 1-888-266-4226

For more information or to order direct visit darkhorse.com or call 1-800-862-0052 Mon.–Fri. 9 A.M. to 5 P.M. Pacific Time

*Prices and availability subject to change without notice

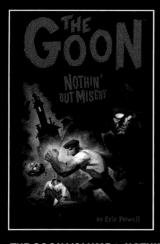

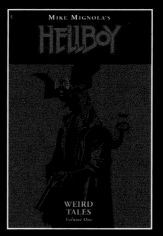

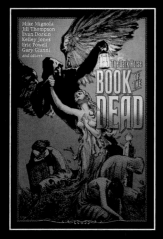

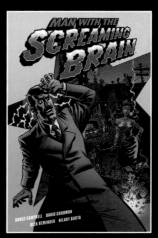

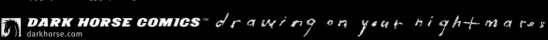